JOHN NOLEN,
LANDSCAPE ARCHITECT
AND CITY PLANNER

LALH

JOHN NOLEN, LANDSCAPE ARCHITECT AND CITY PLANNER

R. BRUCE STEPHENSON

LIBRARY OF AMERICAN LANDSCAPE HISTORY

AMHERST, MASSACHUSETTS

For Andrés and David

Library of American Landscape History
P.O. Box 1323
Amherst, MA 01004
www.lalh.org

Printed in Canada

Library of Congress Control Number: 2021934464
ISBN: 978-1-952620-32-4

Designed by Jonathan D. Lippincott
Set in Galliard

Distributed by
National Book Network
nbnbooks.com

The Library of Congress has cataloged the hardcover edition as follows:
Stephenson, R. Bruce (Robert Bruce), 1955–
    John Nolen, landscape architect and city planner / R. Bruce Stephenson.
        pages cm
    Includes bibliographical references and index.
    ISBN 978-1-62534-079-5 (cloth : alk. paper)
1. Nolen, John, 1869–1937. 2. City planner—United States—Biography. 3. Landscape
architects—United States—Biography. 4. City planning—United States. I. Title.
    HT167.S74 2015
    711'.4092—dc23
    [B]
                                                                                    2014043991

Publication of the paperback edition of

John Nolen, Landscape Architect and City Planner

is supported by the Nancy R. Turner Fund.

CONTENTS

PREFACE

In this rich biography, R. Bruce Stephenson approaches John Nolen (1869–1937) from multiple perspectives, keeping in sight his subject's intellectual grounding in the fields of landscape architecture and city planning. Stephenson makes extensive use of Nolen's professional correspondence and personal letters, which he interweaves with passages from his published writings and reports. The result is a narrative that is both moving and revelatory, a multidimensional portrait of an influential practitioner at the epicenter of the nascent field of city planning.

Nolen came late to his profession. The reform-minded lecturer was thirty-three when he enrolled in Harvard's new department of landscape architecture, a decision catalyzed by the recently published biography of Charles Eliot and Nolen's first visit to Central Park. He identified deeply with Eliot, whose passion for nature he shared, and he also felt closely aligned with Olmsted, the founder, in Nolen's words, of "an art peculiarly suited to American conditions in high service of the American people."

When Nolen opened his office in Cambridge after graduating from Harvard in 1905, he already had an important job in hand—a new park system for Charlotte, North Carolina. He was soon lecturing for large progressive-minded audiences, and he also began publishing, first writing a series of articles about Olmsted and then editing a collection of Humphry Repton's writings. Following Repton's example, Nolen traveled in England and Europe to study gardens, parks, and cities firsthand. Frequent trips abroad throughout his career kept Nolen apprised of city planning developments, especially in Germany and England.

Planning jobs in Savannah, Roanoke, San Diego, and Madison, Wisconsin, came to Nolen during his first decade in practice, and commissions for dozens of model suburbs and industrial villages, many in the South, soon followed. Throughout his long career, Nolen maintained a commitment to providing Americans city dwellers and suburbanites with walkable, well designed, and distinctive places to live. He created company towns, replanned rapidly expanding cities, and, in a few memorable instances, planned new experimental towns, the most fully realized of which is Mariemont, Ohio.

Stephenson's book offers a comprehensive analysis of Nolen's professional achievements, his collegial networks, and perhaps most important, a sense of how Nolen's principles continue to influence planning trends today, particularly those associated with new urbanism. Confronted with the impact of modernism during the final decade of his life, Nolen was appalled by Bauhaus-inspired plans that merged "neighborhoods into a soulless urban mass." Stephenson makes clear that many of Nolen's neighborhoods escaped this fate and that many continue to thrive as a result of his visionary planning principles.

This new, paperback edition of the reprint, first published by LALH in 2015, was inspired by continued interest in John Nolen and his relevance to landscape architects, planners, and all those concerned with the future of small towns in America. I remain grateful to R. Bruce Stephenson for his original study and to LALH senior manuscript editor Sarah Allaback, who worked closely with Stephenson to create an engaging text that would do justice to this important figure.

Robin Karson
Executive Director
Library of American Landscape History

ACKNOWLEDGMENTS

In 1979 I moved to a historic neighborhood in Clearwater, Florida, close to my employer, the Pinellas County Planning Department. My job was challenging and I liked to run to clear my mind. Clearwater was a scenic coastal town, but traffic and a dearth of sidewalks made for a series of dismal outings. My experience changed after I charted a course through Belleair, an attractive community set on an axial grid with a bayfront park, wide sidewalks, small greens, historic homes, and street trees. Over the next few months, my evening run restored my faith in city planning—quality human-scale design could enlighten daily life. I did not learn until much later, however, that John Nolen designed Belleair at the zenith of his career. My faith in planning owes a debt to Nolen.

If this book was long in coming, it was not due to lack of support. Rollins College provided funding and a sabbatical so I could visit communities Nolen designed and institutions holding his papers and plans. Grants from the Florida Humanities Council supported my analysis of Venice, Clewiston, Belleair, Clearwater, and St. Petersburg. Cornell University's John Nolen Research Fund allowed me to closely examine the John Nolen Papers. Elaine Engst and her staff at the Cornell Archives spent hours helping me uncover the mysteries encased in the more than one hundred boxes of correspondence and plans that make up the collection. James Hagler, director of the Venice Museum, and Butch Wilson, director of the Clewiston Museum, gathered an amazing array of historical photos and plans. The staff at the Arthur and Elizabeth Schlesinger Library on the History of Women in America provided access to the papers of the Nolen-Schatte family, a collection of previously undocumented letters. Jonathan Miller, the head librarian at Rollins, was indefatigable in securing historical photos for publication.

A group of inspired citizens were instrumental in helping me evaluate Nolen's work and legacy. Betty Intagalia (Venice), Adele Mehan (Union Park Gardens), Kacey Ratterree (Savannah), Mark Eisen (Madison), and Thomas Hanchett (Charlotte) are dedicated civic champions who celebrate the past to improve their communities. Hanchett, executive director of the Museum of the New South, is also an excellent scholar and readily shared his insights.

This book is also an outgrowth of research shared at academic panels and symposiums over the last decade. I am thankful for the acumen of a dedicated group of scholars including Mervyn Miller, Rob Freestone, Chris Silver, Mary Corbin Sies, Jon Peterson, Robert Fishman, Millard Rogers, Emily Talen, Arne Alanen, David Mollenhoff, Charles Warren, Kristin Larsen, William Fulton, and the late John Hancock. I am also indebted to David Edgell, Victor Dover, Frank Starkey, and D. R. Bryan for sharing how they applied Nolen's principles in their work. Tom Low, who heads the Duany Plater-Zyberk office in Charlotte, was especially helpful, as his ability to interpret Nolen's design technique is unparalleled.

Robin Karson's encouragement and patience turned a cumbersome manuscript into a coherent book. The comments of reviewers and copy editor Mary Ellen Wilson were thorough and sensitive to the material. Sarah Allaback was the perfect editor, coordinating the illustrations and text and fine tuning the prose.

Rick Foglesong, my colleague at Rollins, shared his time and expertise in city planning history to help me tell a better story. My keen-eyed students Caty Coplin, Stacey Matrazzo, Andrew Landis, and James Brantley contributed a dozen photographs. My wife, Myrtho, not only lent her support, but read passages again and again, making this work a family effort. The book would never had been written without the encouragement of Andrés Duany, who early on recognized Nolen's importance and was unfailing in his support. Finally, David Schuyler, a valued mentor, made sure I wrote "the next book."

JOHN NOLEN,
LANDSCAPE ARCHITECT
AND CITY PLANNER

John Nolen (left) and the San Diego Plan, 1926. Courtesy Division of Rare and Manuscript Collections, Cornell University Library.

INTRODUCTION

In 1927, Lewis Mumford identified John Nolen as the one city planner who "realizes where the path of intelligent and humane achievement will lead in the next generation."[1] A pioneer in the emerging field of city planning, Nolen was at the height of his career. He had just completed *New Towns for Old*, a groundbreaking book that both summarized the collective goals of the profession and outlined his plan for guiding America's future urban development.

Mumford understood Nolen's influence as a missionary of city and town planning to be his greatest contribution to the field. After visiting Letchworth, England, in 1906, Nolen became inspired by the first garden city as a model for American development. Over time he adapted its principles—the provision of open space, tree-lined streets, and a variety of housing types—to projects in different regions throughout the country. One of the first practitioners to market the concept of comprehensive planning on a national scale, he communicated his vision through stereopticon slide shows to local civic clubs, in speeches to his peers, in books and reports, in college courses, and at countless public meetings. His audiences included 1,700 African American students at Tuskeegee Institute in Alabama; over two hundred men who came to a parks meeting after work in Madison, Wisconsin; and the attendees of the International Cities and Town Planning Conference in Berlin.[2] He traveled incessantly throughout his career—from Cambridge, Massachusetts, to San Diego, Venice, Florida, Roanoke, and dozens of other American cities and towns, frequently spending months at a time in the field promoting the benefits of the "civic art" of city planning.

By the 1920s, having witnessed two decades of intense urban growth, Nolen had already concluded that comprehensive planning could "have only limited influence on larger places, relieving only the worst civic conditions, ameliorating merely the most acute forms of congestion."[3] Although frustrated by the damage that had already been done—the result of haphazard development, the use of gridiron plans, and local politics that favored short-term financial gain over long-term improvement—Nolen found reasons to be optimistic. The elements of his town and city plans—zoning, the accommodation of pedestrians alongside automobiles and public transportation, and provision for park land—provided a means of grappling with the explosion in population and its requisite urban development.

Nolen had high hopes for what he described as the two main divisions of city planning—replanning existing towns and cities and laying out new communities, either satellites of existing cities or garden cities, which were separate entities in new locations.[4] He communicated his plans for the future to prospective clients by using his most successful and representative projects as examples. The chapters in his 1927 book included plans for an industrial town (Walpole, MA), an industrial city (Kingsport, TN), a village for factory workers, (Kistler, PA), an old seacoast town (Cohasset, MA), a war emergency project (Union Park Gardens, Wilmington, DE), an upscale residential suburb (Myers Park, Charlotte, NC) and finally, an example of "a wholesale migration from cities" to an ideal town (Mariemont, OH). In the varying size, purpose, and geographical range of these examples, Nolen demonstrated his broad concept of town planning—a profession he pioneered and practiced to serve all Americans, from immigrant factory workers to public benefactors.

A pragmatic visionary, Nolen embraced the "marvelous development of the motor vehicle" as part of a future that could be engineered to raise the quality of life, while also working to provide pedestrian accessibility and open space for parks and preserves.[5] Designing "walks and paths and lanes should have special attention" because "few people walk today," he noted, and walking promoted good health and social intercourse.[6] He realized that "highway planning must be changed to meet the new conditions, with correspondingly revolutionary changes in construction."[7] Through foresight, planners could link towns to one another, which would then meet up with cities and ultimately come together in a regional plan. In the 1920s and '30s, Nolen came to believe that such "intelligent and humane achievement" lay within the grasp of those who would make the right choices. He stood apart from many of his peers in his acute understanding of the political issues that needed to be resolved to lay the groundwork for new city and town plans, as he did in his ability to relate to audiences of every social and economic background, regardless of region or race. He targeted real estate developers and building companies, explaining how profits could be made more easily from good design. Perhaps most important, Nolen credited individual civic leaders with the inspiration behind most of his successful plans. Although he was forced to confront the reality of human greed, racism, and corruption, Nolen persisted in his efforts, as well as in his belief in the fundamental goodness of mankind.

Born into poverty and placed in an institution as a child, Nolen consistently considered the poor in his plans for cities. After studying European housing efforts, he became a founding member of the National Housing Association and fought for higher housing standards in the United States. His desire for beauty and fitness was a means of achieving a larger goal, "more of the things that make life worth living." These included "decent homes; children well fed, with fit bodies and active minds; sunlight not obscured by a dense canopy of smoke; reasonable quiet; and, above all, safety from danger and disease."[8] It was this passionate desire to design an environment fostering human well-being that led Mumford to single Nolen out as the foremost humanitarian leader in his field.

At the Nineteenth Conference on Urban Planning in 1927, Nolen presented an optimistic view of the planning profession in a paper titled "Twenty Years of City Planning Progress in the United States, 1907–27." But even as he looked toward the future as president of the conference, Nolen was confronting a personal financial crisis. Beginning in the 1920s, he expanded his practice with a new office in Florida, an achievement he advertised with a poster titled "Florida 'in the making,'" which included four city plans and over fourteen town and neighborhood commissions. Just a few years later, however, his once promising investment in planning Florida's new towns and cities appeared to be crumbling, as real estate values plummeted and the speculative ventures that had underwritten his work dissolved. He was soon forced to close his Florida office, sustain significant financial losses, and leave without completing the grand plan he had envisioned. Although he maintained his optimism, at least in public, Nolen's practice never fully recovered.

When Nolen died in 1937, his longtime associate Justin Hartzog recalled his ability to communicate with a wide range of audiences as an attribute worthy of emulation. "He struggled to implant new ideas in the practical mind, to crystallize the dreams of the visionary mind, and to check the rashness of the unprepared mind." Hartzog recalled that Nolen was easily approachable and made time for "the earnest student, the ambitious technician, the harassed public official, or the besieged public benefactor."[9] His facility in relating with others, a skill he diligently honed to market his cause, would prove his greatest asset as a planner. Through his efforts to further his mission of city planning, Nolen also established an international network of allies, including English garden city advocates Ebenezer Howard and Raymond Unwin, and he brought their concept of town planning to the United States. Nolen's translation of these garden city principles would prove an enduring contribution to the history of American city planning, influencing urban development throughout the country in his day and our own.

1

THE RISE OF AN URBAN REFORMER, 1869–1902

On July 14, 1869, Matilda Nolen gave birth to her third child and first boy, John. The family lived in central Philadelphia, where John's father, John Christopher "Shay" Nolen, owned and managed a small hotel. The City of Brotherly Love was hardly the wholesome, green country town William Penn had envisioned when planning it two centuries before. Fraudulent elections, cholera epidemics, crime, and opportunism marked the booming post–Civil War years in the city of over 600,000 inhabitants. One of the world's leading industrial centers, Philadelphia was also the home of a powerful and corrupt political machine controlled by James McManes, the Republican Party boss who translated votes into jobs and government contracts. In 1870, for example, voters approved funds to build a new city hall, and though construction began the next year, twenty-one more years passed before the project was finished. Political corruption, graft, and inefficiency pervaded municipal governance during McManes's reign.[1]

Shay Nolen was a willing participant in the rough world of Philadelphia politics, and after the 1870 election, he was determined to thwart McManes. New legislation had allowed the ruling party to register voters, and Republicans flooded the polls with repeat voters using fictitious names. In protest, Nolen joined a group of Democrats who marched on the Nineteenth Ward courthouse to lodge their complaints. Inside the courthouse's locked doors, armed guards protected Judge Alexander Crawford, who was overseeing a group of court officials certifying the returns. Nolen and a small cadre of supporters forced their way into the building. After a tense confrontation, Crawford shot Nolen, and three days later, the thirty-five-year-old father of three died. Nolen's funeral service was heavily attended; he was buried on October 16 at St. Mary's Cemetery. Afterward, the family struggled, for the young widow had minimal support from her extended relations.[2]

Little is known of John Nolen's early childhood other than that he lived in near poverty and both of his sisters had died by the time he turned eight years old. The financial panic of 1873, which was centered in New York and Philadelphia, intensified Matilda Nolen's hardships. Her situation improved when she married Caleb Aaronson, but Aaronson refused to provide for his stepson. After Matilda appealed to the Children's Aid Society for help and the nine-year-old child was accepted into Girard College, a residential school for orphaned boys, she moved to Newark, New Jersey.[3]

Girard College was named for Stephen Girard, a merchant-banker who epitomized the municipal leadership of the early republic as well as the philanthropic spirit of the city. The Frenchman had risen from humble beginnings to join Philadelphia's merchant class. Girard brought talent, experience, and fiscal acuity to a city shifting from a mercantile to an industrial economy, and public service accompanied his financial success. During these years, Philadelphia broke new ground in humanitarian reform. By the 1830s the city offered institutions for rehabilitative incarceration, mental illness, physical disabilities, and, owing directly to Girard, the education of fatherless boys and orphans.[4]

Reportedly the richest man in the United States, Girard willed the majority of his estate to the city. Girard College, which opened to one hundred students in 1848, was his most significant gift, the largest charitable donation of its time. Enclosed by a ten-foot wall, the forty-three-acre campus occupied a rise on the city's western edge, where the Greek Revival architecture reflected the school's nonsectarian civic values. Like many reformers of his day, Girard was a deist, and an early backer of what was then called organic education. For this prominent philanthropist, the "fairest of Utopias" rested on "the simple tradition of the citizen," words Nolen underlined in his copy of Henry Ingram's 1887 biography of Girard.[5] Nolen would later comment that "before the time of Emerson and the Concord philosophers, Girard was an advocate of plain living and high thinking."[6] (Fig. 1.1)

Girard College's mission was to produce self-sufficient, civic-minded young men to work in Pennsylvania's factories. But shortly before Nolen arrived, a new curriculum was introduced that combined vocational training with the liberal arts, so, in addition to learning how to operate factory machinery, the inquisitive boy also studied history, literature, moral philosophy, foreign languages, botany, mathematics, art, and theater. Along with a steady diet of

Fig. 1.1. Founders Hall, Girard College. Photograph by Matt Honea, 2012.

republican values plain but wholesome food was provided, and academics were balanced by a regimen of exercise and recreation.[7]

Nolen prospered in this orderly institutional environment. An avid reader, he excelled in literature and history. Girard and Benjamin Franklin were his early heroes on a list that came to include Samuel Morse, Mark Twain, and William Cullen Bryant. European history introduced a world far beyond Philadelphia that captured Nolen's imagination. He found the Italian Renaissance especially intriguing and later in life would become a devoted student of the period. In his adolescent years, Nolen also developed an interest in the arts, performing Shakespeare, learning the basics of drawing, and gaining an eye for painting and architecture. He became adept at public speaking and acquired a proficiency in French and German that would become a valuable asset later in life when he regularly traveled to Europe. Although Girard College offered no formal religious training, the Bible was studied, and lessons of sacrifice, hard work, and benevolence, presented from a broad Protestant perspective, helped reinforce the school's civic mission. Classical texts, Enlightenment treatises, and Transcendentalist essays were also assigned to teach that humans were blessed with reason and that thrift, discipline, and honorable intent allowed a free people to prosper and live in harmony.[8]

From his first year at Girard, Nolen found a special joy in nature. Two hours per day were allocated to recreation; students had access to a playground, an athletic field, a swimming area, and woods near a farmhouse, barn, and gardens. Nolen came to see how the outdoors brought "sanity to human affairs" and would later describe himself as a "nature lover."[9]

In 1884 Nolen graduated first in his class and earned an apprenticeship in the iron industry, though he chose instead to work as an office boy for Girard president Adam Fetterolf. Over the next year, Nolen took a series of drawing courses in his spare time. The pleasing forms he sketched illustrated his artistic ability and no doubt spurred his belief in "the need for art in life as one of the durable satisfactions."[10]

At eighteen, Nolen went to work as a clerk for the Girard estate, which was overseen by Philadelphia's Board of City Trusts. George E. Kirkpatrick, the estate's superintendent and a Girard alumnus, quickly took a liking to the new employee. A genial man without children, Kirkpatrick mentored Nolen, encouraging the young man's growing ambition. Nolen began considering a career in public service but realized that he would need a university degree—something unheard of for a Girard graduate. He saved his money, devoting his free time to self-education, and on his twenty-first birthday, a party of twenty-two guests (including Kirkpatrick) joined in celebrating Nolen's future, a "kingdom within, full of light and hope," as the invitations read. Frank Zesinger, Nolen's best friend from Girard, presented him with the Ingram biography, which Nolen highlighted extensively while preparing for the entrance exam to the University of Pennsylvania's Wharton School of Finance and Economy. He scored well and, in the fall of 1891, entered the university with junior class standing.[11]

In the early 1890s, the Wharton School was at the forefront of educational reform. In 1881 Joseph Wharton, the cofounder of Bethlehem Steel, established the first collegiate business school to encourage engagement across academic disciplines. Students needed such training, Wharton believed, if they were to become leaders capable of ameliorating the damaging fluctuations of the American business cycle. The financial panics that began in 1873 and ran through the end of the century forced a reappraisal of the nation's laissez-faire economic system. In Nolen's lifetime, the standard of living had risen, but wealth was spread unevenly and the gap continued to widen between the wealthiest Americans and the working class. The bifurcation of society into contesting parties of labor and capital threatened republican values and social stability.[12] Both the fear of class warfare and faith in progress informed teaching at the Wharton School.

Wharton was modeled on German universities, which wedded government policy to higher education. Courses in economics, sociology, and public administration fostered innovative applied research that attracted bright young American graduate students. Early Wharton graduates Edmund J. James and Simon Nelson Patten earned doctorates at Martin Luther University of Halle-Wittenberg under the direction of Johannes Conrad, who argued that state- and university-trained experts must direct urban expansion and coordinate public and private investment to procure a "fit" society. The two returned to the United States and the Wharton School convinced that government had an ethical duty to improve living conditions for its citizens.[13]

At the Wharton School, James and Patten championed a view that the physical environment and society were interdependent and that systematical planning could improve society in general.[14] Experiments in applied research at Wharton in the early 1900s reflected a staunch faith in the "gospel of efficiency."[15] James, as Wharton's first director, marketed the new school by hosting symposiums and inviting Philadelphia's business leaders and civic reformers to mix with faculty and students. James's approach to resolving utility and transportation dilemmas appealed to both groups. In the dialogues that ensued, the school raised the prospect that experts could bring efficiency to municipal government.[16]

While James emphasized pragmatism, Simon Patten was constructing a provocative concept of social theory. In his view, it was the human species' cooperative predisposition that produced civilization, and this inner monitoring system, the "civic instinct," should be nurtured to achieve the full potential of industrial capitalism.[17] The United States was achieving an unprecedented standard of living, but Patten thought it imperative to balance investment between private interests and the public good. Encouraged by Patten to nurture the civic instinct, procure profits, and advance social evolution, Nolen learned to turn theory into practice, especially when it came to urban reform.[18] Later in life he would, like other students of Patten (including Walter Weyl, Rexford Tugwell, and Benjamin Marsh), lead reform movements based on their teacher's maxim to "make a better use of the world and reach a higher civilization."[19]

In addition to Patten and James, Nolen was influenced by the historians James Robinson and John B. McMaster. The German-trained Robinson claimed that Nolen was his best student at the University of Pennsylvania.[20] Robinson would later join Charles Beard and Vernon Parrington in the vanguard of the so-called New History movement, which pioneered the concept of a usable past.[21] Through Robinson, Nolen was introduced to Beard, and he maintained contact with both men into the 1930s. McMaster, a historian who taught at the University of Pennsylvania from 1883 to 1920, was best known for writing an eight-volume history of the United States that chronicled the rapid and unruly ascent of industrial capitalism. Under his tutelage, Nolen explored the increasingly volatile relationship between property rights and the government's obligation to protect the public health, safety, and welfare. He wrote a term paper for McMaster documenting the conflict over the expansion of the public domain in the American West, where national forests and parks were being set aside in the early 1890s.[22] This research laid the groundwork for Nolen's honors thesis on the Philadelphia Gas Works and introduced the future city planner to the tools government could employ when acquiring private property for the public good.[23]

Nolen's abiding interest in history, especially the Italian Renaissance, was not unusual; by the 1890s, a "Renaissance complex," the notion of a culture that inspired receptiveness to beauty and humane concerns, had permeated artistic and intellectual circles in the United States.[24] In his copy of Philip Schaff's volume *The Renaissance* (1891), Nolen underscored the sentence: "The humanist saw the finger of God in reason, in science, in nature, in art and taught men that *life is worth living*."[25]

Nolen's Ivy League education was hard won—aside from a small scholarship, he supported himself by working as a gardener at the Girard estate.[26] He took a businesslike approach to his studies and moved crisply through the Wharton academic schedule. Modest almost to a fault, he realized how far he had risen, but was not satisfied. "I shall try harder than ever to make good use of my time and devote myself diligently to study for I am not very 'apt' and must make up for it by work," he wrote as his 1892 New Year's resolution.[27] At this point in his life, Nolen had only a vague idea of a vocation. He had thoughts of becoming a teacher or a professor and even broached the idea of returning to the University of Pennsylvania as a dean. That he could consider such a position revealed how his life had turned, with doors opened to opportunities he could barely have imagined before entering the university. His good fortune was aided by a genial nature and sober idealism, traits identified in the caption under his photo in the university yearbook: "A modest blush he wears, not formed by art; free from deceit his face, and full as free his heart."[28]

Despite a schedule dedicated to work and study, Nolen was not a recluse. He attended football games, joined a fraternity, and began a romance with Barbara Schatte, whom he would later marry. And he was not without guile. "Crafty John," as his closest friend Franklin Edmonds called him, had a streak of hedonism that was endearing to a close-knit group of Wharton students.[29] He had a gift for putting others at ease and was apparently adept at reading people, a skill not uncommon to children who must fend for themselves at an early age. Nolen also spoke his mind; in his senior year he placed third in the all-college debate. He served as president of the Wharton School Council, and, along with Edmonds (who won the debate), he founded, edited, and published the *Wharton School Bulletin*. On June 16, 1893, Nolen graduated "with distinction." Others receiving this accolade included Edmonds and Thomas S. Gates, who in 1930 would become president of the university.[30] The *Philadelphia Times* reported that Nolen was "a singularly bright young man and holds to a marked degree the confidence of many good people."[31]

In the summer of 1893 the nation was in a severe recession, and unemployment neared twenty percent, so Nolen returned to a summer job at

was located in the central Catskills north of Tannerville, New York. Onteora accommodated three hundred visitors in sixty cottages and a spacious inn. Nolen oversaw the running of the inn and care of the grounds. Onteora was "wild and natural," he had written the previous summer, "far from ostentatious or showy and yet everything that is beautiful and lovely is truly appreciated, especially from an artistic standpoint."[32] (Fig. 1.2)

Wheeler was a skilled gardener, interior decorator, and designer who became best known as an advocate of the Arts and Crafts movement. In 1881 she collaborated with Louis Comfort Tiffany to lighten the somber interior of Samuel Clemens's new mansion in Hartford, Connecticut, and two years later the pair refurbished the public rooms in the White House. In 1893 Wheeler helped design the interior of the Woman's Building at the Chicago World's Fair. That year Onteora celebrated its tenth anniversary. The Catskills retreat

Fig. 1.2. Onteora Inn, early 1890s. Courtesy Onteora Club.

Fig. 1.3. Onteora Procession, early 1890s. Courtesy Onteora Club.

was unlike anything the young Ivy Leaguer had encountered. In her desire to "live a wild life" each summer, Wheeler celebrated the ideals of classical civilization with a pagan flourish. There were costumed Arcadian processions with children dressed like woodland gods and young women in flower-trimmed gowns carrying sheaves of blossoming grasses. Neighboring property owners were not quite sure what to make of "the band of enthusiastic idiots." Wheeler described how the group was "always—perhaps unconsciously—trying to resist the encroachment of convention at Onteora, and perhaps it was this desire which gave all our gaieties a tinge of something which belonged to the ideal, classical or imaginative periods."[33] (Fig. 1.3)

A healthy dose of gender equity also fueled Onteora. A coterie of Wheeler's female friends, including writers Mary Mapes Dodge and Susan Coolidge, built cottages and were instrumental in creating a sanctuary that celebrated humanist thought and nature worship for both sexes. Residents hiked or painted outside during the day and spent their evenings conversing under the stars, dancing, singing, and reciting poetry or reading aloud. By 1887 an inn had been expanded to accommodate the growing stream of visitors that included Columbia University English professor Brander Matthews, painter Carroll Beckwith, actress Maude Adams, critic Mariana Griswold Van Rensselaer, editor Richard Watson Gilder, and writers John Burroughs, Hamlin Garland, and Samuel Clemens.[34]

Working in the Catskills provided Nolen with lessons that rivaled anything taught in the Wharton School, and overseeing the inn tested his administrative skill and patience.[35] Although he had mastered the basics of horticulture while tending the Girard estate's manicured grounds, Onteora demanded a different type of care. There was little need for clipping or mowing; instead, Nolen was instructed to highlight the mountain scenery and supplement its beauty.[36] No record remains of Nolen's landscape duties at the retreat, but the mix of horticulture and native landscape design that Wheeler practiced there is documented in her book *Content in a Garden* (1901). On a quarter-acre half-moon-shaped site, she fashioned a succession of bloom that celebrated the subtlety of the seasons. The mountain meadows were her inspiration, "as one never finds a clearly cut outline, a sharp departure from one tint to another."[37] She laced her garden with native species including Quaker lady, wild columbine, gentian, mountain laurel, azalea, and rosebay rhododendron. Working at Onteora, Nolen gained an appreciation for landscape gardening. It was a discipline that required assessing existing conditions before drawing plans, he wrote a decade later, one that should respect "the fundamental principles of art and the laws of nature."[38]

Although Nolen did not record his landscape duties, he wrote profusely about his treks through the Catskills. More than a half century before, the Hudson River School painters Asher B. Durand and Thomas Cole had spent a summer painting the surrounding landscape. Nolen retraced their steps, taking in grand mountain views: "A beautiful green rolling valley, dabbled only here and there by human habitations" and set off by "the most perfect aesthetic mountain lines . . . irregular, yet grandly graceful," as he wrote to his future wife in 1894. Over time, Nolen's interest in the outdoors intensified as he contemplated, like so many artists and writers before him, the value of sublime nature, describing "these dear mountains, the beautiful woods of Onteora. Clear, bright, pleasant air and everything *perfectly peaceful*." He extended his hiking regimen to take in panoramic views of the Hudson Valley from sites such as the Catskill Mountain House, which Cole had painted. One evening, watching the sun "sink quietly down into the middle of the Catskills" from Lake Mohonk, he experienced an intimate feeling of transcendence and stayed in his small boat well into the night to view the lake in the starlight.[39] (Fig. 1.4)

Spending most of his free time immersed in nature, Nolen came to see the world in a different light. He wrote to Barbara Schatte after tramping through the wild that he doubted "anyone appreciates the recreation of life more than

Fig. 1.4. Thomas Cole, *A View of the Two Lakes and Mountain House, Catskill Mountains, Morning*, 1844. Courtesy Brooklyn Museum.

I." The young man also observed the inner workings of human nature, discussing the essence of beauty, the value of art, modes of literature, and gardening with Onteora's sophisticated guests. High in the Catskills he had encountered the best of what life had to offer, and he had also discovered the source of inner peace. "How happy people should be who have as much as the people have who are here. And yet they do not impress me as being particularly happy. I have come to the conclusion that contentment does not come from what we have, but from what we are; not from without, but our inner life."[40]

In late September 1893, Nolen returned to Philadelphia determined to find a profession devoted to cultural and social improvement. Edmund James opened the door to the young man's ambition, appointing him assistant secretary to the American Society for the Extension of University Teaching, which James oversaw in addition to directing the Wharton School. Nolen received a $1,000 salary and joined college friends Franklin Edmonds and Cheesman Herrick in this early experiment in adult education. Although the pay was low, the position was well suited to someone eager to make his mark in the world. It had the added benefit of a November first starting date, which allowed Nolen to make a trip to the Chicago World's Fair.[41]

The World's Columbian Exposition captivated Nolen along with millions of other visitors. "It opened my mind to all that is grand and beautiful

and good in the world," he declared. Like t[...]edecessors half a
millennium before, the architects, sculptors, [...]scape architects who
created the White City revealed the benefits of collaboration in civic art. Formal groupings of neoclassical buildings and sculpture were set within a system of parks and plantings designed by Olmsted himself. Late in life, Nolen
wrote that the White City's aesthetic harmony was the product of "a supreme
design" that effectively allocated the placement of buildings "before a single
construction wall was laid."[42]

If the White City's architectural style was overtly classical, its mix of
romantic nature and classical architecture was uniquely American.[43] The
Wooded Island that Olmsted designed for the serpentine lagoon running
from Lake Michigan to the center of the fairgrounds was, in essence, a sacred
grove and a testament to the Arcadian ideal in American design tradition. The
Beaux-Arts movement undoubtedly influenced the architect Daniel Burnham
and his compatriots, but Olmsted's design proved "it was possible for an artist to reconcile the pagan rite with the Christian festival, the satyr with the
saint," according to the Yale urbanist Christopher Tunnard.[44] The White City
offered a glimpse of the future, a place made livable by mixing the wild and
domestic, the sacred and profane. (Fig. 1.5)

Fig. 1.5. *Wooded Island,* Chicago World's Fair, 1893. Photograph by N. D. Thompson Publishing Co. Author's collection.

The brilliant [illegible] their Italian [illegible] and land [illegible] backdrop of Lake Michigan helped initiate the [illegible] erican Renaissance as classical ideals merged with artistic [illegible]al achievement. American civic art was forming a commanding identity. Like other visitors to the White City, Nolen could not believe "the world held so many wonders" after examining the latest marvels of science and industry. He was especially drawn to the Palace of Fine Arts. He wanted to spend an additional week there, but his new job waited. He left Chicago with a new confidence that stirred his ambition and filled him with a "deep desire to do something in this great universe which is going socially onward."[45]

Nolen and Barbara Schatte had met in 1890 at a party hosted by the Perot family in their spacious home in Ardmore, a streetcar suburb of Philadelphia. A wealthy, childless couple, the Perots had taken in Barbara and her two older sisters in 1881, two years after they were orphaned. When the Schatte girls entered their teen years, the Perots invited suitable young men to meet them at supervised Sunday events. Nolen and Frank Zesinger, his close friend from Girard, attended such a party and were drawn to the younger sisters. Zesinger married Emma in 1892; his friend's courtship proceeded at a slower pace.[46]

In 1891, after her high school graduation, Barbara took a job teaching at the James Forten School, a central Philadelphia institution for African Americans and Jewish immigrants that was tied to the Settlement House movement.[47] Nolen was impressed by the noble endeavor. Over the next two years, Schatte and Nolen grew close. She attended his university graduation with the Perots and, after the ceremony, presented him with biographies of Daniel Webster and Henry Clay, books that would occupy a prominent place in his growing library.[48]

Nolen's new job with the American Society for the Extension of University Teaching provided a quick entry into the field of civic reform. Established in 1890, ASEUT was modeled after the English University Extension founded seventeen years before at Cambridge University by R. D. Roberts, who created a center of study to end the monopoly that wealthier classes held on higher education. Roberts wanted to provide laborers with an intellectual foundation to improve their standing and repel "the charge of ignorance which is ever being hurled against the working classes." The Cambridge program transformed those who attended. Upon completion of the night school program, one graduate wrote, "I feel as if I had been a prominent member of a highly civilized community." After its success at Cambridge, the Extension of University Teaching opened a new campus in London. It had a different clientele—business clerks and artisans—but the goal rem▮▮▮▮▮same: "provid-ing busy adults a systematic education of the universi▮▮pe."[49]

In Philadelphia, the ASEUT built its program on the London model, offering a broad liberal arts education to young men and women employed in the trades and business. This effort grew in concert with the outpouring of educational initiatives in the 1890s, including compulsory school atten-dance, lending libraries, debate societies, public lectures, and the Chautauqua. The "Peoples' University," as ASEUT came to be called, fed the appetite of citizens hungry for intellectual challenge.[50] "It is the greatest machinery for enlightening the public," James wrote.[51] For Nolen, it was an opportunity to meet other reformers.[52]

The extension courses offered an alternative to the rote university lec-ture; instructors sought to create interest in subjects rather than simply impart information. The history of classical Greece and Rome, the Renaissance, Eng-lish and French literature, and the writings of John Ruskin were typical of the course offerings, which featured six weekly lectures followed by an interactive "conversational class." The idea that the liberal arts could exert a broad civiliz-ing influence can be traced to Ruskin, one of the most prominent intellectuals of the Victorian era.[53] Nolen became well acquainted with Ruskin's pedagogi-cal principles, which he used to illustrate the ASEUT mission. In his *Annual Report of the Secretary* for the year 1900, Nolen wrote about students finding "opportunities for happiness and for service" when they "see the meaning of the universe" and come "to understand and appreciate art and nature; to enjoy beauty; to see things in their proper relation." Nolen helped establish ASEUT programs in Pennsylvania, New Jersey, and Washington, D.C.; by 1900 more than 180,000 citizens in fifteen states had taken courses.[54]

After the death of her second husband, Nolen's mother returned to Phila-delphia in January 1894 and set about making up for lost years, as her son became the center of her life. Nolen and Frank Edmonds regularly visited her apartment for home-cooked meals, and she provided John with domestic comforts he had rarely experienced. Despite spending much of his youth in an institution, Nolen embraced his mother's attention without bitterness and joined her in creating a life that met needs long denied. The two formed an enduring relationship, as Matilda became a cornerstone in the new family her son would form.[55]

In 1894 Nolen's ASEUT contract expired. But the young reformer had proven his worth, and James hired him to a permanent position as assistant executive secretary and doubled his pay. Secure with his new personal and financial stability, he was ready for marriage. "I do not claim that I am worthy of you, but I ask you to see if you can love me as I am, and Barbara the love that is in me, _____ ote in a long letter to Schatte.[56] The note led to a _____ ed by the Perots, and a formal marriage proposal. There v___ ts between the two, and their letters grew more heartfelt. "What a noble thing true love is," Nolen wrote, "and how it elevates either man or woman, the heart and soul life is deeper and truer than any other. How incomplete the life of a man or woman seems without the opposite. Home is our nearest approach to heaven."[57] Barbara accepted Nolen's proposal October 20, 1894, a date the couple celebrated the rest of their lives. The wedding was set for the spring of 1896 in Ardmore.[58]

After James accepted a position with the University of Chicago and Frank Edmonds headed to Cornell on a graduate fellowship in 1895, Nolen received another raise and additional responsibility. Along with administering ASEUT's regional outreach, Nolen began editing the *Citizen*, the organization's journal. Over the next five years, he reviewed a wide range of articles and developed a particular interest in municipal affairs. He also assumed the role of moderator in the conversation classes, collaborating with professors from Harvard, University of Pennsylvania, Princeton, University of Chicago, and Oxford. He worked alongside W. E. B. Du Bois and Woodrow Wilson, reunited with James Robinson and John McMaster, and developed close friendships with ASEUT's regular lecturers Edward Howard Griggs, Cecil Lavell, and Earl Barnes.[59]

By 1895 Nolen was making a name for himself in reform circles. In May he delivered his first public address at the Girard College commencement, "Stephen Girard: Municipal Statesman." To Nolen, Girard epitomized the municipal statesman, the man who used his standing to improve the lives of others, especially the less fortunate. Combining pragmatic intelligence and principled behavior, Girard had identified a civic ideal and, in Nolen's words, "made it a reality." Since Girard's death, the challenge of the industrial city had become more pressing. To establish a blueprint for the future, Nolen said, experts must place "civic faith" on a rational foundation. Then municipal statesman could forge a city that was as healthy as it was just, where "every man would be both laborer and capitalist." "We might then be tempted to believe in the words of St. John," Nolen declared, "that we saw the Holy City, the New Jerusalem, coming down from God out of Heaven."[60]

The quest to utilize civic faith to build a New Jerusalem—a city of optimal design that fostered health, altruism, and civic loyalty—was a common refrain among urban reformers.[61] The new generation of university-trained experts was determined to build a heavenly city on secular dimensions. They had an evangelical streak, but they were also pragmatic and their optimism was well founded: investments in sanitary sewer and water systems had stymied cholera, utilities were routinely regulated and service improved, and public parks were common.[62] Nolen's position with ASEUT allowed him to hone his interest in urban reform, and as he encountered the wider world, he began to study systematically the innovations that were raising the standard of urban life in the United States and Europe.

After his Girard speech, Nolen traveled to the Seventh Annual Conference of University Extension at Oxford, satisfying a long-standing wish to visit Europe. Touring the English countryside, he encountered a nature aesthetic different from that at home. The picturesque scenes did not have the wild splendor of the Catskills; rather they revealed a human hand active for centuries. Ordered hedgerows and fertile fields blended to create a landscape beautified through agrarian husbandry. He also took in the masterpieces of the eighteenth-century English landscape architects Lancelot "Capability" Brown, William Kent, and Humphry Repton. After the conference, he spent a week in London and then Paris. The French capital, in its belle époque, appealed to his artistic nature and became a favored destination in future travels. In addition to exploring the English landscape and French urbanism, Nolen was plotting the route of his honeymoon.[63] (Fig. 1.6)

John and Barbara Nolen married on April 22, 1896, at St. Mary's Epis-

Fig. 1.6. An example of the English landscape style Nolen emulated. Photograph by Thomas Warren Sears, 1906. Courtesy Division of Rare and Manuscript Collections, Cornell University Library.

copal Church in Ardmore. The Reverend Hudson Shaw, an ASEUT lecturer from Oxford University, assisted the local pastor in performing the marriage rites, and Frank Edmonds served as best man. After the reception the couple headed to the Princeton Inn, gathering cherry blossoms and violets on their way. They spent their time after dinner at Nassau Hall listening to a concert and then visited with Princeton president Woodrow Wilson and his wife before retiring to a honeymoon suite. The next afternoon, thirty friends and family members saw the Nolens off on a six-week European voyage. The cruise was intoxicating, but they spent too much time enjoying the ocean view and suffered severe cases of windburn, yet found humor in looking "like lobsters-boiled." Docking at Liverpool, the newlyweds set off for Wales, after which they journeyed to Stratford-on-Avon, Oxford, York, Edinburgh, and the Lake District. A voyage to Brussels was followed by trips to Cologne and finally Paris. They left the continent intent on returning, especially to Germany, where Barbara had relatives and where John was determined to study.[64]

While the Nolens were abroad, the Perots were overseeing the construction of a new home in Ardmore, where Nolen had purchased a lot. Christened "Blytheham," the spacious two-story Colonial Revival structure was designed by Thomas P. Lonsdale, the architect for the Pennsylvania Building at the Columbian Exposition and a graduate of Girard College.[65] A five-minute walk from the train station, the house was on a 60-by-225-foot lot where Nolen could test his skills as a landscape gardener. Limited to a landscaping budget of $25 a year, Nolen chose perennial and native plants. He bounded the property with a dense line of shrubs to enclose the 50-by-80-foot lawn, and planted thirty trees to frame the house. Along the foundation a layer of low-lying shrubs and a liberal planting of vines served to visually connect the home with its setting. Nolen supplemented the plantings with hardy native species obtained from the nearby woods. Fruit trees—apple, peach, plum, pear, and cherry—and gooseberries, currants, white and red raspberries, and blackberries provided the family with a healthy bounty. In addition, the kitchen garden yielded peas, beans, corn, radishes, lettuce, tomatoes, and celery. Most of the labor was performed by Nolen and his wife, except when aided by the occasional tramp they hired and housed.[66]

Nolen wrote an article in 1905 for *Country Life in America* that described the grounds of Blytheham, noting the contentment and cheer that gardening offered.[67] In addition to supplementing the family's food supply, the landscape was designed so that each room looked out on an idyllic setting. The time spent gardening nurtured Nolen's civic and artistic interests. Envisioning a personal Eden and laboring to make it a reality created beauty, and it also defined the attributes of a good citizen. These labors were rewarded

Fig. 1.7. Blytheham, Nolen's house in Ardmore, Pennsylvania. From *Country Life in America* (August 1905).

professionally, as well. When Nolen opened his landscape architecture practice, Blytheham's gardens and parklike landscape helped earn some of his first commissions. (Fig. 1.7)

Their work together creating Blytheham also solidified John and Barbara's partnership. From the first, the couple agreed to live within their means and "to seek beauty in things which are useful, to have everything simple, plain and good; to avoid things which require great care and labor; to provide hospitality, cheerfulness and variety in housekeeping."[68] In four decades of marriage, the Nolens' dedication to these virtues endured, setting a tone for an amiable home life. They raised four children who went on to graduate from Harvard, Stanford, and the Massachusetts Institute of Technology. Over time, their hospitality became the basis of a thriving network of family and friends that stretched across the United States and Europe.

In 1897 the four-year economic downturn finally ended and Nolen's professional prospects improved. He was elected executive secretary of ASEUT, and the additional administrative responsibilities meant less travel and more time at home. In early 1898 their first child, John Jr., was born. Despite job security and a growing family, Nolen grew increasingly restless. ASEUT's mission of academic outreach was stimulating, but he had begun contemplating a career infused with art and tied to the land. He visited available farm properties with the hope that his landscape gardening skills might transfer

Fig. 1.8. Edward Howard Griggs, 1903. Courtesy Division of Rare and Manuscript Collections, Cornell University Library.

to agrarian husbandry. Returning to Europe also crossed his mind. Studying there, he thought, would be "one of the highest pleasures."[69] When Nolen turned thirty in 1899, his interest in changing careers intensified.

Fortunately, he received sage advice from his colleague and good friend Edward Griggs, with whom he also shared close ties. The families vacationed together, lent each other money when times were hard, cared for each other's children, and provided emotional support at critical moments. Griggs, who struggled with clinical depression, valued Nolen's "unfailing understanding" and "loyal friendship."[70] The two men also shared a love of the outdoors and occasionally spent a week hiking in the mountains of Vermont and New Hampshire. (Fig. 1.8)

Griggs, a professor of ethics at Stanford before heading east, was the ideal companion for the ambitious administrator. One of the most popular lecturers of his day, Griggs was praised for his "easy, flowing style, rich in imagery, full of allusions to history, literature, and art."[71] Nolen moderated discussions of his friend's classes, including Cities of Italy and Their Gift to Civilization, Goethe's *Faust,* and Painters of Florence. The men spent hours in private discussion, delving into the moral basis of government, the relationship between art and civic life, and the essence of beauty.[72] They were both staunch humanists, and Griggs led Nolen to see life as an art that reached its highest form in self-expression.[73]

Nolen and Griggs also shared a fascination with the Italian Renaissance. Like their fifteenth-century predecessors, they rejected doctrinaire religious beliefs. Nolen thought orthodox religion had devolved into a faded esoteric experience that could not address the challenge of modern life. Christianity, he believed, must give way to a "New Humanism."[74] Indeed, *The New Humanism* (1899) was the title of Griggs's first book, which Nolen quoted liberally in both his personal correspondence and the promotional tracts he wrote for ASEUT. Griggs believed moral values should be based on scientific reasoning and the same classical values that had inspired the Italian Renaissance. Lives devoted to reason, beauty, and civic duty would ensue, and just as in fifteenth-century Italy, the merging of capitalism and humanism would advance the American Renaissance.[75]

Griggs, who spent two years in Europe before writing *The New Humanism,* urged Nolen to take a sabbatical and study abroad. The administrator needed little prodding. In 1901 he took a year off from his work at the society and enrolled at the University of Munich. It was a defining decision. In the early twentieth century, Germany was a center of intellectual ferment, and after his experience there, Nolen's life would never be the same.[76]

Before departing, Nolen received counsel from his former professor James Robinson, then at Columbia University. Robinson encouraged him to travel outside Germany and study the Middle Ages before devoting himself to the Renaissance. Frank Edmonds also offered advice, telling his friend to "bring home the culture of Erasmus" and "not lose the patriotism of a Lincoln."[77]

On June 22, 1901, the Nolen family set sail for Hamburg, planning to visit family in Saxony.[78] After two weeks touring Germany, the Nolen and Griggs families met for an extended holiday in the Swiss Alps, which included hikes in the mountains.[79] After their sojourn, Griggs wrote a pantheistic essay, "The Ministry of Nature," which Nolen would later quote in his first city plan.[80]

Nolen visited Lucerne, where, walking its clean streets, he found an unmatched aesthetic unity. Railways and major roads ran in tandem to minimize crossings. Buildings sited at a uniform distance from the street provided the backdrop for civic structures placed at prominent points. He discovered clean and orderly working-class neighborhoods that stood in sharp contrast to the fetid ghettos of Philadelphia. Public gardens and parks were pleasant and easily accessible, especially via the tree-lined esplanades paralleling the public waterfront. A decade later, in his plan for Madison, Wisconsin, Nolen would recall how Lucerne's artistic layout incorporated scenic views, which

Fig. 1.9. Lucerne, Switzerland, c. 1906. Courtesy Division of Rare and Manuscript Collections, Cornell University Library.

provided a dramatic background to a city designed by "an ingenious and studious people."[81] (Fig. 1.9)

The family settled in Munich two weeks before the university opened. Nolen spent much of his free time in the public library reading German newspapers and preparing for his classes in Italian painting, the history of the Renaissance, and German art and architecture, a course taught by Arthur Weese. Aware of Nolen's passionate interest in urban reform, Weese introduced him to German experiments in city planning, which dated back to the 1870s, when Otto von Bismarck constructed a more cohesive industrial nation. Because Germany lacked an abundant supply of land and natural resources, efficiency was sought, and the state empowered city officials to zone land for particular uses. Complementary studies identified the placement of utilities, parks, and transportation systems, and public investments were prioritized.[82]

In 1893, the Viennese architect Camillo Sitte was part of the jury for a competition to design a new plan for Munich. Author of *City Planning According to Artistic Principles* (1889), Sitte was a critic of Paris's Beaux-Arts formalism who championed the concept of "organic design." Sitte was responding to Georges-Eugène Haussmann's efforts to transform medieval Paris into the City of Light; in the process, twenty thousand homes in medieval neighborhoods were razed.[83] In the late 1860s, Vienna had followed the Parisian model with its Ringstrasse plan, and Sitte, a young architect at the time, despaired over the loss of public and religious landmarks. His book traced the source of urban vitality to the historic city's streets and public spaces. Sitte would influence the first generation of professional planners, including Raymond Unwin and Nolen, to merge organic design with Renaissance principles in the practice of the art of city planning.[84]

Nolen's professor Theodore Fisher, who had helped implement the Munich plan, introduced his American student to the "Sittesche Schule" of design.[85] Nolen was soon studying the relationship between private buildings, plazas, and public greens and gaining a working knowledge of "civic art." In 1902 he came to appreciate the broader field of city planning after attending the second International Housing Congress in Düsseldorf. The German industrial center must have seemed like a Wharton School project for an ideal city—arranged to conserve resources, limit waste, house workers in sanitary environs, and move traffic and goods efficiently.[86] Düsseldorf illustrated, Nolen later wrote, "the scientific basis and painstaking thoroughness which underlie German city planning."[87] (Fig. 1.10)

Nolen's interest in civic art and urban planning intensified as he adapted to life in Germany. He regularly attended plays, the opera, and concerts, and

Fig. 1.10. Dusseldorf Housing Project. Courtesy Division of Rare and Manuscript Collections, Cornell University Library.

Fig. 1.11. Worker Housing in Frankfurt, Germany. Photograph by B. A. Haldeman, 1911.
Courtesy Division of Rare and Manuscript Collections, Cornell University Library.

beer gardens also had appeal. The Bavarian capital's rich public life surpassed anything he had experienced in England or the United States. His small family embraced the local culture; they celebrated Christmas in Bavarian fashion and sang traditional holiday songs in German. They spent New Year's in the nearby mountains enjoying walks through pine forests and a memorable sledding expedition. Living in Germany confirmed Nolen's belief that investment in the public good—from subsidizing worker housing to efficiently placing utilities—was integral to improving urban life.[88] (Fig. 1.11)

In March 1902 the family headed south, eager to escape the cold and visit Italy. In Florence, Nolen immersed himself in the wonders of the city's art, architecture, and history, savoring the Tuscan spring at the time E. M. Forster began writing *A Room with a View*. Early in the book a chaplain leading a group of English tourists exclaims, "In these days of toil and tumult one has great needs of the country and its message of purity. Andate via! Andate presto, presto! Ah, the town! Beautiful as it is, it is the town."[89] Forster's "message of purity" resonated on both sides of the Atlantic. Nolen understood that the future lay in planning both the city and the countryside. He saw how the placement of Tuscan cities and towns echoed the natural topography and enhanced the civic realm. Given the explosive growth of the American city, it was essential to emulate this organic method of planning.[90] After dedicating himself to the study of the Italian Renaissance, he was determined to practice an art that could delight and serve America's rising urban population.

Nolen had arrived in Europe with a general concept of civic art and urban reform; he returned to the United States grounded in the nascent discipline of city planning. Sailing from Genoa in early June, he could only hope a door would open to his ambitions. The key to a new life awaited in the form of a homecoming gift—the president of Harvard's new book, *Charles Eliot: Landscape Architect* (1902). It was a biography of his son, "a lover of nature and his kind who trained himself for a new profession."[91]

Fig. 2.1. Central Park. Photograph by John Nolen, 1908. Courtesy Division of Rare and Manuscript Collections, Cornell University Library.

2

LANDSCAPE ARCHITECT, 1902–1905

Reading *Charles Eliot, Landscape Architect* stirred Nolen's ambition and spirit. "President Eliot's book is sacred," he proclaimed in a letter to Alan Harris, an Englishman associated with the university extension.[1] The handsomely illustrated biography and anthology recounted the life of a lover of nature, planner, and park advocate. Before his death at age thirty-seven, Charles Eliot had expanded his expertise to include regional park planning, and his work led to the establishment of the Trustees of Public Reservations, the nation's first land conservancy. Nolen, who turned thirty-three in July 1902, was impressed with Eliot's accomplishments. By summer's end, he found himself considering attending Harvard University to study landscape architecture. In September, after an event in New Jersey with the American Society for the Extension of University Teaching, Nolen made a special trip to explore Central Park and contemplate his future.[2]

As he walked across Sheep Meadow in the late afternoon, Nolen noticed how the placement of shrubs, trees, and grass created a play of light and shadow similar to the effect of a Jean-Baptiste-Camille Corot painting. At twilight he discovered the park's center, the Ramble, crossed its rugged terrain, and emerged by the lake. (Fig. 2.1) "Central Park is more beautiful than I thought—so hilly and rocky—and if I can I shall get another glimpse," he wrote to his wife.[3] Nolen did not return on that trip, but his wanderings through the park and Eliot's example convinced him to leave ASEUT and take up landscape architecture.

It was Eliot's life experience, as much as his skill as a practitioner, that inspired Nolen to become a landscape architect. Like Nolen, Eliot lost a parent at a young age. He was nine years old when his mother died and his father assumed the Harvard presidency. Over the next eight years, the shy, awkward first son grew apart from his father. The boy began to regain a sense of security and self-confidence after his father remarried in 1877. In addition to developing a relationship with his stepmother, he began pursuing the "strenuous life" to combat what he called a "'shrinking' habit." Hiking and boating ventures, coupled with drawing and mapping exercises, gave the teenager direction and fostered an interest in applying his artistic skills. While a student at Harvard he spent two summers camping near Mt. Desert, Maine, and was finally able to shake free of his personal malaise.[4]

After graduating from Harvard in 1881, Eliot decided to practice landscape architecture, a profession that was then hardly known outside Boston and New York. With the blessing of his father, an advocate of pragmatic education, he embarked on a course of study in agricultural chemistry, horticulture, applied zoology, applied entomology, and farm management, followed by a practicum in topographical surveying.[5] After a year of "practical gardening" at Harvard's Bussey Institute, he secured the first apprenticeship in Olmsted Sr.'s office.[6] Eliot's quiet nature, discipline, and artistic sensibilities won over his often harried mentor, who had moved his office to Brookline in 1883. The elder man appreciated his apprentice's blossoming talents and encouraged him to build on his skills as a writer. In 1885 Eliot decided to study landscape gardening in Europe. He spent a year analyzing a spectrum of landscapes, sending his studies back to Olmsted's office in a series of letters that were later edited by his father for publication in *Charles Eliot, Landscape Architect*. Eliot became one of the era's most articulate critics, an idealist who inspired a generation of landscape architects.[7]

Eliot returned to the United States and entered private practice in 1886, an opportune time for members of his field. Beginning in the early 1880s, Boston's explosive growth pushed long-standing civic issues to the forefront of the municipal agenda. Elite citizens in Boston and Cambridge were investing in improving the arts, the civic landscape, and public health, and their patronage allowed the Olmsteds and Eliot to pursue landscape design.[8]

In 1891 Eliot joined the journalist Sylvester Baxter, a champion of Edward Bellamy's widely read utopian novel *Looking Backward* (1888), to lobby for the creation of a metropolitan park board.[9] A year later, Eliot was named lead consultant to the newly formed Metropolitan Park Commission in Boston. The group was chaired by Charles Francis Adams, son of former president John Quincy Adams, and Baxter served as commission secretary. Eliot's genius was to integrate and extend earlier plans and projects for the Boston region into

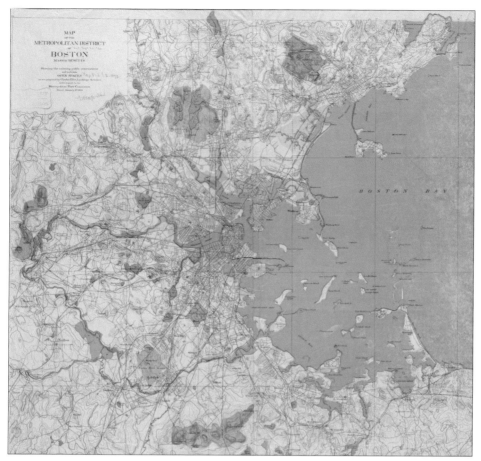

Fig. 2.2. Map of the Metropolitan District of Boston. From *Report of the Board of Metropolitan Park Commissioners* (January 1893).

a study titled *Report of the Board of Metropolitan Park Commissioners* (1893). The report's text, maps, and hand-drawn illustrations presented the vision of an "Emerald Metropolis" where parkways linked a variety of parks running from Revere Beach to outlying natural preserves, or "reservations."[10] (Fig. 2.2) The reservations were utilitarian as well as beautiful, especially where native forests surrounded lakes that were part of the Boston municipal water supply. Eliot dismissed the notion that because lands were "wild" they should be left untouched. A series of drawings showed how improvements, including selective logging to open views and replanting decimated stands of native forest, could enhance the vitality of the landscape and the visitor's experience.

The timing of the report could not have been worse. As the nation slid into a four-year depression beginning in 1893, the Metropolitan Park Commission's funds shrank, slowing the implementation of Eliot's plan.[11] After Eliot's death Baxter kept the project alive, and in the early 1900s it came to

Fig. 2.3. Charles River Esplanade. Courtesy Division of Rare and Manuscript Collections, Cornell University Library.

fruition. Stands of native forests were preserved and, after a new dam was completed in 1910, promenades were built along the Charles River where mud flats once existed. (Fig. 2.3) Bostonians came to partake of the more "congenial outdoor life"[12] that Eliot envisioned, and landscape architecture evolved along the path he helped pioneer. His program of self-education provided the basis for Harvard's curriculum, while the *Report of the Board of Metropolitan Park Commissioners* became a prototype for city and regional plans in the United States and Europe.[13] It was also a work of moral persuasion that inspired such visionaries as Lewis Mumford and Ian McHarg.[14]

Olmsted Sr. and Eliot had defined the profession of landscape architecture, and John Nolen was determined to advance their legacy. In early 1903 he applied to Harvard University's Department of Landscape Architecture. "My experience in selecting the profession is not unlike Charles Eliot's," he wrote.[15] For both men, landscape architecture was a calling as much a profession. It was a means to work in the outdoors and to practice an art predicated on advancing the public good. The committee that reviewed Nolen's application was impressed: an Ivy League degree, a semester at the University of Munich, a decade as a college administrator, and experience as a landscape gardener. Nolen had recently published "Aid from University Extension Methods," an article for the *Library Journal* emphasizing informing the "intelligence of public opinion" as indispensable to social progress.[16] The Philadelphian's interest and success in promoting civic affairs appealed to the young Harvard faculty, which was looking for students who could sell the profession as well as practice it. Nolen was awarded a $300 scholarship and second-year undergraduate status with the condition that he enroll in a summer school drawing class.[17]

Nolen accepted the offer, but with some trepidation. Barbara had recently given birth to their second child—also named Barbara—and selling his beloved Blytheham to move a growing family to a rented home in Cambridge tested his resolve. Yet, he had habitually taken calculated risks to move ahead in the world. Keeping to Girard's creed of simplicity, civic-mindedness, and moderation had served him well, instilling him with a tempered optimism and a quiet confidence. These attributes stand out in Nolen's resignation letter to ASEUT: "I look back with the greatest satisfaction notwithstanding that my attainments are moderate; I believe I have been able, through persistent and well-directed effort, to contribute something of value to the society."[18]

His colleagues Edward Griggs and Cecil Lavell strongly supported their friend's decision to leave the society. "Heading to Harvard—'the land of promise'—a dream come true," Griggs wrote, adding: "My best wishes go with you, dear fellow. It's a kind of beginning of the 'new life' isn't it?"[19] Starting anew would be, Lavell noted, "ever happier than [staying] with the Extension."[20] Once Nolen took up residence in Cambridge that August, there was no looking back. "I fasten my mind steadfastly upon the new life and its glorious promise of usefulness, contentment, health, and independence."[21]

On August 28, 1903, three weeks before Nolen started classes, Olmsted Sr. died. The great reformer had founded the profession of landscape architecture, and the Harvard faculty was determined to safeguard his legacy while charting a path for the future. Nolen's arrival was well timed. As the historian Jon Peterson writes, Nolen "burst upon the scene, almost as if he were a gift of the gods, sent to replace the prematurely deceased Charles Eliot, who, had he lived, might have led the profession."[22]

When Nolen entered Harvard, landscape architecture was a promising but fledgling department. In 1896 Harvard's president Charles W. Eliot and Nathaniel Southgate Shaler, dean of the Lawrence Scientific School, had decided that the younger Eliot, then in the firm of Olmsted, Olmsted, and Eliot, would teach the first course in landscape architecture. But Eliot's untimely death the next year altered their plan. In 1900, Charles W. Eliot established the nation's first four-year degree program in landscape architecture in memory of his son. Frederick Law Olmsted Jr. and Arthur Shurcliff were the program's first instructors, and Shaler presided as dean.[23] The department's charge was to instruct students in the technical elements of land analysis and the principles of design to prepare them for professional practice;

the curriculum followed the general course of study that Eliot had devised as a self-taught student of landscape architecture fifteen years earlier.[24] Classes in architecture, forestry, engineering, horticulture, geology, and botany supported a two-semester landscape architecture course and practicums taught by Olmsted Jr. and Shurcliff.[25]

Olmsted Jr. served as chair, shuttling between his private practice in Brookline and the Department of Architecture where the new program was headquartered. He held the Charles Eliot Chair of Landscape Architecture, a professorship established by Nelson Robinson, who also funded the construction of Robinson Hall, where the department was housed. By 1903 the program's first two graduates, Henry Vincent Hubbard and Charles Downing Lay, were already earning commissions. The next year, Hubbard joined the faculty, one that was steeped in practice and committed to establishing an academic discipline. They had all worked in the Olmsted office, and the firm's projects in Boston and New York provided an extended classroom.

Upon taking up his studies at Harvard, Nolen described how his interest in the past inspired his ambitions. "The word 'Athens' stirs ones imagination and awakens one memory as only a few words can. The combination of the ancient Greek—his love of beauty and of health, and above all his *perfect balance* is one that we need as much as ever today."[26] Fortunately for Nolen, the city of Boston, the "Athens of America," was pursuing a reform agenda enlivened by classical ideals. The Boston Public Library epitomized these ambitions. Designed in 1895 by the New York firm of McKim, Mead, and White, the Beaux-Arts structure inspired a generation of architects. Harvard and the Massachusetts Institute of Technology provided a wellspring of local talent in the fields of architecture and landscape architecture. Guy Lowell, the scion of a Boston Brahmin family who designed landscapes as well as buildings, typified the genius of the time. His 1902 book *American Gardens* was consulted by a generation of landscape architects eager to find inspiration from the Italian Renaissance for their own work.[27]

The ancient Greeks and Romans brought urban civilization to new heights, finding meaning and sustenance in a fertile countryside, and Bostonians were determined to do the same.[28] This desire to reconnect with the forests and fields helped bring Eliot's vision to fruition. While Nolen was at Harvard, the Metropolitan Park Commission acquired 9,300 acres of parkland in seventeen municipalities, including over fifty acres of waterfront along the region's three main rivers, bringing new opportunities for recreation, nature study, and aesthetic appreciation to a population eager to enjoy the outdoors.[29] Early-twentieth-century reformers were no longer content with offering passive recreation to anxious urban dwellers; they wanted to produce a fit populace and shape human behavior toward civic ends.[30] Social justice was also part of the equation, as Eliot had written: "what would be fair, must first be fit."[31] The goal, then, was to clean, order, and sanctify a discordant environment that inhibited human progress, an agenda that reformers pursued with religious devotion.

"The country is manifestly at the dawn of a great civic awakening," Sylvester Baxter proclaimed in 1902 after reviewing plans to improve the public landscape in Boston and New York.[32] This "civic awakening" spread from the urban Northeast with a zeal that matched the religious awakenings of the early eighteenth and nineteenth centuries. It grew into a full-fledged crusade to save democracy under the banner of progressivism, which was dedicated to reforming the urban environment and its institutions.[33] Frederic C. Howe summarized the situation in *The City: The Hope of Democracy* (1905): "The corruption, the indifference, the incompetence of the official and the apathy of the citizen, the disparity of wealth, the poverty, vice, crime, and disease, are due to causes economic and industrial. They are traceable to our institutions, rather than the depravity of human nature. And in consequence the city will no longer be an incidental problem. It has already become the problem of society and the measure of our civilization."[34]

The planning of cities based on the concepts of utility and conservation was part of Nolen's education at the Wharton School. Under President Theodore Roosevelt, conservation moved from an ideal to public policy. During his administration more than two million acres of forests, parks, monuments, and wildlife refuges were placed in the public domain, and laws were established to strengthen the ability of federal agencies to protect such lands from exploitation. Conservation, perhaps the purest expression of progressivism, encapsulated the desire to refurbish Americans' relationship with the land. By 1900 reformers were laboring to shape a landscape that would be more sustaining for future generations and more representative of a people who value both the right to property and the quality of the land they hold in common. Conservation wove a new morality into the national fabric, and protecting natural resources was pursued by progressives with the same fervor as urban reform.[35]

Nolen's class at Harvard counted eleven students, but he seems to have formed his closest relationships with the faculty, men of similar age and ambition. Nolen was then thirty-four years old, Olmsted Jr. and Arthur Shurcliff were thirty-three, James Sturgis Pray, a former assistant in the Olmsted firm, was thirty-two, and Henry Hubbard was twenty-eight.[36] It was a talented group, though untested. As dean, Nathaniel Southgate Shaler, a geologist by training, tied the department's mission to an emergent environmental ethic. Shaler was a respected spokesman in the field of conservation, and his final book, *Man and the Earth* (1905), called for responsible land stewardship in the face of increased industrialization.[37] In his first year at Harvard, Nolen offered his own assessment of the situation: "Only nature could check the modern rush for money."[38]

Initially Nolen chafed over the long hours spent indoors rather than in the field. His disenchantment fell away, however, when he entered Olmsted Jr.'s classroom.[39] Under the department chair's guidance, he learned to integrate the fields of horticulture, forestry, architecture, and civil engineering. His first course with Olmsted Jr., Landscape Architecture I, surveyed the evolution of the discipline from an art to a profession. Olmsted traced the origins of landscape architecture to the gardens of ancient Rome, and he also discussed the influence of landscape painting.[40] Nolen became aware of artists from Claude Lorraine to Thomas Gainsborough, whose work reflected the reverence for the natural world that Alexander Pope extolled in his poetry.[41] J. M. W. Turner's paintings were discussed as spectacles of light and shadow, his hazy views inspiring contemplation.[42] The era's fascination with the sublime appealed to a society desiring natural beauty but committed to industrial progress. For John Ruskin, who praised Turner and whose *Modern Painters* was required reading in the course, nature revealed moral law, "the perfectness and beauty of the work of God."[43] Ruskin advocated immersion in nature to find truth, a chief tenet of the philosophy behind the emerging profession of American landscape architecture.

In the early twentieth century, students of landscape architecture no longer analyzed painted scenes to learn design technique, as Eliot had done under Olmsted Sr.'s tutelage.[44] However, landscape painting did inspire aesthetic sensibilities. After the Landscape Architecture I course, Nolen was determined to lecture on the subject, for he felt it was essential to elevate "public taste" and lead it "in the right direction," as he wrote to Alan Harris.[45] Nolen had met Harris in London through ASEUT, and the Englishman became a mentor. The two exchanged long letters on the attributes of the well-designed city and good art. Harris also paid for Nolen's subscriptions to professional journals such as *Der Städtebau* and sent Nolen photos of urban scenes and reproductions of landscape paintings. After hanging a Corot print from Harris over his desk, Nolen felt duly inspired to continue his studies. Corot's unaffected naturalness and realistic depiction of rural life not only epitomized good art for Nolen, but also expressed the joyful humanism he hoped to elicit in the places he designed.[46] (Fig. 2.4)

The Italian Renaissance garden was the next subject introduced in the course. Its "remarkable development of form and symmetry," Olmsted Jr. noted, reflected a fundamental shift in human consciousness.[47] In contrast to the cloistered medieval garden, the late-fifteenth-century gardens

Fig. 2.4. Nolen included the Jean-Baptiste-Camille Corot painting *Pastorale* (1873) in one of his presentations, c. 1906. Courtesy Division of Rare and Manuscript Collections, Cornell University Library.

adorning Florentine villas offered vistas that encouraged the contemplation of the horizon. These gardens often contained a *bosco sacro*, where a statue of Pan, the epitome of wild nature, stood on the edge of a stand of trees. The *bosco* hinted at the new desire to step beyond civilization and explore nature's wildness.[48] The growing interest in outdoor recreation demanded a new pattern in the development of American cities. Creating an aesthetic equilibrium between the built and natural environments was the task of the landscape architect, and the Italian Renaissance garden was the starting point—even though Olmsted Jr. lamented that the subtlety of these gardens was lost to the "crudeness characteristic of our people today . . . who could only appreciate geometric design."[49]

After receiving an introduction to classical and Renaissance gardens, students analyzed the contrast between Versailles and the informal gardens designed by William Kent, Lancelot "Capability" Brown, and Humphry Repton. The course concluded with an overview of Olmsted Sr.'s most important commissions, including the Emerald Necklace, Central Park, Prospect Park, Mount Royal Park, and the parks and parkways of Buffalo. After identifying the "controlling purpose" of each plan, students assessed the project's accessibility, physical characteristics, quality of scenery, and economic value. The instructor included an array of slides illustrating how each plan had come to fruition.[50]

Another highlight of Nolen's first year was Denman W. Ross's course in design theory. Ross was a painter, art collector, and lecturer. His seminal work, *A Theory of Pure Design: Harmony, Balance, and Rhythm* (1907), extended Ruskin's thesis of "truth to nature" by offering a "formalistic aesthetic," a series of universal design principles used to assess works of art. He combined the analysis of historical precedents with recent discoveries in psychology and biology to help students evaluate artistic composition. A leader in his field, Ross proposed establishing a Graduate School of Design at Harvard in the mid-1920s, a decade before Joseph Hudnut, the dean of the Harvard School of Architecture, used the same term in his scheme to replicate the German Bauhaus in Cambridge. A devotee of the Renaissance, Ross assigned texts by Leonardo da Vinci, and his model for graduate education was the Accademia delle Arti del Disegno, which flourished in fifteenth-century Florence.[51] "Art is life," Ross told Nolen's class, "for it is only through expression that we realize our ideas and ideals." Whether in ancient Greece or twentieth-century America, good art inspired virtue, the essence of republican civilization.[52] "Art for life's sake, not art for art's sake" became a central tenet of Nolen's practice, and it originated with Denman Ross.[53]

In his first year at Harvard, Nolen also learned about trees, shrubs, and groundcovers, the composition of soils, and topography. Ross provided the template to translate this knowledge into plans that highlighted natural features. Nolen's drawing skill was improving, and he had an aptitude for harmonizing the varied components of a landscape into a balanced design. Confident in his ability, he decided to pursue a master of arts in landscape architecture at the conclusion of his second semester. That summer, he also started his own practice.

Nolen earned his first commission from Joseph Fels, one of Philadelphia's leading industrialists and an ASEUT benefactor. After planning improvements for the grounds of Fels's large Westside soap factory, Nolen found work in Ardmore. Thanks to lobbying by the Perots, he earned contracts to design landscape plans for several private residences.[54] With a new stream of income, the Nolen family ended a period of austerity, and by summer's end they had settled into a rented home in a quiet neighborhood near the Cambridge Public Library. There were regular outings to Revere Beach and Franklin Park, Harvard was an easy walk, and John and Barbara were tending a sizable garden. Although finances were still tight, the family camped for two weeks on Orr's Island in Casco Bay, Maine. Ever the entrepreneur, Nolen gained a client while there and came back the next summer with a landscape plan for a residence on nearby Bailey Island.[55]

Nolen returned to Harvard that fall more confident in his skills. In September he was elected president of the Landscape Club. Much to his delight, he was enrolled in a battery of practical courses: forestry, planting design, and Landscape Architecture II, which incorporated a series of field studies. At last, he noted in a letter to Harris, he was applying his knowledge outside the classroom.[56] Olmsted Jr. expected students in the Landscape Architecture II course to be well acquainted with a park system's components: boulevards, parkways, urban squares, neighborhood parks, scenic reservations, and rural parks. The Emerald Necklace was their laboratory. Nolen prepared a series of reports that culminated with a detailed assessment of Franklin Park. The lay of the land held "much of the sylvan grace that is idealized by such landscape painters as Claude Lorrain, Constable, and Corot," he noted, but city officials had not fully implemented the plan Olmsted had drawn twenty years before. It was time to follow through and "pay the debt owed to the creative mind of Frederick Law Olmsted." Nolen also assessed a series of urban squares—Winthrop Square, Foothill Square, Broadway Square, and Chelsea Square—and produced a proposal to link the parks of Worcester, Massachusetts, with a new parkway system.[57] (Fig. 2.5)

The semester's highlight was a tour of Central Park and Brooklyn's Prospect Park led by Olmsted Jr. Any misgivings Nolen had about the lack of pragmatic application in the Harvard curriculum vanished after this outing.[58] Prospect Park's ninety-acre Long Meadow seemingly stretched beyond the horizon, and for Nolen, perusing it on a clear autumn day was more like a religious experience than academic study. Four decades after Calvert Vaux and Olmsted Sr. had executed their plan, masses of trees were reaching maturity to create an idyllic escape. "I have never seen such coloring, the tupelos, the maples have a glory beyond mention," Nolen wrote.[59] The Long Meadow epitomized designs that fostered "the genius of place," the guiding principle in the second-year landscape architecture course.[60] (Fig. 2.6) The ability to highlight a site's definitive features—rocky outcroppings, shorelines, wooded hills, and grassy meadows—without undue embellishment was a skill

Fig. 2.5. Franklin Park. Photograph by John Nolen, 1904. Courtesy Division of Rare and Manuscript Collections, Cornell University Library.

Fig. 2.6. Long Meadow. Photograph by John Nolen, 1904. Courtesy Division of Rare and Manuscript Collections, Cornell University Library.

practiced in ancient Rome and raised to an art form by Capability Brown, Humphry Repton, and Olmsted Sr. Nolen was taught to dispense with flower-beds and formal gardens to create a naturalistic appearance. Stunted and diseased trees were to be removed and indigenous trees and shrubs planted to ensure the integrity of nature. "Modification around natural limitations" was allowed, provided the designer did not detract from the existing beauty. When it came to land subdivision, a team of experts was required. "Cooperation between the landscape architect and the architect" was essential," Nolen wrote in his class notes.[61]

A centerpiece of the Harvard curriculum was Olmsted and Vaux's 1868 plan for the Chicago suburb of Riverside. The model suburb was a staple problem in Olmsted Jr.'s exams, for which students were asked to subdivide land based on functional and aesthetic considerations. Riverside occupied a 1,600-acre rectangular site on a commuter rail line nine miles west of Chicago. (Fig. 2.7) The floodplain of the Des Plaines River was enveloped in a park, a green backbone that ran roughly north to south through the community. At the park's juncture with the rail line, the town center was laid out on a grid parallel to the east–west railway, but the rest of Riverside broke from the

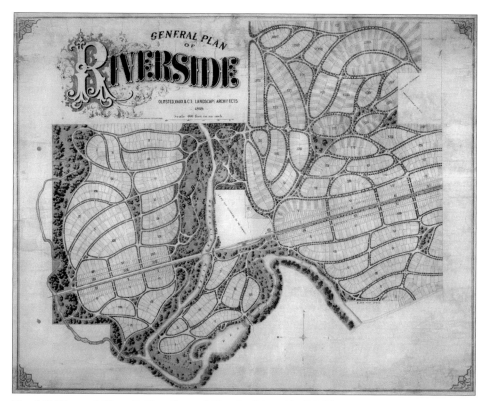

Fig. 2.7. Olmsted, Vaux & Co., General Plan for Riverside (1869). Courtesy Riverside Historical Museum.

traditional arrangement. A curvilinear system of roadways conformed to the site's topography, helping to accentuate natural drainage patterns. Small triangular parks were placed at intersections, and linear green spaces ran between neighborhoods. Riverside offered a prototype for channeling the rising flood of urbanization. Designing suburbs required the application, Olmsted Sr. wrote, of "the arts of civilization."[62]

During his last semester, Nolen began to define landscape architecture in his own terms. "The quiet escape and mental refreshment and enjoyment, which can only be derived from the quiet contemplation of natural scenery, is found only in a large, rural park," Nolen wrote in his class notes. But he then added, "I question this statement."[63] Since exploring the open spaces and woods at Girard College, Nolen had experienced design and nature on a variety of scales. In Europe he indulged his senses in public gardens. At Blytheham he labored to create an Arcadian retreat, and in Cambridge he turned a small yard into an edible delight. Even the walk to Harvard each day held promise, a time to observe subtle seasonal shifts and take in remnants of the natural landscape. Nolen appreciated Olmsted Sr.'s maxim to "re-create," but having spent most of his childhood in an institution, he had a different concept of recreation. Girard College allocated basic necessities in utilitarian fashion, a regimen that, Nolen believed, created community and inspired virtue. Among Harvard's landscape architects he would champion a "democracy of recreation" to ensure that children and adults were provided with the opportunity to experience the outdoors.[64] Nolen wanted the public to interact with nature, not just contemplate its artistic beauty. In 1905 he stood some distance from his colleagues, most of whom focused on aesthetics rather than utility in the practice of their profession.[65] (Fig. 2.8)

Nolen's pragmatic predilection was apparent in his analysis of Cambridge's Winthrop Square, a 90-by-150-foot historic green centered on a Civil War memorial. The public site appeared pleasant enough until one inspected it more closely. Nolen found the shrubbery filthy and the site strewn with "waste paper, leather, rags, cigarettes butts, barrel hoops, old stockings, whiskey bottles, tin cans, old shoes and much worse." Unemployed men occupied its three benches day and night. The only other group to use the space was children, but no play area was offered. Nolen recommended purchasing an adjacent vacant lot to meet the recreational needs of the children and after several more visits he realized the site could serve adults as well. He designated two small sections of the park for trees and shrubs, creating a setting of quiet repose in the heavily populated district.[66] The report he wrote for his class earned him an A+.

By his final semester, Nolen had surpassed the faculty's expectations. His

Fig. 2.8. Central Park. Photograph by John Nolen, 1908. Courtesy Division of Rare and Manuscript Collections, Cornell University Library.

thoroughness and analytical abilities, particularly in the practicums, won the trust of Frederick Law Olmsted Jr. In early 1905, Olmsted Jr. asked Nolen to take on a special project, writing a biography of his father.[67] The following February, the first of four installments of "Frederick Law Olmsted and His Work: An Appreciation by John Nolen" appeared in *House and Garden*.[68] Four projects of varied scope—Montreal's Mount Royal Park, the grounds of the U.S. Capitol, the Schlesinger estate (in Brookline, Massachusetts), and Franklin Park—were systematically analyzed, with an impressive array of photos accompanying the text. If the list represented only a small number of commissions, the articles nevertheless revealed a great deal about the author. Nolen described his subject in terms that might equally apply to himself; Olmsted Sr. was a Renaissance man who valued nature, self-education, and public service. A pragmatic reformer, Olmsted founded "an art peculiarly suited to American conditions in high service of the American people."[69]

In the final installment, Nolen hinted at his own concept of landscape architecture. Olmsted had established a secure foundation, he noted, but the profession must develop by taking on still broader issues ranging from disease mitigation to procuring play areas for children. As the urban landscape became more functional, practitioners should remain dedicated to creating "ennobling environments" that "drew inspiration from nature."[70]

Before he left Harvard, Nolen began collaborating with Olmsted Jr. on a second writing project. As chair of Harvard's landscape architecture department, Olmsted Jr. was determined to establish a set of guiding principles for a budding profession. In the early 1900s, it was common practice for specialized fields to establish criteria for interpreting knowledge and to create procedures for executing duties.[71] The article, "Normal Requirements of American Towns and Cities in Respect to Public Open Space," presented the means to meet the profession's goal of providing the "opportunity for exercise and for the enjoyment of outdoor beauty." The park system was divided into seven components: boulevards, parkways, city squares, playgrounds, neighborhood parks, large parks, and nature reservations. Integrating the different park types into a comprehensive system limited inefficiencies and ensured that "clear thinking" predominated. This was essential if the profession was to develop, the authors concluded, "a widening of aims, a finer discrimination, and expansion of the ideas of service."[72]

In the spring of 1905, Nolen was not only writing, but also preparing for the birth of another child, completing his degree, and building his practice. Two months before graduation, Charles W. Eliot recommended Nolen for what would become his first civic commission. To the student's great pleasure, Olmsted Jr. excused him from final exams to pursue "productive work" with the Park and Tree Commission of Charlotte, North Carolina.[73]

3

CHARLOTTE, LETCHWORTH, AND SAVANNAH, 1905–1907

In April 1905, George Stephens, the secretary-treasurer of the Park and Tree Commission in Charlotte, had contacted the president of Harvard to find a reputable landscape architect who could design a model park system for North Carolina's largest city. After receiving Nolen's name, Stephens wrote to the novice practitioner describing the opportunity and requesting a fee schedule. Nolen's rate of $25 a day plus expenses was more than expected, but with references from Charles W. Eliot and Horace J. McFarland, president of the American Civic Association, Stephens convinced the commissioners to award Nolen the contract.[1]

Stephens had high hopes for the fast-growing Piedmont region. A year before hiring Nolen, he had been instrumental in establishing the Charlotte Park and Tree Commission, one of the first such organizations in the South. There were only two city parks—Vance Square, established in 1890 on land granted to the municipality after the closure of the U.S. Mint building—and Settlers Cemetery, but the decision to build a new municipal reservoir outside of town presented another potential park site.[2] (Fig. 3.1) To generate enthusiasm for the new project, Stephens looked to Charlotte's most respected civic leader, Daniel Augustus Tompkins.[3] In a presentation to the Board of Aldermen, Tompkins convinced civic leaders to support a park commission and allot funds for improving the abandoned reservoir, which later became Independence Park.[4]

Arriving in Charlotte in mid-June, Nolen encountered a "real southern town, hot everywhere, squalid in parts, but as the South goes not unpromis-

Fig. 3.1. Settlers Cemetery. Photograph by John Nolen, 1906. Courtesy Division of Rare and Manuscript Collections, Cornell University Library.

ing."[5] With a population of 20,000, Charlotte was a center of banking and a key rail depot for the Piedmont's textile industry. The city's rapid urbanization and rising prosperity had galvanized talk of a New South, but Charlotte was still characterized by a rural mindset, poverty, and legal apartheid. The aldermen had created the park commission with a stipulation barring African Americans from city parks, except for nurses caring for white children.[6] (Fig. 3.2) Nolen found the state of race relations unsettling, but had little time to ponder Jim Crow laws.[7] After meeting his host, George Stephens, Nolen immersed himself in the history of the commission and its efforts to create a viable park system.

Fig. 3.2. Downtown Charlotte. Photograph by John Nolen, 1906. Courtesy Division of Rare and Manuscript Collections, Cornell University Library.

On his second day in Charlotte, Nolen was up before dawn and ready to venture into the surrounding countryside with two commissioners to inspect potential sites. The first to mount his horse, Nolen was suddenly off at a dead gallop. "Hanging on like grim death," the novice equestrian traveled a mile down Charlotte's busiest street before the horse suddenly stopped and its rider jumped off. Nolen had mounted his patron's steed by mistake, and after a good laugh the journey proceeded. He spent the next two days on horseback examining farmland, lakes nestled between foothills, and a forest of live oaks mixed with magnolias and hickories. In town, Nolen studied the land set aside for Independence Park and a series of smaller scenic parcels. At the end of the week, he presented his findings to the commission.[8]

Nolen, the "well known Northern landscape artist," as the *Charlotte Observer* reported, proposed the creation of a system of parks. He presented a prioritized list of sites, which were located in a three-mile area between the downtown and the countryside. The investment in forests, lakes, and rolling landscape offered more than aesthetics; it represented a business expense. And the returns—higher property values, the mitigation of environmental damage, and a healthier population—were priceless. He offered several options for parkland acquisition, including issuing bonds, fee simple acquisition, and property assessments, but the cooperation of landowners would be most important.[9] Stephens had donated land for Independence Park to enhance an adjacent real estate project, and the Park and Tree Commission willingly accepted Nolen's advice.

The creation of Independence Park marked an important first step for the Charlotte commission. The sinuous seventeen-acre site held "great beauty," Nolen reported, particularly in its pleasant views of the surrounding countryside. His preliminary plan showed a system of curving walkways and an informal planting pattern designed to enhance the natural setting. The commission unanimously approved the plan before moving on to discuss the creation of a city park system.[10] After the meeting, Nolen was ebullient. He enjoyed working with Stephens and even contemplated opening a branch office in Charlotte.[11] But the venture would have to wait—he had little time to do more than read the newspaper's account of his presentation before hurrying back to Cambridge for commencement ceremonies.

On June 27, 1905, Nolen graduated from Harvard with a master of arts in landscape architecture, with President Theodore Roosevelt in attendance. He immediately opened an office at Harvard Square and also enrolled in a summer-term public speaking course at Harvard. Despite being a respectable orator since his debating days at the University of Pennsylvania, Nolen felt he lacked a special gift for speaking. At the American Society for the Extension of University Teaching he had learned to organize and moderate public lectures, but now as a consultant he occupied center stage. To present his message more engagingly, Nolen began experimenting with using a stereopticon in his lectures. Projecting glass lantern slides onto a screen, he could show an audience the coordinated lines of a park plan and images of landscape masterpieces that unveiled the potential of a project or site. By August Nolen had started building a slide collection that would eventually number in the thousands.[12] His presentations became an art form, integrating aesthetic images and technical drawings to illustrate the value and benefits of his plans. (Fig. 3.3)

Having completed projects in Pennsylvania, Maine, New Hampshire, Massachusetts, and New Jersey, Nolen was ready to focus on Charlotte.[13] "My first and best love is the South," he claimed upon returning to North Carolina in October 1905. The region's natural features, cultural barriers, and rural ways were a source of fascination: "The fields of cotton and the separation in the schools and in the trains of white and colored people made me realize that I was really *South*!"[14] Traveling through the Appalachians, he was taken by

Fig. 3.3. John Nolen, c. 1908. Courtesy
Wisconsin Historical Society.

the beauty of the landscape. Near Asheville he encountered twenty- to thirty-
foot-tall rhododendrons and laurels growing wild, causing him to wonder
"what a sight it must be in June."[15]

Nolen made a special side trip to see Biltmore estate, the 120,000-acre
property in the Appalachian high country laid out by Olmsted Sr. for George
Washington Vanderbilt in the 1890s.[16] He was interested less in the grand
house than in the beauty and utility of Olmsted's landscape and spent over
six hours on horseback taking in gardens, farms, and forest. Having recently
completed his article on Olmsted, Nolen especially appreciated the grounds:
"What a wonderful genius the elder Olmsted was!" he wrote to his wife. "The
more I know of him the lower I bend the knee: infinite genius and infinite
pains characterize all his work." Yet despite his admiration, he was determined
to take inspiration from, not copy, the great man's example.[17]

Upon returning to Charlotte, Nolen presented his completed plan for
Independence Park to the commission; the informal layout reflected Tom-
kins's directive to create a system of serpentine walkways, to place trees where
they had been lumbered, and to leave everything else as it was.[18] He also
drafted a plan to augment Vance Square by adding a regimen of trees and
shrubs to the formal setting. (Fig. 3.4) His final project, a landscape plan for

Fig. 3.4. Vance Park. Photograph by John Nolen, 1906. Courtesy Division of Rare and Manuscript Collections, Cornell University Library.

Settlers Cemetery, used curved walks and strategically sited cedars, oaks, and pines to create a shady, tranquil setting.[19]

With Vance Park, Independence Park, and Settlers Cemetery, Charlotte now had the foundation for establishing a full-fledged park system. There was, however, more enthusiasm than funding. The Park and Tree Commission's annual appropriation from the city was $1,000, barely enough to pay a consultant, much less finance the acquisition of large sites.[20] Despite the obstacles, Stephens remained undeterred. He believed Nolen's message of progress and beauty would eventually take hold, and to keep the Harvard expert in Charlotte, Stephens commissioned him to create a landscape design for his new home.[21] Once Charlotte's leading citizens observed this work, Stephens expected them to hire Nolen, and then the park commission would be inclined to establish a park system.[22]

In Charlotte, Nolen was confronted with the region's deep-seated racism. On his second day in town he attended a theater production of "The Clansman," based on Thomas F. Dixon Jr.'s best-selling novel of the same name.[23] It was an unabashedly racist portrayal of Reconstruction, replete with self-interested, plotting Yankee politicians, and Ku Klux Klan members clad in white robes carrying blazing crosses, on thundering hooves and leaving a pile of black corpses in their wake. The play drew rave reviews from the local press, but Nolen thought it "one-sided and an unworthy appeal to passion and prejudice." As the curtain fell, he was caught off-guard by the audience's resounding applause. "The people here are all stirred up about it and I am sure it will work infinite harm," he wrote to his wife. "Poor people, if they could only see that it strikes at their weakest point. My eyes are more open than ever before."[24]

During the remainder of his stay in Charlotte, talk of the play dominated conversation. At a dinner party hosted by civic leaders, Nolen was seated next to Dixon. He thought the playwright was misguided but also found him polite, well spoken, and charismatic. After the meal, Nolen was called upon to share his opinion of the play.[25] According to the *Charlotte Daily*, "Mr. John Nolen, of Boston, spoke briefly, but pleasantly. He said he felt himself the most ignorant man in that party; that he was born since the war and has lived all his life North. The most interesting thing to him about the play here was its effect on the Southern audience."[26] It was an unforgettable evening, both fascinating and repelling. The South was an enigma to Nolen; its culture was imminently American but marred. The experience engendered a new appreciation for home. "Hugs and kisses in greater number than this space allows," he wrote to Barbara. Two days later he wrote another letter exclaiming, "What advantages we have in Cambridge!"[27]

The Charlotte park initiative gained momentum when a fresh slate of officials swept into office in the fall of 1905; in addition, a city commission style of government had replaced the Board of Aldermen. The commission's members now represented banking, insurance, and real estate interests, and they looked more favorably upon investing tax dollars in municipal projects such as roads and utilities that would aid the business community.[28] With his Harvard credentials and visionary plans, Nolen emerged as an able spokesman for urban reform in Charlotte. The Queen City was pining for respectability, and its citizens had "long been susceptible to persuasive prophets from the far country, especially those with impressive degrees and accents."[29] "Mr. Nolen and the CPTC are trying to bring some harmony of development for the private properties of the city," the *Charlotte Observer* reported in October.[30] Indeed, the effort to regulate urban expansion was a common theme in the nation at this time.[31]

Before returning to Cambridge, Nolen gave a public lecture to an audience of four hundred. Slides of Italian Renaissance villas and their gardens flashed before the crowd, as Nolen noted the historical roots of the desire to experience the pleasures of the countryside. With the adoption of a comprehensive park plan, citizens could enjoy extended vistas, "boscos," intimate gardens, and celebratory spaces, and city officials could order future development that harmonized with the landscape. Nolen also documented the value of using trees and shrubs from nearby forests and glens. He explained that native plants required less fertilizer and watering than exotic species and were hardy enough to withstand the region's extremes of heat and cold. A native landscape was not only resilient, but also had a distinct tone and texture. "The missionary of beautiful back yards and breathing places," the *Observer* reported, concluded the presentation by quoting Ralph Waldo Emerson: "The most poetic of all the occupations of real life, the bringing out by art of the native but hidden grace of the landscape."[32]

The address was well received. Seven prominent citizens hired Nolen to design landscape plans for their residences. In January, he returned to press the issue of comprehensive park planning, delivering another lecture and writing an editorial, "The Land of Promise," urging citizens to tithe to fund parks. "The task of making the city convenient, healthy, and beautiful" was a work of civic "faith," he declared, and it demanded the "willingness to appropriate small sums regularly and cheerfully."[33]

After leaving Charlotte, Nolen traveled on to Greenville, South Carolina, where the *Daily News* described him as the "happy combination of the artist and the engineer." His straightforward idealism and slides of the evocative landscapes of Turner and Corot mesmerized his audiences. To illustrate his points, Nolen presented the usual fare of Italian, French, and English gardens, as well as urban parks in Boston and New York. He also noted that the "back to nature" movement was spreading from its northern base, as shown by school boards and popular magazines endorsing the study of nature and outdoor recreation. This trend would intensify, Nolen concluded, when access to healthy activity and scenic lands became an expectation of urban life.[34]

Nolen's call to reconnect to nature and the land spoke to enduring southern values. The region was still largely rural, and cities were more closely tied to the countryside than were their counterparts in the North.[35] The connection was moral as well as physical. Shortly after the nation's founding, Thomas Jefferson described "the cultivators of the earth" as the nation's most independent, virtuous, and cherished citizens.[36] The land was the South's greatest resource, and transforming portions of the city into parks struck a chord for a people eager to reestablish their cultural prominence. Infusing the lush beauty of the southern landscape into the city, Nolen reasoned, could produce a lifestyle the North would never match. These principles appealed to the proclivities of his audience, and although he did not immediately earn a commission in Greenville, he did plant a seed. Two decades later, the Greenville City Council, along with the municipal governments of Charleston and Columbia, South Carolina, would hire him to prepare a city plan.[37]

After publication of "Frederick Law Olmsted and His Work," Nolen had begun lecturing on a regular basis. His first public talk, "The Beauty of Unspoiled Nature," was delivered at the Boston Public Library in February 1906. Landscape architecture was evolving in response to the demands of the modern industrial city. Cultural adaptation defined the profession, and to make this point, Nolen contrasted Olmsted Sr., the "park planner for the people," with André Le Nôtre, the "gardener of the king," who created Versailles to please Louis XIV and reveal the power of divine rule. A strict geometry overruled nature to create an ornate landscape filled with artificial objects: parterres, allées, fountains, statues, great canals, and labyrinths. By contrast, in the "strongly democratic nineteenth century," Olmsted Sr. analyzed the land's existing conditions and made them the basis of his design. In the early twentieth century, advances in civic art and conservation drew upon "the beauty of unspoiled nature" to meet the new mandate for outdoor recreation.[38] The *Boston Evening Transcript* published the speech, but unfortunately the paper focused on the accomplishments of Olmsted Sr. rather than Nolen's central point: the innovation infusing the practice of landscape architecture.[39]

Thanks to Edward Griggs, however, Nolen was given a second chance to state his case, this time in Montclair, New Jersey. Griggs had moved to Montclair in 1902 and was soon engaged in the town's affairs. He helped found the Municipal Art Commission and orchestrated its sponsorship of Nolen's address. The lecture, titled "Outdoor Art," presented an agenda to improve the urban landscape. Nolen recounted how the country's rapid urbanization had led to the neglect of private landscapes and public grounds. Society had an obligation to repair damaged sites, he noted, and to create parks and gardens that celebrated a community's "natural conditions." Nature was humanity's common denominator—the very foundation of culture—and the human prospect hinged on cultivating and deciphering this elemental resource. "Nature antedates all the arts and sciences," Nolen proclaimed, "and without knowledge of nature, the history and development of man is incomprehensible." He showed slides of Olmsted-designed parks, presenting them as the nation's crowning achievements, but claimed that too many open spaces in metropolitan New York and Boston were "neglected." With "art everywhere else," Nolen declared, "its application" must proceed "in our outside surroundings."[40] This time Nolen's message resonated. The Municipal Art Commission asked him to return to discuss a civic improvement plan, and in 1909 he would design his first town plan for Montclair.

At Tompkins's request, Nolen visited Biltmore again in 1906 and wrote an article for the *Observer* about the experience. "Mr. John Nolen Becomes Eloquent over What He Saw at the Famous Estate" extolled the beauty of

Fig. 3.5. Biltmore Village. Photograph by John Nolen, c. 1906. Courtesy Division of Rare and Manuscript Collections, Cornell University Library.

Olmsted's gradual transitions in the vast landscape, the use of native vegetation, and the sophisticated planting compositions that enlivened the senses and refreshed the mind.[41] He took a separate trip to Biltmore Village, which Olmsted also designed. At the rail stop, a brick plaza was the point of confluence for the fan-shaped street plan. Shops and residences built in the English Tudor style ringed the plaza and trees lined the streets.[42] (Fig. 3.5) Nolen took a number of photographs that would appear in later town plans.

As Nolen expanded his professional practice, he found it difficult to obtain authoritative texts on landscape gardening and park design. He urged the American Society of Landscape Architects to sponsor the republishing of classic texts in the field. After considerable conversation with the organization's president, Samuel B. Parsons Jr., he met with George Mifflin, one of the founders of the Houghton Mifflin publishing company. In April 1906 Mifflin agreed to publish a series of classic gardening texts in conjunction with the ASLA.[43] Nolen would edit the first book, *The Art of Landscape Gardening* (1907), a compendium of Humphry Repton's *Sketches and Hints on Landscape Gardening* (1795) and *Observations on the Theory and Practice of Landscape Gardening* (1803).

The Art of Landscape Gardening was an instructive, richly illustrated book. (Fig. 3.6) Following Nolen's introduction, overlays depicted color renderings of before-and-after landscapes. Repton's musings on the interplay of light and shadow, the formation of vistas, and the selection of trees to accentuate architectural style revealed his detailed knowledge. Nolen traced the origins of modern practice to Repton's predecessors William Kent and Capability Brown. According to Nolen, in challenging "the absurdities and excess of formal gardening," Kent and Brown became overzealous and destroyed grounds of great beauty. The "sound and rational" ways of Repton, who integrated their advances with attributes of the formal style, came to right this "unbalanced reaction."[44] Nolen identified with Repton, whom he considered a "practical man": "Like his American successor, Olmsted, he held no sympathy for a design that did not provide for plain necessities of human living."[45] Through systematic record keeping, Repton established a set of fixed principles to improve the professional practice of landscape gardening.[46] These principles—unity, harmony, and variety—set the standard for Olmsted's practice, and Nolen was intent on adapting them to meet the demands of urban life in the twentieth century.[47] (Fig. 3.7)

Following Repton's example, Nolen began a systematic study of city planning to identify the standards of practice for the new profession. He sailed to

Europe in summer 1906 with the landscape architect Thomas W. Sears, who had provided photos for the *House and Garden* articles on Olmsted.[48] Nolen wanted to apply his findings, where appropriate, to his practice in the United States.[49] After settling in London, the two men visited Letchworth, the first garden city, developed in 1903 in the Herefordshire countryside, thirty-five

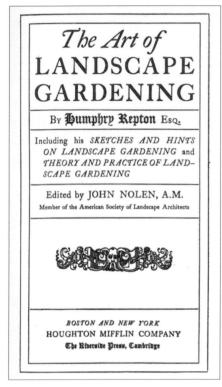

Fig. 3.6. Title page, Humphry Repton, *The Art of Landscape Gardening* (1907).

Fig. 3.7. Humphry Repton landscape. Photograph by Thomas Warren Sears, c. 1906.

Courtesy Division of Rare and Manuscript Collections, Cornell University Library.

miles north of London, according to plans Ebenezer Howard had envisioned in his influential 1898 treatise, *To-morrow: A Peaceful Path to Real Reform.*[50] The garden city promised health, convenience, and community—a new order of living. Citizens would be drawn from the congested cities of industrial England to, Howard wrote, "the bosom of our kindly mother earth, at once the source of life, of happiness, of wealth, and of power."[51]

To-morrow had a practical edge not found in the era's popular utopian texts. Its author linked liberty and profit to a cooperative land ownership system that he called "common sense socialism."[52] Howard's genius was to chart the steps, provide the language, and establish a form—the garden city—to offer an alternative to London's speculative, laissez-faire development. Mixing the best attributes of town and country, Howard planned communities of 6,000 acres to accommodate 30,000 to 50,000 residents, with development concentrated on 1,000 acres and the remainder devoted to agriculture, forest preserves, and parks. Garden cities would be laid out in interconnected constellations linked by rail to each other and to London. Howard also championed a vision of social equality. "The object," he wrote, "is to raise the standard of health and comfort of all true workers of any grade." A limited dividend company would fund construction and reinvest profits into the community to promote "the natural and economic combination of town and country."[53] The historian David Schuyler writes that Howard's vision stood out "from the hundreds of other utopias imagined toward the end of the nineteenth century" because of its "combination of the visionary and the practical, the radical tradition and the essentially conservative ideal of the harmonious community."[54]

The impact of "the middle way," as Howard called it, was immediate. Eight months after his book was published, the Garden City Association was formed; in 1901 the noted attorney Ralph Neville assumed its chairmanship and brought in Thomas Adams, a young Scottish architect, to serve as full-time secretary. Adams organized two well-attended conferences that presented the model company towns of Bourneville and Port Sunlight as precursors of the garden city. This initiative emphasized the practical tilt of Howard's ideas and led to the republication of his text in 1902, with slight changes and a new title, *Garden Cities of To-morrow.* That same year, Neville convinced a team of industrialists to form the First Garden City Pioneer Company to build a model town, and in 1903 land was purchased on a rail line thirty-five miles from London. Architects Raymond Unwin and Barry Parker were hired to interpret Howard's schematic diagrams and plan the first garden city.[55]

Although committed to Howard's concept, Unwin and Parker were also

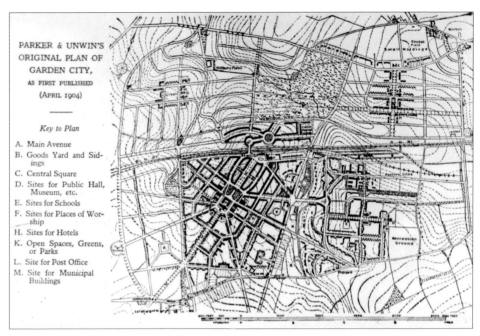

Fig. 3.8. Letchworth plan, 1904. Courtesy Division of Rare and Manuscript Collections, Cornell University Library.

inspired by Camillo Sitte.[56] The medieval English village was the model for the vernacular architecture they fashioned to invoke a sense of order and stability. The architects also carefully sited the community by analyzing the soil and topography to identify the most appropriate areas for development, preservation, and agriculture. Streets and neighborhoods were aligned to ensure efficient movement and provide access to nature, business districts, and civic institutions. Unwin also valued the Beaux-Arts approach, as demonstrated by his use of axial avenues terminating at the town center.[57] The first garden city was a herald of the future, a rational model to direct the expansion of the industrial city. (Fig. 3.8)

The very fact that Letchworth was built according to a plan brought it renown, but it never became the community Howard had envisioned. The economics of real estate development proved inimical to his cooperative land ownership scheme. Yet even though the first garden city was not a model of social reform, it demonstrated the efficacy of expert physical planning.[58] Nolen claimed it was the "Perfect City." (Fig. 3.9) He noted that industry and housing were efficiently aligned, but Letchworth's real promise lay in fostering a sense of community through civic design. From Letchworth, Nolen traveled on to London, where Sears developed his film, including several photographs of landscapes designed by Repton.[59] After just a day in the city, they continued on to France.

On the way to the Paris Opera House, Nolen had a chance encounter with James Robinson, his former professor. The meeting led to an evening with Robinson and the American architect Ralph Adams Cram discussing art and Japanese and English gardens. Nolen spent the remainder of his time in Paris analyzing parks and gardens, including Luxembourg Gardens, Vaux-le-Vicomte, and Fontainebleau. In late August, he returned to Lucerne and Interlaken after a four-year absence. There, Sears photographed the outdoor concert hall and promenades crowded with tourists, images that would later be used to illustrate Nolen's early city plans.[60] Munich was the final destination. A meeting was arranged with Alan Harris, and Nolen led a daylong tour. Visiting old haunts recalled happy associations and provided an opportunity to assess the progress made in implementing the city's plan. Nolen and Sears would stay on in the Bavarian capital, attending the Oktoberfest festival before heading home.[61]

Returning to Cambridge in mid-October, Nolen felt a joyful reunion. His trip to Letchworth would cause him to reconsider his practice and focus on the importance of town planning, particularly the potential for incorporating landscape architecture into garden city design. But for now, he settled his affairs and spent the next several weeks among family. With three children under the age of twelve, he and Barbara decided to rent a larger residence on Avon Place in a quiet Cambridge neighborhood abutting an old orchard.

Fig. 3.9. Letchworth. Photograph by Thomas Warren Sears, from Montclair Town Plan, 1909.
Courtesy Division of Rare and Manuscript Collections, Cornell University Library.

It was within walking distance of Harvard Square, a block from Peabody Elementary School, and a trolley ride from the beach at City Point. Well supplied with play spaces and sidewalks for roller skating, the neighborhood was perfectly suited for a family with children. Nearby Avon Hill provided a winter sled run, and the Nolen house became the triage center for neighborhood children complaining of bumps and bruises. In this nurturing environment, Nolen experienced a joy he had not known as a child. The bonds of thrift, simple decency, and common recreation engendered what his children later called "the Happy Family."[62] (Fig. 3.10)

Nolen returned to full-time consulting in mid-November, continuing work on a series of small projects he had begun before leaving for Europe. Although his practice was profitable, he was growing increasingly frustrated that so few clients fully appreciated his efforts.[63] He was looking for a large public commission, and while in Europe had mulled over a letter from George Baldwin, a civic leader in Savannah, Georgia.[64] The city was considering hiring a landscape architect to consult on a series of projects.[65] Nolen pursued the lead, and in late November of 1906 he headed south to assess Savannah's park system.

Fig. 3.10. Avon Place, Cambridge, c. 1910. Courtesy Division of Rare and Manuscript Collections, Cornell University Library.

Upon arriving in Savannah, Nolen was captivated by the mild climate and tranquil setting. "It is a beautiful day here," he wrote home on Thanksgiving, "bright sun shining, fresh warm wind blowing, church bells ringing and the live oaks, great big fellows, and palmettos making all out of doors look almost as green as summer with us."[66] Over the next week, he documented Savannah's "peculiar wealth," the investment procured from the city's oak-shaded historic squares, broad avenues, and well-placed churches and public buildings.[67] Indeed, James Oglethorpe's 1733 plan had introduced a pattern new to the English colonies. The basic elements of the neighborhood—public squares, narrow local streets, and short blocks—structured an aesthetically pleasing and walkable living environment.[68] A half century had passed since the establishment of the city's large public outdoor space, Forsyth Park. Nolen took a series of notes to prepare a proposal for a comprehensive park plan, completed the report in Cambridge, and sent it to Baldwin, a founding member of the Savannah Parks and Tree Commission.[69] In March 1907 a letter from P. D. Daffin, the commission's chairman, requested that Nolen come to Savannah for an interview.[70] The SPTC was impressed with Nolen's resume of southern commissions and hired him to design a single park on an 80-acre site on the city's southern boundary. Baldwin had come to realize that obtaining approval for a comprehensive park plan would involve considerable effort.[71]

Nolen returned to Charlotte to deliver a lecture at the Academy of Music. Since his first presentation in North Carolina two years earlier, the landscape architect had become a more accomplished speaker with a broad vision of urban reform. He was now speaking out on city planning, and the "civic awakening" had inspired a litany of interrelated reforms, from procuring potable water to adopting housing codes. But the issue closest to Nolen's heart was the welfare of children. In 1906 he had become a founding member of the Playground Association of America, which was dedicated to structuring the socialization of youths through organized play.[72] A year later the organization's journal, *Recreation Magazine,* redefined recreation. The leisurely pursuit of "re-creation" that Olmsted Sr. had envisioned now included time devoted to active play and organized sports. Parks were still places to luxuriate in nature, but they should also provide space for children to participate in vigorous, healthy pursuits.[73] Nolen described the need for recreation areas to be "beautiful and well-equipped," as well as near the homes of the children who used them. According to Nolen, "In the planning of our cities, the children have too often been left out—they are merely places for adults to live and do business in, yet we know that if the opportunity for play is denied, the stunting and perversion of child life are absolutely inevitable results."[74] As

Fig. 3.11. Photograph by John Nolen used to illustrate the need for areas devoted to active recreation, c. 1906. Courtesy Division of Rare and Manuscript Collections, Cornell University Library.

the country's leading advocate for active recreation, Nolen explained that the concept of the park was changing.[75] Investments in recreation belonged in the same class of improvements as "streets, water, lights, and transportation. . . . They are indispensable. No enlightened city, hopeful of its future can afford to be without them."[76] (Fig. 3.11)

Despite Nolen's advocacy, the Charlotte city commission continued to delay funding of a park plan. Nolen shifted his focus back to Savannah, where Baldwin was making progress. During the summer of 1907 he completed his park plan. (Fig. 3.12) Formerly called Jefferson Davis Park, in honor of the president of the Confederacy, its name was changed to Daffin Park by city leaders eager to capture northern investment. Nonetheless, Daffin Park would remain segregated and inaccessible to African Americans.[77]

Nolen's plan reflected the site's topography and Baldwin's directive to provide sports fields and a parade ground.[78] (Fig. 3.13) Traditional European elements—a tree-lined mall, terminating vistas, an amphitheater, and a *bosco sacro*—were integrated into an American setting, where a forest surrounded playgrounds and athletic fields. Shade trees bordered the rectangular site, and plans included the planting of an additional 1,500 native trees and 12,000

Fig. 3.12. Daffin Park site. Photograph by John Nolen, 1906. Courtesy Division of Rare and Manuscript Collections, Cornell University Library.

shrubs. Four rows of live oaks bounded the mall that ran through the middle of the park on its most level ground. Basin pools were to be placed at the mall's termini, and from these points short diagonal walkways, lined with oaks, elms, and magnolias, ran to the corners of the park, forming triangular sections on each end of the mall. The plan also followed Denman Ross's directive to harmonize opposing ideals in artistic form. A site for a school lay on direct axis with a grove of 295 native pines, the canopy species for much of the surrounding region.[79] The parade ground, which doubled as a baseball field, was the largest space, occupying most of the park's northern half; a field house, track, and swimming pool were sited on its eastern edge; and a band

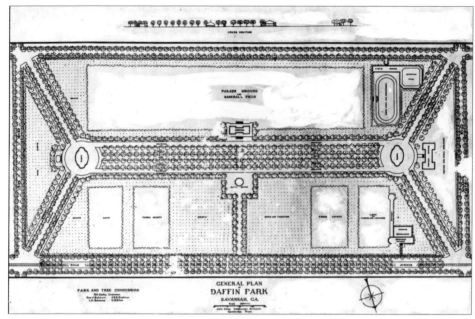

Fig. 3.13. Daffin Park plan, 1907. Courtesy Division of Rare and Manuscript Collections, Cornell University Library.

Fig. 3.14. Daffin Park mall. Photograph by Caty Coplin, 2012. Courtesy Division of Rare and Manuscript Collections, Cornell University Library.

Fig. 3.15. Daffin Park. Photograph by author, 2006.

shell, flanked by an open-air theater, lawns, and groves, served as the focal point of the southern half.

The plan received immediate approval from the park commission, and trees for the park border and the mall were soon planted. Over time, the mall evolved into a beautiful linear walk shaded by live oaks offering a cool respite from the oppressive summer heat. (Fig. 3.14) In the half century after World War II, Daffin Park became "everyone's backyard," a scenic landscape that accommodates picnics, strolls, and an array of sports.[80] Since the park's inception, city officials have worked to honor Nolen's plan, and Daffin Park remains close in form and spirit to its designer's original intentions. (Fig. 3.15)

Daffin Park marked a turning point in Nolen's career. It was a substantial undertaking that gave him the standing to take on a series of larger projects, primarily in the South. Although he never prepared a full-fledged park system for Savannah, his association with Baldwin earned him one of his most important commissions, a contract to prepare a comprehensive city plan.

4

CITY PLANNER, 1907–1908

By 1907 John Nolen was developing a new tool to order the twentieth-century American city. His comprehensive plan, which typically included a park plan, civic center plan, and rudimentary transportation system, spoke to the progressive concern for the public good; President Theodore Roosevelt had proclaimed that property was subject to regulation "to whatever degree the public welfare may require."[1] A range of issues now fell under the purview of city planners: the subdivision of land, siting of civic buildings, and conservation of resources, as well as considerations related to recreation, transportation, public health, and social justice.[2] "Imagination, courage, and public spirit" were the ingredients, Nolen declared, to "provide for the future by intelligence and foresight."[3]

Nolen was given an opportunity to share his ideas about comprehensive planning in 1907 when Sarah Johnson Cocke, president of the Women's Civic Betterment Club in Roanoke, Virginia, hired him to draft a city plan.[4] Nolen came recommended by George Baldwin, who had been pleased with his work in Savannah. After the club raised the money to hire Nolen, the city council appointed a Committee on Civic Improvement, whose all-male members would serve as liaison for the project.[5]

Nolen arrived in Roanoke in April of that year. The city of 37,000 residents, located at the southern end of the Shenandoah Valley, was a key depot for the coal industry. An isolated crossroads before the Norfolk and Western Railway constructed a rail terminus and repair facility in 1882, Roanoke became the principal point of transfer for rail traffic between the western

Virginia coalfields and Norfolk's shipping yards. In three years its population jumped from 1,000 to 5,000, reaching 18,000 in 1892 and doubling again by 1907. Serious problems accompanied this rapid urbanization. The city had a dismal sanitation record, crowded schools, tangled street connections, no public library, and no parks or playgrounds. "It is a big job to remodel a city, especially where so much has been done exactly wrong," Nolen noted in his initial appraisal. Yet, he noted, "the people seem more ready to go ahead than at Charlotte."[6]

The reason was Sarah Johnson Cocke. Originally from a prominent Georgia family, she had become a leading figure in Atlanta society. After the death of her first husband, in 1903 she married Lucian H. Cocke, Roanoke's mayor from 1882 to 1884. Three years later she founded the Women's Civic Betterment Club, which became the vehicle for placing civic beautification and public sanitation projects on the municipal agenda.[7] Soon after Cocke led a women's boycott of downtown grocery markets plagued with fetid conditions, the city council passed a food inspection ordinance. Empowered by this victory, she convinced prominent local families to pay a team of consultants from Baltimore to evaluate the city's health record. Their report, *Sanitary Roanoke*, recommended constructing a new water and sewage system, paving and cleaning streets, scheduling regular health inspections, and securing a potable water supply. Roanoke's path to urban reform was hardly atypical in the early 1900s. The city planning movement was indebted to women who lobbied for parks, safe water supplies, street cleaning, and sanitation improve-

Fig. 4.1. Roanoke Market Square, c. 1907. Courtesy Division of Rare and Manuscript Collections, Cornell University Library.

ments. Their success led them to endorse a broader set of reforms, from city planning to child labor laws, which stoked a wave of social change.[8]

Nolen spent a week compiling his initial analysis of Roanoke and concluded that a new approach to civic investment was required, especially in the chaotic Market Square area.[9] (Fig. 4.1) Before heading back north at the end of the month, he delivered a lecture sponsored by the women's club. Many obstacles lay ahead, but Roanoke's prime location—bounded by valleys, mountains, and rivers—fueled Nolen's belief that Virginia's third-largest city could set a benchmark for the nation's "Renaissance of civic affairs."[10] He returned to Roanoke for two weeks in July and left with a stockpile of material, including topographical maps, Board of Trade reports, and scores of photos.[11] He was able to focus on preparing his first comprehensive city plan because his small office in Cambridge had expanded, employing a part-time secretary as well as a horticulturist named Daniel Clark. By late August, Nolen had assembled his maps, surveys, and field notes into *Remodeling Roanoke,* a forty-page report with sixty illustrations.[12]

Nolen did not mince words in documenting the evils of Roanoke's rapid expansion. He criticized earlier developers for ignoring topographical features, a practice that had resulted in an "inconvenient and wasteful" urban pattern. (Fig. 4.2) In addition to problems with flooding and traffic circula-

Fig. 4.2. Downtown Roanoke. Photograph by John Nolen, 1907. Courtesy Division of Rare and Manuscript Collections, Cornell University Library.

tion, the municipality had failed to adequately allocate public services such as water, sewer, and transit to a large portion of the population. Roanoke's future prosperity, as Nolen explained, would depend not only on industrial production but also on meeting the basic needs of the working class and the "full requirements of child life." He concluded that "there has been no realization yet of the great possibilities of city-making," and provided his own vision in the form of a city plan, regional park plan, civic center plan, and a thoroughfare system design. He buttressed his report with quotes from Olmsted Sr., Olmsted Jr., Jane Addams, Theodore Roosevelt, William Morris, Edward Griggs, Andrew Carnegie, Simon Patten, Patrick Geddes, Charles W. Eliot, and Charles Eliot.[13]

Remodeling Roanoke argued that citizens—regardless of class or race—should be provided essential services and humane living conditions.[14] Nolen was no stranger to poverty, but the squalid conditions of Roanoke's African American community shocked him. The landscape, "dotted over with ramshackle negro cabins that hung insecurely on the side hills," created "an almost intolerable situation," he wrote. "It would scarcely be possible to make a worse disposition of that section than the existing one either from the point of view of the public or the present unfortunate occupants. For every reason—economic, sanitary, aesthetic, humanitarian—active steps should be taken to radically change the character of the city in the Old Lick section."[15] (Fig. 4.3) Nolen's desire to improve living conditions among black residents encom-

Fig. 4.3. African American neighborhood, Roanoke. Photograph by John Nolen, 1907. Courtesy Division of Rare and Manuscript Collections, Cornell University Library.

passed a strain of reform seldom seen in the Jim Crow South. For southern progressives, segregating the races constituted reform, and the judicial doctrine of "separate but equal" justified their actions.[16] But the photos of the African American enclaves that appeared in *Remodeling Roanoke* documented the inequality of the city's distribution of wealth and resources. Nolen's report introduced city planning as a rational process that addressed every aspect of the city and all segments of the population with the goal of creating a fit environment.

To allay concerns that city planning was effective only in the urban North, he set *Remodeling Roanoke* within the context of Virginia history, presenting a reprint of the 1699 Williamsburg plan as a model for his Civic Center Plan. Five municipal buildings were configured on a central square in an arrangement that emphasized the new city hall. (Fig. 4.4) Set on high ground with

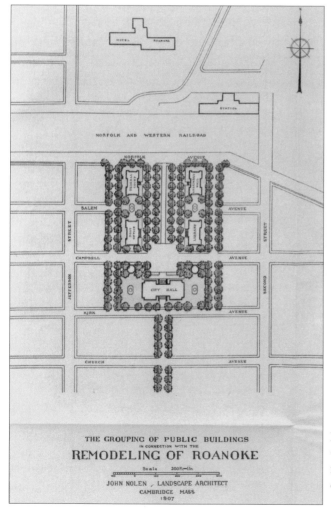

Fig. 4.4. Roanoke Civic Center plan, 1907. Courtesy Division of Rare and Manuscript Collections, Cornell University Library.

a commanding view, the civic center was also within walking distance of the central train station. Building such a civic center, Nolen argued, would not only give Roanoke a new "dignity and appropriate beauty," its "ennobling influence" could crystallize civic impulses into "action for the public good."[17] In *Remodeling Roanoke*, an artist's rendering of the University of Virginia illustrated how harmoniously arranged buildings had a "noble effect" on a free people. Celebrating Jefferson's legacy was good politics in Virginia, but economics also played an important role. The civic center's compact, accessible site would make the conduct of city business more convenient and efficient.[18]

The framework for Nolen's comprehensive city plan was its transportation system. (Fig. 4.5) In Roanoke, thoroughfares would radiate from the civic center to the urban edge, where they merged with parkways paralleling Tinker Creek and the Roanoke River. Encircling roughly two-thirds of the city, the proposed parkways formed a twelve-mile greenbelt that determined the boundaries of future urban expansion. In addition to upgrading recreational opportunities, the parkways bordered floodplains that, if preserved, would mitigate flooding and improve sanitary engineering.[19] As a means of improving Roanoke's haphazard circulation system, Nolen provided a schematic diagram of a hierarchical transportation network with four roadway types:

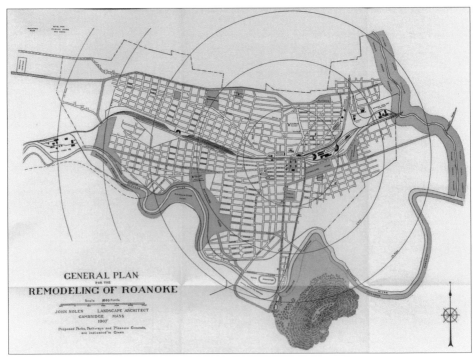

Fig. 4.5. Roanoke comprehensive plan, 1907. Courtesy Division of Rare and Manuscript Collections, Cornell University Library.

suburban, main city avenues, parkways, and important residential streets. The roadways were scaled to meet the demands of their respective primary users: pedestrians, carriages, automobiles, and streetcars. (Fig. 4.6)

Nolen considered street trees integral components of road design. "Trees in the city have great value for health in improving the quality of the air, for comfort in furnishing welcome shade from the burning heat of the sun, and for beauty in the glory that they often impart when well grown to an other-

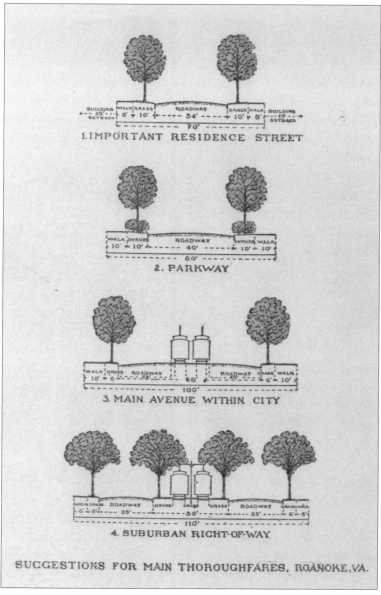

Fig. 4.6. Roanoke street scheme, 1907. Courtesy Division of Rare and Manuscript Collections, Cornell University Library.

wise commonplace street," he wrote. "Paris has over a hundred thousand trees on its streets and boulevards outside of its parks and gardens, and they penetrate to the very heart of the business district."[20] In an effort to increase the number of street trees in Roanoke, Nolen made them integral to the transportation network, the civic center plan, and the park system. Planting strips containing shade trees paralleled ten-foot-wide sidewalks to make the pedestrian experience safer and more enjoyable.

Remodeling Roanoke presented a vision of a green city where nature was part of daily life. In the report, Nolen quoted Edward Griggs's observation that "Nature has its own unapproachable grandeur, beauty or mystery," representing "one of the subtle secrets of exulted and harmonious living."[21] For the many immigrants from the countryside, parks also provided opportunities to socialize and respite from daily toil. Playgrounds and playfields were also of "inestimable value."[22] To meet the needs of diverse populations, Nolen placed two- to three-acre neighborhood parks and playgrounds in each of the city's four wards. A thirty-acre riverfront "Recreation Park" with swimming beaches and athletic fields was sited on a promenade connected to a parkway. Investing in a park system created value, he argued, and each park

Fig. 4.7. Proposed site of Roanoke Riverfront Park. Photograph by John Nolen, 1907. Courtesy Division of Rare and Manuscript Collections, Cornell University Library.

increased the worth of the next until the system was complete. A photograph of a square in Savannah with the caption "The Parks of Savannah, established through the foresight of Oglethorpe, have today a valuation of 5 million dollars" brought home the point.[23] Well-worn images from Nolen's lectures also accompanied the report, including photos of Bostonians enjoying the Charles River Reservation, which Nolen actually considered less beautiful than the Roanoke River. (Fig. 4.7)

The Boston parks inspired Nolen's most far-reaching proposal, a system of "public reservations" and parkways running between Roanoke and Tinker Mountain. (Fig. 4.8) Among the "rich gifts of nature" proposed for acquisition, Mill Mountain was the priority.[24] Located two miles from the downtown, it offered panoramic views to the Blue Ridge range and held the potential to meet the city's long-term recreational needs. Preserving the 1,740-foot mountain would also secure a major source of potable water. Crystal Spring flowed

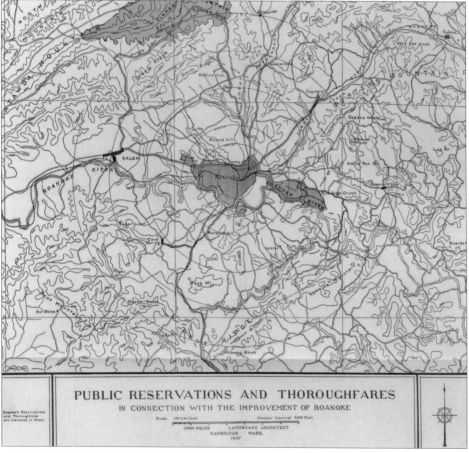

Fig. 4.8. Roanoke Regional Park plan, 1907. Courtesy Division of Rare and Manuscript Collections, Cornell University Library.

from the mountain's base, yielding five million gallons of pure water each day. Given Roanoke's history of water-borne disease, Nolen reasoned, "it is imperative that the people possess the mountain."[25]

In 1907 comprehensive city planning was a nascent field and Nolen had few examples from which to draw. He looked to J. Horace McFarland, who had catalyzed the "Great Awakening" of Harrisburg, Pennsylvania, for a strategy for bonding Roanoke's debt to fund the plan's implementation.[26] A noted author and civic reformer, McFarland had united activists and experts, including Warren H. Manning, author of the Harrisburg plan.[27] Like Roanoke, the Pennsylvania capital had experienced rapid population growth, and its water supply was threatened by the pumping of untreated sewage into the Susquehanna River. McFarland and civic activist Mira Lloyd Dock convinced the city's business elite to hire Manning to prepare a comprehensive improvement plan. Manning made recommendations for dredging the river to securing a safe supply of potable water and he also designed a citywide park system.[28] The passage of a $1 million bond issue funded the proposed improvements, and within five years the results were significant. The rehabilitation of Wetzel's Swamp exemplified the success of Harrisburg's investment. In 1901 forty percent of the city's sewage seeped into the swamp. Five years later, it had become a tranquil setting of parkland and lake and was rechristened Wildwood Park.[29]

In November 1907, *Remodeling Roanoke* came before a joint meeting of the city council and the county Board of Aldermen. Nolen's plan was well received. Over the next five years, the council invested in parks, procuring a secure water supply and expanding the sewage system. But the more far-reaching elements—a civic center, transportation system, and regional parks—were ignored because the council did not want to take on bonded debt to fund improvement projects. The city had no Horace McFarland to rouse public opinion and draw national attention. For real estate investors, city planning proved to be an encumbrance, and manufacturing and industrial expansion remained the cure-all for local problems. Rather than structuring growth or improving the living conditions of the poor, municipal funds underwrote schemes to advance real estate interests and build factories.[30] By 1910 *Remodeling Roanoke* was effectively shelved.[31]

Nolen's proposal to correct the abysmal conditions in the African American community was also disregarded. Using tax dollars to relieve the squalor of the disenfranchised was anathema in a society where a third of the population could not vote, lived in constant fear of violence, and had only rudimentary public services.[32] Over time Nolen would chip away at the inequities of segregation, but he never again documented a city's failure to meet the basic needs of African Americans as openly as he did in his first city plan.

Recognized as an important prototype among urban reformers, *Remodeling Roanoke* helped Nolen lay the groundwork for his city planning practice. It became a standard reference in McFarland's American Civic Association publications, and the noted Scottish city planner Patrick Geddes reprinted the Roanoke plan in his book *Cities in Evolution* (1915).[33] Nolen found his first city plan to be an excellent marketing tool, noting that when competing for commissions, "it was worth everything to have the Roanoke Report."[34] Moreover, *Remodeling Roanoke* was not entirely forgotten in the city for which it was created. In 1928 city officials paid Nolen handsomely to draw a new comprehensive plan, one that went well beyond his previous work in its detail and complexity.[35] However, the revised plan was also filed away in the municipal archives, owing to the financial tumult of the Great Depression. (Fig. 4.9)

Nolen's plans were rediscovered in the mid-1990s, when city officials voted to prepare another new city plan. *Remodeling Roanoke* inspired the effort, and in 1997 the American Planning Association honored Nolen's initial plan with its National Historic Planning Designation. In Roanoke's new plan, adopted in 2001, *Remodeling Roanoke* provided the basis for three key initiatives: the creation of the Roanoke River Greenway, the preservation of Mill and Tinker Mountains, and the Market District revitalization.[36] An investment of $65 million was made to rejuvenate the degraded Roanoke River and build a twenty-six-mile recreation trail on its border. In the effort to showcase Roanoke as a green city, the city council voted to place most of Mill Mountain under a protective conservation easement.[37] (Fig. 4.10)

By the spring of 1907 Nolen had become a widely recognized city planner of interest to civic leaders across the country. That May, George Marston, of the San Diego Chamber of Commerce, asked him to apply for a commission to produce a new plan for the city.[38] Nolen sent a draft of the Roanoke city plan, along with letters of recommendation from J. Horace McFarland, Edward Griggs, George Stephens, and George Baldwin. Nolen was acquainted with the Southern California city through Samuel B. Parsons Jr., who had designed City Park (later renamed Balboa Park), its premier public green space. In Nolen's opinion, San Diego was struggling to undo the shortsightedness of past generations. A "well-considered, appropriate comprehensive plan," he wrote Marston, would ensure the city reached its potential.[39]

The San Diego commission was highly coveted. Nolen was competing against George Kessler, the consultant who had designed Kansas City's celebrated park system, Warren Manning, and the Olmsted Brothers. Each of the consultants had drafted comprehensive plans, but Nolen's quick response

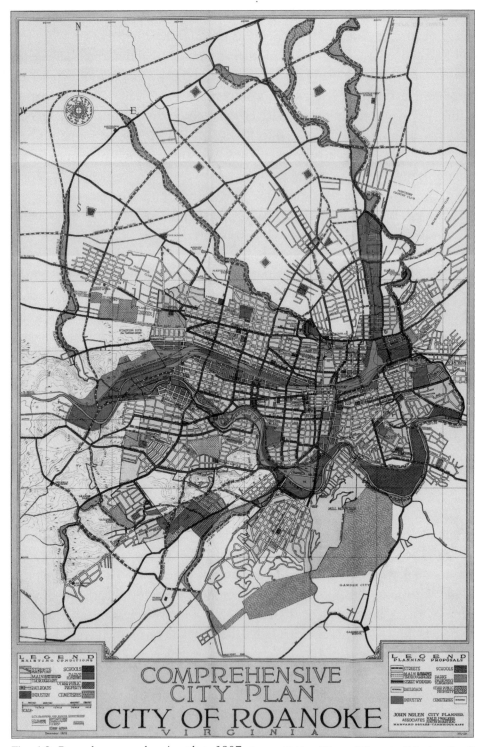

Fig. 4.9. Roanoke comprehensive plan, 1907. Courtesy Division of Rare and Manuscript Collections, Cornell University Library.

Fig. 4.10. Roanoke River Greenway and Mill Mountain. Photograph by the author, 2012.

and assessment of local conditions impressed Marston. In August Nolen signed a contract with the San Diego Chamber of Commerce for a standard $1,000 fee and expenses.[40]

Nolen expected to head west in October, but financial problems threatened to scuttle the trip. Though his annual income of $2,500 was sufficient, he was struggling to pay his bills. Payment for the Daffin Park project had been delayed, and with the cost of running an office, association dues, and project marketing, Nolen found it difficult to break even. He asked several acquaintances for a $1,000 loan, which he promised to repay with interest over a two-year period.[41] Edward Griggs advanced Nolen the money. Since leaving ASEUT, Nolen had continued to promote Griggs's lectures, and Griggs was happy to help his friend.[42]

Fig. 4.11. Kansas City Parkway, c. 1925. Courtesy Division of Rare and Manuscript Collections, Cornell University Library.

The San Diego commission opened Nolen's eyes to the extent and variety of the western landscape. He used the trip to visit some of the country's most important cities and natural wonders, making associations and personal connections that would broaden his practice. In Kansas City, he examined the progress made in implementing Kessler's 1893 park plan, the blueprint for one of the nation's premier park systems. Nolen was especially impressed by the curving parkways that bordered creeks and wove around the bluffs overlooking the Missouri River.[43] (Fig. 4.11) While there, Nolen addressed a gathering of civic associations, praising their accomplishments and encouraging them to follow Chicago's example and make playgrounds a requisite for every neighborhood.[44] At this event, Nolen likely met J. C. Nichols, a real estate entrepreneur who, a decade later, would hire him to draft a preliminary plan for Country Club Plaza, a model urban development on Kansas City's Ward Parkway.[45] In his last book, *Parkways and Land Values* (1937), Nolen devoted a chapter to Kansas City, illustrating the lessons he learned in 1907.[46]

Traveling across the Rocky Mountains, Nolen was mesmerized by the range of autumn colors. The monumentality of Salt Lake City, with its wide streets laid on axis with the resplendent Mormon Temple also impressed him. He admired the "fortitude, the devotedness, the piety, and the simplicity of the Mormons," but that did not mean he would join the faith, he wrote his wife.[47] Stopping in Napa Valley, Nolen felt as if he were in Italy and was surprised when the locals spoke English. He toured San Francisco's Golden Gate Park before heading to Los Angeles, where rampant traffic and the city's disjointed public spaces left him eager to move on. On finally reaching San Diego, he was stunned by the union of mountains and sea. It was "one of the most beautiful places on God's earth . . . a fairyland of palms, and lovely flowers, of green earth and blue sea, of sunshine and fresh breezes."[48] From his room at the Coronado Hotel, he imagined himself looking out over the Clock Tower in Venice and rhapsodized that Southern California was "our Italy."[49]

Nolen spent two weeks in San Diego, logging up to one hundred miles a day to study the region, often in the company of George Marston. (Fig. 4.12) A self-made man devoted to civic beautification, Marston was the driv-

Fig. 4.12. Colonel Ed Fletcher, George Marston, and Nolen (left to right), 1908. Courtesy San Diego Historical Society.

ing force behind San Diego's park and urban planning initiatives. In 1902, while in New York on business, Marston had paid Samuel Parsons from his own funds to draw a plan for City Park, a 1,400-acre tract about a mile and a half from the coast. In 1905, as the chairman of the newly established San Diego Park Commission, Marston arranged for George Cooke, Parsons's former partner, to serve as superintendent of City Park and oversee its $20,000 budget. Having secured the future of the park, Marston turned his attention to urban planning.[50] Marston and Nolen hit it off immediately. Crisscrossing San Diego County's 3,200 square miles, they encountered a range of scenery—beaches, promontories, mesas, and canyons—and must have enjoyed discussing the future of the city against this impressive natural backdrop.[51]

Nolen spent three days hiking in the Cuyamaca Mountains, east of the city, with a small group that did not include Marston. They followed a mountain stream and camped by an ancient grove of western live oaks. At the higher elevation Nolen was captivated by the Coulter pine, a fire-tolerant species with the largest cone of any pine.[52] (Fig. 4.13) Settling back at the Coronado to draft a preliminary report, Nolen was struck by San Diego's unmatched climate. Residents lived "out-of-doors more hours of the day more days in the year than in any part of the United States." For the thousands suffering from "nervous prostration," San Diego was the cure.[53] But even though the climate and scenery were ideal, the civic landscape was mediocre. There were "no wide and impressive business streets, practically no open spaces in the heart of the city, no worthy sculpture," Nolen wrote. With the exception of City Park, the basic elements of a park system—parkways, neighborhood parks, and playgrounds—were missing. There was a wealth of natural resources, but unless action was taken, they would be lost.[54] Nolen's harsh assessment was not unexpected. During his time in San Diego, he reiterated these points in countless lectures that left him feeling as if he had "spoken with every citizen in the county."[55]

San Diego: A Comprehensive Plan also presented a framework to guide development and repair the damage inflicted during the frenzied real estate boom of the 1880s.[56] In 1887 real estate firms subdividing land successfully lobbied for a city charter that platted newly annexed land on narrow 25-foot-wide lots to increase the amount of salable property. In the next two years land was subdivided and sold at a furious pace; nineteen thousand parcels were bought up in get-rich-quick schemes. In 1889 San Diego's population reached 40,000, but with the collapse of the real estate market, it plummeted to 16,159 within a year.[57] The population had risen again to 30,000 by 1907, but municipal officials were still sorting out the ownership of lots sold to investors now scattered across the country. Moreover, the platting of land

Fig. 4.13. Coulter Pine. Photograph by John Nolen, 1908.

Courtesy Division of Rare and Manuscript Collections, Cornell University Library.

had been inconsistent at best and illegal at worst, including some partially submerged oceanfront properties that were sold to hapless investors. Countless empty lots stretched from the city to the desert's edge, "platted through the energy of real estate agents."[58] Laid out on a rectangular grid, the street network ignored topographical constraints and cut through hills and filled in valleys and canyons at great expense to taxpayers and the environment. Reforming the subdivision of land was essential, and Nolen's plan presented principles to guide future development.[59]

Despite past errors, San Diego had the potential to become a distinctive twentieth-century city by drawing income from a new source of wealth—tourism. By the early 1900s urban tourism had become a staple industry in Los Angeles as well as San Diego.[60] Nolen envisioned a modern "pleasure city," a place to indulge one's senses in a setting blessed by nature. He believed that San Diego could rival the cities of the Riviera, provided it developed a

Fig. 4.14. Nice, France, public waterfront. From Nolen's photomontage, 1908. Courtesy Division of Rare and Manuscript Collections, Cornell University Library.

striking waterfront that was accessible to the public. To illustrate his improvement plan, Nolen created a photomontage of the waterfronts in Menton, Nice, and Monte Carlo on the Côte d'Azur in France.[61] (Fig. 4.14) Docks, wharves, warehouses, and industry were relocated to special zones to improve business efficiency, and the rest of the coast would be dedicated to enhancing civic life. Bay Front Plaza was the centerpiece of a system of promenades and parks, a definitive public space offering stunning views of the Pacific Ocean.[62] (Fig. 4.15) Following Beaux-Arts protocol, Nolen designed a boulevard to connect the plaza to a civic center half a mile away. (Fig. 4.16) This alignment was both functional and symbolic, placing the seat of government on axis with a grand plaza sited to view a sublime nature. (Fig. 4.17) The plan was ambitious. It would require purchasing a block of vacant land on a major thoroughfare (D Street) to build the civic center, which included a new city hall, county courthouse, and federal building sited on a civic green. For the architecture, Nolen wanted to employ a Mediterranean style that expressed the city's Spanish heritage. A second waterfront park, the Esplanade, was placed on axis with City Park. Twelve hundred feet wide, it housed an open-air theater, art museum, and aquarium surrounded by small parks and gardens planted with species native to Southern California.

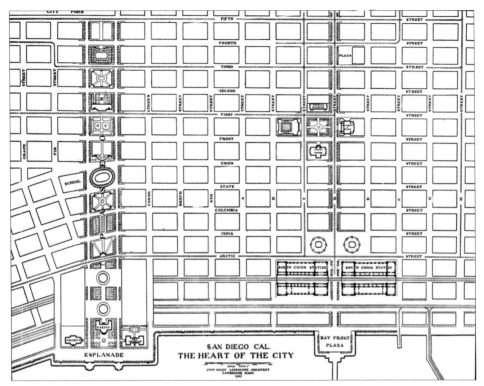

Fig. 4.15. San Diego Bay Front Plaza, rendering, 1908. Courtesy Division of Rare and Manuscript Collections, Cornell University Library.

Fig. 4.16. San Diego Bay Front, rendering, 1908. Courtesy Division of Rare and Manuscript Collections, Cornell University Library.

The downtown was the point of origin for a wide-ranging park system. A beach preserve was sited at Point Loma, a peninsula that stretched seven miles into the bay. Because San Diego had no public beaches, creating this preserve would set an important precedent.[63] With its unmatched climate and ample supply of sandy, curving coastline, San Diego could reap returns unimaginable

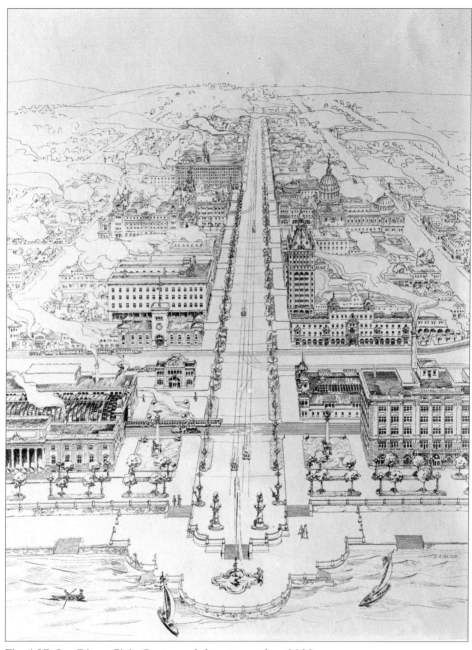

Fig. 4.17. San Diego Civic Center and downtown plan, 1908. Courtesy Division of Rare and Manuscript Collections, Cornell University Library.

Fig. 4.18. Torrey Pine. Photograph by John Nolen, 1908. Courtesy Division of Rare and Manuscript Collections, Cornell University Library.

in the Northeast. Parkways would link the waterfront parks to a preserve on Mount Soledad, the foothills overlooking Mission Valley, and a series of forest remnants, with Torrey Pines Reserve being the most significant. Located twenty miles north of the downtown, the reserve is home to the rare species *Pinus torreyana*, which thrives on cliffs overlooking the Pacific Ocean. The tree's long needles and distinctive cones give it a graceful picturesque form, and it is found only in Southern California xeric coastal uplands.[64] (Fig. 4.18)

Nolen believed that securing nature's "aesthetic wealth" was crucial to the city's future. Land prices were relatively low, and given the city's size, the thousand acres identified for acquisition was not extensive. The public debt could be bonded to fund the park system, and the return would be "so great," Nolen wrote, that the choice "is embarrassing."[65]

In prescribing a solution to the city's traffic problems, Nolen was less confident. The popularity of the automobile in Southern California forced him to confront a difficult issue. In Los Angeles, the car was an important yet disruptive force. San Diego still had time to plan, but during the "home rush," traffic was already a problem.[66] Nolen's solution was to make the automobile a unit within a system. Multimodal thoroughfares with 150- and 125-foot

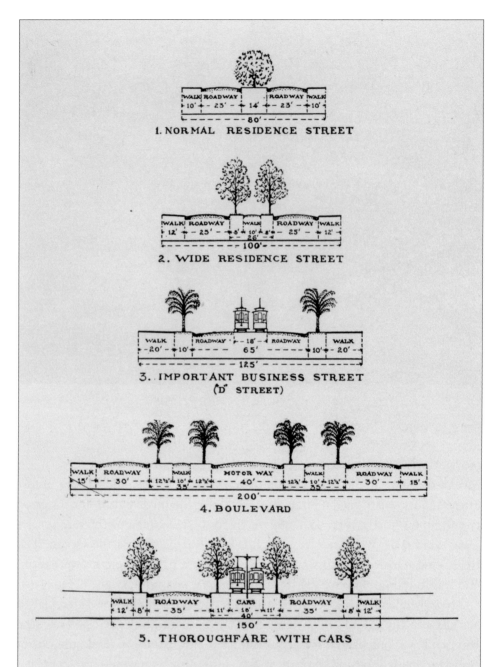

Fig. 4.19. San Diego street scheme, 1908. Courtesy Division of Rare and Manuscript Collections, Cornell University Library.

right-of-ways incorporated streetcars, automobiles, sidewalks, and street trees. To limit the automobile's impact in neighborhoods, Nolen recommended reducing 80-foot residential right-of-ways to 60 feet to accommodate 23-foot road widths, sidewalks, and street trees.[67] (Fig. 4.19)

The thoroughfares linked a continuum of public spaces planned to extend from the urban core to the city's periphery. Neighborhood centers—pedestrian-scaled environments with cafés, small businesses, and apartments—were placed at transit stops and important intersections. Sidewalks allowed pedestrians to travel safely from their homes to neighborhood centers. Walking was, Nolen wrote, "a delightful form of recreation and one of the most effective encouragements to profitable social intercourse."[68] Three types of play areas were proposed: sand lots for preschoolers, playgrounds located next to primary schools, and tracts of sports fields for older children.

In planning an American Riviera, Nolen paid little attention to the social issues he addressed in Roanoke. *San Diego: A Comprehensive Plan* presented the "pleasure city" that civic leaders desired. Nolen belived that the future would be "determined less by what people do in the few hours they are 'officially at work' than in their many hours of free time."[69] Park recreation bred virtue and good health, in his view, and San Diego was designed to model these traits.

Immediately after the completion of *San Diego: A Comprehensive Plan*, George Marston founded the Civic Improvement Association to champion its implementation.[70] The group was chaired by Julius Wangenheim, president of Commerce and Trust Bank. In the spring of 1908, the plan was printed in pamphlet form and disseminated among civic leaders. Wangenheim was cautiously optimistic about its acceptance. The national economic downturn that had begun in 1907 had spared Southern California, but San Diego's good luck ended that summer.[71] Bond sales for road improvement projects dropped dramatically and a half million remained unsold, making it impossible to issue new bonds. Nevertheless, Wangenheim and Marston continued to publicize the plan and enlist "the support, as far as possible, of every class and every member of the community."[72] Nolen's plan was printed in the *San Diego Union* on New Year's Day 1909, but in this time of economic reversal, the initiative fell on deaf ears. With so much uncertainty, there was little desire to spend scarce funds on grand civic projects.

In response to the financial crisis, Marston focused on reforming municipal government, and in 1909 he orchestrated the creation of California's first commission-style government. He brought Nolen's plan before the new body, but failed to secure a majority vote. After the economy rebounded, however, Marston again appeared before the city commission with proposals to implement portions of the plan. This piecemeal approach was effective, and in 1911 voters approved measures to acquire parks, build playgrounds, and improve streets in line with Nolen's recommendations. The city commission also restricted industrial uses along the waterfront to areas designated in the plan. However, Marston failed to secure the reform of land subdivision, which was opposed by powerful interests profiting from the demand for Southern California real estate. In 1912 San Diego's two major newspapers, the *Union* and the *Tribune,* came out against city planning, spurring Marston to run for mayor in 1913 and again in 1917 on a city planning platform.[73] Although he was twice defeated, Marston's campaigns kept *San Diego: A Comprehensive Plan* on the public agenda.[74] Over the next decade, officials established Torrey Pines Reserve and Collier Park on Point Loma, and subdivision reform was pursued by a small group of private developers. The Mission Hills neighborhood was the most notable example of Nolen's influence: roads followed the topography, vistas were plentiful, and small parks created a definitive sense of place.[75] In the ensuing years, Nolen periodically returned to San Diego as a consultant and reviewed the Olmsted Brothers' plan for City Park, renamed Balboa Park for the 1915 Panama–California Exposition. In 1926 Nolen was hired to draft a second comprehensive plan, as he had for Roanoke. It followed the outline of his initial effort.[76]

Nolen's *San Diego: A Comprehensive Plan* was a seminal work. At the time, city planning was still an experimental field, but Nolen's call for municipal reform raised standards and inspired action. His analysis and vision earned the respect of his peers as well. Land subdivision and transportation networks conformed to local topography, while urban development was allocated to the "naturally most fit" areas. Building on Eliot's model, Nolen molded a future city around the natural setting of the region. The preserves of forest, mountain, bay front, beach, and canyon identified in *San Diego: A Comprehensive Plan* differentiated it from European efforts. After San Diego, the Cambridge office began receiving requests from an increasingly reform-minded clientele.

5

CITY PLANNING IN
AMERICA AND EUROPE, 1908–1911

In January 1908 Nolen received a letter from John M. Olin, president of the Madison Park and Pleasure Drive Association, describing a unique opportunity.[1] Inspired by the German model of higher education, the "Wisconsin Idea" was employing faculty expertise to advance government reform.[2] Olin hoped to create a partnership between the university and the city by hiring Nolen as a professor who could offer a course in landscape design and also work as an urban planner in Madison.[3] After meeting with Charles H. Haskins, a Harvard history professor who had also taught at the University of Wisconsin, Nolen decided to discuss his prospects with Howard Griggs. He concluded it best to keep his full-time practice in Cambridge but to offer his consulting services to Madison.[4] Olin still wanted Nolen to relocate, but Nolen insisted that he needed to remain in Cambridge to take on "the big civic improvements sweeping the country."[5] After a flurry of letters, Olin structured a contract to Nolen's satisfaction. As consultant he would earn $3,200 a year for three years (the equivalent of a University of Wisconsin faculty salary), and Olin would manage projects for Nolen with the University of Wisconsin, the state Park Board, the state Board of Control, and the city of Madison.

In choosing to accept the offer, Nolen recognized the promise of the Wisconsin Idea and the opportunity to further ideals he valued. In the early 1900s, Wisconsin was known as "the laboratory of democracy" largely because of its charismatic governor, Robert M. La Follette Sr. "Fighting Bob" was a politician of heroic proportions: muscular in build, a skilled orator, egalitarian in vision, and incorruptible.[6] After his election in 1901, his administration instituted the nation's first direct primary and curbed the influence of the powerful railroad and lumber corporations.[7] By the time he left Madison for the U.S. Senate in 1906, La Follette had a string of accomplishments none of which was more important than the Wisconsin Idea. Together with Charles Van Hise, his classmate and later president of the University of Wisconsin, La Follette championed the notion that the university could become the nation's first "German University," an institution of higher education dedicated to improving the service and function of government.[8] Van Hise led a restructuring of the school's governance system and curriculum, prompting faculty (including economist Richard T. Ely, a classmate of Simon Patten and Edmund James in Germany) to invest in government reform.[9]

Nolen arrived in Madison in April 1908. After an initial meeting with Olin, he described his client as "a rather grim-visaged gentleman, very plain spoken but fair." Olin's "savage looking eye" was also well trained, as Nolen learned when the two men examined Madison's parkways and scenic landscapes.[10] On his second day in the Wisconsin capital, Nolen delivered the keynote address at a grand Madison Park and Pleasure Drive Association event. Governor James O. Davidson and other municipal officials attended, but Nolen was more impressed by the two hundred men of all classes who arrived directly from work for a parks meeting. It was a long evening, with a social hour, dinner, presentation of reports, and speeches preceding Nolen's talk, "Beauty and Order in State and City."[11] He opened with a quotation by former president Grover Cleveland: "Nature has made it a law that everyone is in need, mentally and psychically, of relaxation in the open air." In Madison, the MPPDA had crafted a living work of art—a park system—just as a sculptor "turns the block of marble into a figure that seems almost to breathe with life." According to Nolen, Madison's "organic" reform needed to be extended so that the entire city was made a work of art. Nolen declared that Madison, with its history of public/private initiatives, could become a model city.[12]

The address was well received. "John Nolen gave an excellent impression and proved himself a fine builder of words as well as of parks," the *Wisconsin State Journal* reported.[13] The oration and its message surpassed Olin's expectations. By then, Nolen had become a passionate advocate of the Wisconsin Idea as well as the leader of a growing national practice. He was spending six months a year traveling and wondered if he had extended himself too far. "This life is entirely too busy to suit me," he wrote to his wife from Madison. "I hope it will slow down after awhile."[14] Over the next two weeks, Nolen started a series of projects: a subdivision plat and landscaping plans for the University of Wisconsin, the Home for Feeble-Minded Children in Chippewa Falls, and the State School for Dependent Children in Sparta.[15]

Nolen returned to Wisconsin in November 1908. After crisscrossing the state for two weeks, he spent a lonely Thanksgiving in a Madison hotel.[16] He devoted the next week to assessing the city, and the results were not encouraging: too few playgrounds, streets marred by wires and utility poles, a dump near the state capitol, and factories encroaching on the lakefront. Just as in Roanoke and San Diego, "haphazard growth" was the culprit. Nolen set out to reform a landscape muddled by "individual wealth and community poverty."[17] (Fig. 5.1)

In early December he presented his findings in an MPPDA-sponsored address, "Madison in the Making." He explained how planning could rectify the city's problems and laid out the procedure to complete and adopt a city plan. Olin moved quickly on the issue. Within a month, he hosted a meeting devoted to city planning that attracted 350 attendees. There were speeches by the mayor and other officials, but the evening's highlight was a one-hour oration by Olin. He "held his audience spellbound," according to Madison historian David Mollenhoff, while explaining that "the preparation of a comprehensive city plan was not merely . . . an opportunity but . . . an obligation." If "representative" citizens approved of the enterprise, a slate of attorneys and businessmen promised to subscribe $2,500 to cover the cost of publishing the plan. In the spirit of the evening, the group unanimously voted to prepare a city plan under the guidance of a "Committee of Fifty" to include Governor

Fig. 5.1. Madison lakefront. Photograph by John Nolen, 1908. Courtesy Division of Rare and Manuscript Collections, Cornell University Library.

James O. Davidson, Charles Van Hise, and four dozen local businessmen. The committee chair was John Olin.[18]

Olin revised Nolen's contract to include drafting a comprehensive city plan for the MPPDA, and in April Nolen presented his preliminary concepts at the organization's annual meeting. He set three goals derived from German planning practice: highlighting the city's individuality, identifying and prioritizing municipal improvements, and expanding the recreation system. German reform was prized in Madison for inspiring the Wisconsin Idea, and Nolen sold city planning as the "Wisconsin Ideal." Following Germany's lead, he recommended that Madison acquire facilities for physical exercise, additional nature preserves, and a more efficient urban structure. It would become a model city, a prototype for directing public and private dollars to increase both profits and standards of living.[19] (Upon his return to Cambridge, Nolen reworked this speech into an address, which he would deliver in May at the First National Conference on City Planning in Washington, D.C. Nolen's presentation was timely. At this groundbreaking event, German reform was the central topic.)

Before returning east, he spent a week with three state park commissioners assessing properties for inclusion in a state park system. Nolen was in his element exploring Wisconsin's scenic land.[20] The most impressive site was in Door County, a thin peninsula jutting between Green Bay and Lake Michigan. There several thousand acres of wild country ran along the Green Bay shore, highlighted by steep limestone bluffs. (Fig. 5.2) Farther inland, conifer and birch framed views of the islands in the bay.[21] Returning to Cambridge, Nolen pieced together his notes and photographs into a sixty-five-page report, *State Parks for Wisconsin*, which the State Park Commission received in late November.

State Parks for Wisconsin broke new ground at a time when the majority of states had yet to invest in parks.[22] Nolen's report included letters of support from Charles W. Eliot, J. Horace McFarland, Jacob Riis, and Sylvester Baxter. John Muir, who had attended the University of Wisconsin and helped found the Sierra Club, was quoted in the introduction: "Thousands of tired, nerve shaken, over civilized people are beginning to find wildness is a necessity."[23] In 1908 Muir was a best-selling author and an American icon, the man who hiked and camped with Theodore Roosevelt and kept the loquacious president spellbound with his storytelling.[24] As a writer, Muir drew heavily from Henry David Thoreau, even making a celebrated pilgrimage to lay flowers on the naturalist's grave.[25] Nolen paired Muir's quote with several lines from Thoreau's essay "Walking." Thoreau's vision of a sublime nature defined a unique aspect of American culture that Roosevelt had come to personify. With the passage of the frontier, the president initiated a crusade to preserve wilderness and expand opportunities to enjoy the outdoors.[26] That spring,

Fig. 5.2 Peninsula State Park site. Photograph by John Nolen, 1908. Courtesy Division of Rare and Manuscript Collections, Cornell University Library.

Roosevelt convened the first meeting of the nation's governors, challenging them to establish forests and parks that could be integrated, where possible, into the federal system.[27] *State Parks for Wisconsin* was the first response to this initiative, a far-reaching vision to preserve "the wild and beautiful places of Nature."[28]

Wisconsin's abundant scenic land included five hundred miles of Great Lakes coastline, with sections rivaling the pristine beauty of Maine, precipitous bluffs on the banks of rivers and lakes, remnants of virgin hardwood forests, and rolling countryside comparable to the Berkshires in Massachusetts. Sylvester Baxter described the state as on the verge of becoming the "New England of the West," a place "known for its enlightened policy," but Nolen was not so optimistic.[29] He saw that, without state intervention, a significant segment of Wisconsin's population would be cut off from nature and destined to suffer "physical and moral suffocation."[30] Nolen developed criteria to evaluate potential park sites based on their size, cost, and accessibility. Landscape quality also had to be determined; high grades were given to properties with a mix of hilltops and mountains, lakes, bayfronts, riverbanks, and

Fig. 5.3. Dalles State Park site. Photograph by John Nolen, 1908. Courtesy Division of Rare and Manuscript Collections, Cornell University Library.

Fig. 5.4. Devils Lake Park site. Photograph by John Nolen, 1908. Courtesy Division of Rare and Manuscript Collections, Cornell University Library.

Fig. 5.5. Peninsula State Park, 2012. Courtesy Friends of Peninsula State Park.

woodlands. *State Parks for Wisconsin* proposed establishing four parks total-ing over 11,000 acres to "refresh and strengthen and renew tired people."[31] (Figs. 5.3, 5.4)

After he submitted his report, Nolen moved on to other projects, but his work continued to influence the state, as well as his own professional work. The State Park Commission unanimously supported Nolen's report, and in June 1909, assemblyman Thomas Reynolds sponsored a state park bill that passed easily. Funds were allocated and three of the four parks Nolen identi-fied were established by 1917: Peninsula State Park, Devils Lake, and Wyalus-ing State Park.[32] (Fig. 5.5) *State Parks for Wisconsin* inspired Nolen's keynote address to the 1909 American Civic Association conference. It also led him to write an article on parks, solicited by Simon Patten, for *The Annals of the American Academy of Political and Social Science*.[33] Described as a "landmark state park plan," *State Parks for Wisconsin* was a model study that led to an increase in state-owned land devoted to parks throughout the country.[34] In 1936 C. H. Schaeffer, the director of parks in Florida, used it to guide the expansion of his state's fledgling park system.[35]

In early 1909, New York housing advocate Benjamin C. Marsh announced the convening of the First National Conference on City Planning, an event that would bring together the nation's foremost planners and help Nolen to advance his own ideology about urban planning as civic art. Although the meeting was originally scheduled for April, Frederick Law Olmsted Jr. asked Marsh to push the date back, noting that April was an especially busy month for landscape architects. The request masked a deeper concern, however: Olmsted Jr. feared that Marsh would argue for the total acceptance of German city planning. This, he believed, would doom the fledgling movement. The First National Conference on City Planning was moved to late May, and it became a test of wills between two influential men with very different views of the future for American cities.[36]

Marsh, a zealous young reformer and University of Pennsylvania graduate, was the executive secretary for the Committee on the Congestion of Population in New York. The committee's members were mostly social workers and housing reformers who, between 1905 and 1907, were coping with record immigration into Ellis Island. As the teeming neighborhoods of Manhattan's Lower East Side continued to swell, city planning was seen as a tool for relieving congestion and dispersing populations throughout the city. Marsh, a student of Simon Patten, wanted city planners to focus on alleviating urban poverty and improving housing in the inner city.[37] In his conference address, he itemized the failures of the real estate market to supply decent worker housing. It was time for the government to intervene and adopt the German planning model. Implementing a state-authorized planning system was the only way to strengthen municipal governments that regularly capitulated to speculative interests.[38] Marsh's speech drew a mixed response. The idealism was laudable, but he seemed more interested in instituting a crusade against predatory real estate speculators than forming a professional organization.[39]

Olmsted Jr. spoke the next day. Like Marsh, he valued European reform; he had spent the winter of 1908–9 in Germany studying advances in land zoning and suburban neighborhood design.[40] Germany, however, had a history of municipal land ownership that was foreign to the United States. And when it came to the highly charged issue of property rights, change needed to proceed incrementally. Reform was essential and experimentation and advocacy must continue, Olmsted stated, but when city planners looked to Germany "it would be very foolish . . . [to] copy blindly what has been done there."[41]

The Marsh–Olmsted debate framed the conference, which gathered forty-three participants from a variety of fields: social work, architecture, landscape architecture, housing, and journalism.[42] "Olmsted is here," Nolen wrote, as were "[Charles Mulford] Robinson, [Harlan] Kelsey, [Andrew Wright] Crawford, [Edward] Filene, [Arthur] Shurtleff, and a lot other city planning people." A torrential downpour reportedly kept President William Howard Taft from attending the opening night ceremonies (politics was the more likely reason), but for those gathered, a common bond emerged as hopes were expressed and expectations rose. "Thoroughly worthwhile," Nolen exclaimed, "something is going to come of it too—much more than any of us thought!"[43]

Nolen sought to find a middle ground between Olmsted and Marsh. Though devoted to German reform, he knew firsthand the difference between implementing a city plan in the United States versus in Germany. American planners needed to be educators capable of elevating the civic mind, not coercing it. Nolen's own life experience, training, and practice in the smaller cities of the South, Midwest, and West put him in a different camp from Marsh; even when prospects were dim, he held fast to civic education as the key to instituting reform. For example, after a lackluster meeting in Marinette, Wisconsin, he concluded there was little hope for the city. Its leaders were "not capable," he thought, "of very fine things."[44] At the same time, however, he believed Americans to be inherently pragmatic. Once they understood the fiscal acuity of planning, he was confident it would become integral to the machinery of municipal government.[45]

At the conference in Washington, D.C., Nolen asked the question, "What is needed in American city planning?" The answer was straightforward: planners must define, measure, and direct progress in a new way. Equating progress with increases in population and wealth was the norm, but the consequences were disastrous. Denuding the environment to accommodate urban expansion was profitable, but it left behind a monotonous landscape that "haunts one like a nightmare." To escape a "formless future," Nolen argued, city plans had to "echo more closely . . . the physical situation and topography." Ordering development on this pattern would create individuality among cities while preserving their ties to the rural countryside. A city plan was both an aesthetic guide and a public accounting ledger, a mechanism for disbursing and tracking monies to fund long-term municipal improvements. With the rising tide of new wealth, investing in necessities such as outdoor recreation, secure water supplies, and public health was not the issue; rather, it was providing for them in an efficient and equitable manner.[46]

Nolen's civic sermon touted the expert's ability to order the city and inspire commitment. Championing an urban vision literally grounded in the lay of the land, city planning was a "civic art" and "above all democratic," Nolen claimed. "It is in no sense exclusive. The public buildings of a city, its green squares, its parks, and playgrounds are enjoyed by rich and poor, the latter probably more than the former. And there is no sense of charity in their enjoyment."[47] The landscape architect's conception of city planning carried the day, and design expertise and a commitment to comprehensive planning became the basis of the nascent profession. German reform would remain a point of study, as practitioners moved into the fields of housing and land use controls.[48]

In the spring of 1910, Olmsted Jr. and Arthur Shurcliff, both professors of landscape architecture at Harvard, were elected chairman and vice chairman of the executive committee for the National Conference on City Planning. Marsh failed in his elective bid for a position on the committee; effectively excluded from the decision making, he soon left the field. The profession maintained its moderate tone, but it was committed to moving urban reform toward democratic ends. To do so, practitioners would have to enlighten real estate and business interests.[49]

As Nolen had anticipated, the National Conference on City Planning had an immediate impact. Within weeks Edward A. Filene, a leading Boston businessman dedicated to social reform, summoned Nolen, Olmsted Jr., Shurcliff, and architect William Coolidge Jr. to discuss Boston-1915, a city planning exposition scheduled to open in the fall.[50] Filene was "a big businessman," according to journalist Lincoln Steffens, "a thinker who said things like an intellectual, but who went and did them like a practical man of business."[51] City planning appealed to Filene, but he thought implementation might require a revolution. Private property was a sacred right, and reformers had to walk a fine line between socialism and civically instituted change.[52]

The Boston-1915 exposition grew out of Filene's decision in 1908 to hire Lincoln Steffens to write a book like his acclaimed *The Shame of the Cities* (1904). The idea was to document Boston's disorder and poor living conditions to spark a public outcry for city planning. Although a manuscript never materialized, Steffens convinced Filene that reformers must have an idealistic vision based on beauty and equanimity. Filene decided that city planning needed a forum to capture public attention. Having recently brokered the merger of the Merchants Association and the Board of Trade to form the Boston Chamber of Commerce, he had considerable influence, and in early 1909 the chamber of commerce voted to underwrite the exposition.[53] After the conference, it formed the Boston-1915 Committee, which included Nolen among its members.

Filene and Nolen were barely acquaintances at the time, but their interest in city planning led to a lasting friendship. Committed to the ideals of self-improvement and public service, they both pursued pragmatic avocations while addressing humanitarian concerns. A quotation by Filene that appeared in the *Saturday Evening Post* decorated Nolen's office: "In the final analysis beauty is the greatest objective in the world but we cannot teach spiritual truths effectively to starving people."[54] Over the years, Nolen would frequently call on "E. A.," but early on he followed in the influential man's wake.

Filene employed his advertising skills to saturate the local media with announcements for the Boston-1915 event. Nolen joined the young German planner Werner Hegemann, along with Sylvester Baxter, Olmsted Jr., and Shurcliff, in setting up the show. In November 1909, 200,000 citizens attended the three-week event hosted by the Museum of Fine Arts in Copley Square. The impressive visual presentation greeting visitors featured fifty-nine paintings and drawings from Daniel Burnham's plan for Chicago. A room was devoted to the Greater Berlin Plan, while Nolen's plans for Roanoke and San Diego appeared in a display on smaller American cities.[55]

The committee also sponsored a lecture series on good government. For Nolen, this meant the efficient expenditure of public funds; that is, for every dollar entrusted to government, citizens should expect "properly ordered streets, decent housing of all the people, dignified and well-arranged public buildings, convenient and appropriate railroad approaches, ample and suitable schools and playgrounds, parks, and public gardens." A city plan could help allocate municipal improvements in a reasonable sequence, but it took individuals with "civic virtue" to implement the plan. Ultimately, it was "not the changed city, but the changed citizen" that counted. This "new attitude, the new patriotism," Nolen announced, would build cities to stand "as a rich heritage to this and many succeeding generations." Such rhetoric filled the proceedings of the exhibition, and many attendees left feeling that the world was changing for the better.[56]

Werner Hegemann returned to Germany in 1909 confident in the success of the Universal City Planning Exhibition to be held in Berlin the next year. As secretary general for the exhibition, Hegemann regularly consulted his American acquaintances, and plans by Olmsted Jr., Nolen, and Burnham were displayed in his home country. This reciprocity of knowledge produced results.[57] In 1913 Hegemann, who had earned a PhD in political science from the University of Munich, returned to the United States as an acclaimed expert. After a cross-country lecture tour, he garnered a series of commissions in the years leading up to America's entry into World War I, including consulting with Nolen on a residential subdivision in Madison. Hegemann became best known for *The American Vitruvius: An Architect's Handbook of Civic Art* (1922), the elegant summary of city planning that he coauthored with American landscape architect Elbert Peets.[58]

Late in life Hegemann pondered the dreams unfurled in Boston. He had envisioned Boston-1915 as the first in a series of exhibitions that would cause a domino effect as countries competed for prominence in urban planning: "The whole world could become engaged in internal improvements and urban rivalry to such an extent that, during the time required for carrying out the civic plans, international peace would rule and even become a permanent guest upon our planet."[59] Indeed, in the years leading up to the Great War, city planning did inspire the notion, however fantastic, that a New Jerusalem lay in the not too distant future.[60]

During the planning of Boston-1915, Nolen was also consulting with Olin on the details for *Madison: A Model City*.[61] After determining that implementation of their grand vision would cost between $6 million and $10 million over a twenty-year period, they decided to submit a proposal for amending the state constitution and changing the public financing system. Olin had mastered this tactic as president of the Madison Park and Pleasure Drive Association. He proceeded to choreograph the passage of two bills in the state legislature: one to restructure Madison's debt and the second, the Wisconsin City Planning Act, to allow local governments to create city planning commissions for overseeing the drafting and implementation of a city plan.[62] The nation's first state planning bill helped build momentum for the project. A planning commission was established in 1910, and *Madison: A Model City* was published the next year. Nolen's 168-page report, essentially a primer on urban planning, listed every city plan in the United States and included 158 illustrative plates. The text was descriptive as well as visionary, outlining the effort to create a "well-ordered, free, organic city" where "science, art, and culture" took precedence and "the hope of democracy" would be realized.[63]

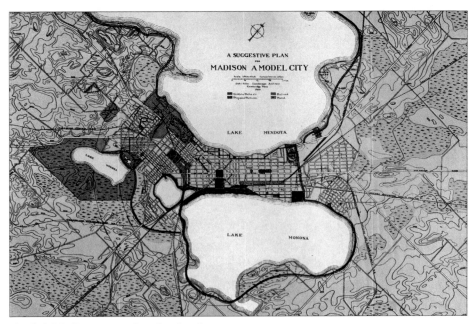

Fig. 5.6. Madison comprehensive city plan. Courtesy Division of Rare and Manuscript Collections, Cornell University Library.

Nolen proposed embellishing Madison's picturesque setting between two lakes with a system of parkways and waterfront esplanades linking city, country, and campus. (Fig. 5.6) The state capitol, under construction since 1907, was the focal point. A thirteen-acre rectangular green, Capitol Square, bordered the statehouse, which would tower above the existing structures. To safeguard its prominence, approaches and building heights would be regulated. A formal tree-lined mall, running between the capitol and Lake Monona, demarcated what was becoming Nolen's trademark: an axial boulevard connecting the seat of government to a natural feature. (Fig. 5.7) From the building it was only a short walk to the lake, with its scenic views.[64]

The capitol was the pivotal point of the street network. Beyond it, there were too many street crossings and a frustrating inconsistency in road widths, exemplified by State Street, the principal connection between the capitol and the University of Wisconsin. (Fig. 5.8) The right-of-way was too narrow, and

Fig. 5.7. Capitol Mall, rendering. Courtesy Division of Rare and Manuscript Collections, Cornell University Library.

Fig. 5.8. State Street, Madison, c. 1910. Courtesy Division of Rare and Manuscript Collections, Cornell University Library.

Fig. 5.9. State Street, Madison, with planned improvements. Courtesy Division of Rare and Manuscript Collections, Cornell University Library.

adjacent buildings were varied distances from the street. Nolen suggested widening the right-of-way from sixty-six to one hundred feet to provide space for a double-track streetcar system, excluding all automobile traffic. To highlight the terminating vista, utility lines were to be buried and a Beaux-Arts scheme would order the placement of buildings. (Fig. 5.9) Improving State Street would also strengthen the tie between the city and the university. With twenty buildings on 350 acres, the University of Wisconsin played a vital role in the life of Madison, and it must not become, Nolen wrote, "an isolated institution." He proposed lining the routes to the school with gardens and landscape amenities, including a linear park hugging the shoreline of Lake Mendota on the far edge of the campus. The two largest nature preserves, the 1,000-acre University Forest and a 200-acre arboretum, were to be outdoor laboratories for students and faculty as well as aesthetic amenities for the public.[65]

The Capitol Mall and the University Forest, located along Lake Wingra, would be the linchpins in the interconnected park system. (Fig. 5.10) Most of the proposed parks lay on or near lakefronts, and playgrounds were assigned to each neighborhood. The model Nolen used for them was Russell Square, a Chicago playground designed in 1904 with play areas for preschoolers and school-age children, as well as ball fields for teenagers and young adults. In listing the benefits of active recreation, Nolen emphasized its role in child-

Fig. 5.10. Madison park plan. Courtesy Division of Rare and Manuscript Collections, Cornell University Library.

hood development, crime deterrence, and mitigating the "morbid temperament" caused by a "sedentary life."[66]

By 1911 working-class housing was at the forefront of city planning agendas.[67] In *Madison: A Model City*, Nolen juxtaposed photographs of unsightly tenements with planned European working-class neighborhoods to illustrate that poor housing quality was a function of a real estate market driven by "ignorance, caprice, and selfishness." This problem was not restricted to a single class; it infected the entire land development system, as "the present character of American city suburbs bears abundant testimony," Nolen wrote.[68] Reform was a technical as well as an ethical challenge. Most often, subdivisions were laid out on a geometric grid that ignored environmental constraints, and the most common problems were flooding and soil subsidence. Round Top Hill, a neighborhood in Madison, illustrated how a site's natural topography could be incorporated into a subdivision plan. (Fig. 5.11) With urban expansion increasing, land subdivision needed regulation, Nolen concluded, even if it "interfere[d] with property rights."[69] In addition, funds should be set aside to purchase parks and road right-of-ways in advance of development. To explain the benefits of municipal land ownership, the report included an appendix itemizing the value of public lands in German cities. The prototype for the Wisconsin capital, however, was Lucerne, Switzerland, a city that offered all the public amenities Nolen desired: "a happy development of lake frontages for public use; a rational street system; a freedom from nuisances; a wise and reasonable regulation of railroads and private buildings; the careful planting and protection of street trees; an abundance of recreation areas and public gardens of all sorts; practical and beautiful sites for public buildings, art galleries, museums, and music halls; comfortable and sanitary housing."[70]

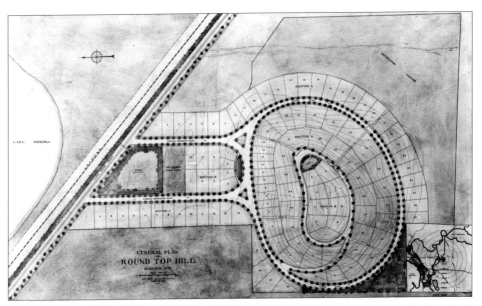

Fig. 5.11. Round Top Hill subdivision, 1911. Courtesy Division of Rare and Manuscript Collections, Cornell University Library.

To implement his plan, Nolen recommended a civic education campaign like the one in Chicago, where the Burnham plan was required reading in high school.[71] *Madison: A Model City* never received the press and widespread support that accompanied Burnham's plan, but it did inspire action. Funds were secured to improve Capitol Square, and Nolen designed a landscape plan patterned after the one Olmsted Sr. had drawn for the grounds of the nation's capitol. A three-tiered system—terrace, lawn, promenade—aligned the park and statehouse along the cardinal points of the compass.[72] Elaborate plantings placed at the termini of the four promenades highlighted the symmetrical quadrilateral design; to avoid repetition each quadrant featured a different plant palette.[73] (Fig. 5.12)

Once work began on the square in late 1912, Madison legislators pushed to implement the Capitol Mall plan. The state legislature gave the go-ahead for officials to negotiate with property owners in the six-block area between Lake Monona and the capitol. A sixty-foot building height limitation was deemed reasonable, but when discussion shifted to acquiring key parcels for public buildings, the initiative dissipated. The $7 million invested in the new capitol discouraged legislators from raising additional tax dollars to fund, as one Milwaukee editor put it, "Madison's money madness."[74] Support for Nolen's plan waned, but its broad vision continued to germinate. In 1920 attorney Michael B. Olbrich, president of the MPPDA, convinced the city planning commission to reprint *Madison: A Model City*. Olbrich led by example; in 1923 he privately

Fig. 5.12. Wisconsin Capitol, planting plan, 1912. Courtesy Wisconsin Historical Society, WHS 5766.

purchased 3,500 feet of lakefront property and donated it to the city. (Fig. 5.13) By the end of the decade, he had secured funds to establish Olbrich Botanical Garden and Olin Park, a waterfront park with a stunning view of the city. In addition, the University of Wisconsin added twenty acres to its lakefront preserve, as Nolen had suggested. In 1923 the state also instituted his recommendation to limit the height of structures on Capitol Square, and government buildings fronted Monona Avenue largely as Nolen planned, highlighting the grandeur of the statehouse and creating a premier civic space. Automobile traffic was limited on State Street, which became the tree-lined link between the capitol and the university that Nolen had envisioned.[75]

Fig. 5.13. Olbrich Park. Photograph by Andrew Landis, 2011.

Madison: A Model City marked a turning point in Nolen's career—his practice was secure and his expertise acknowledged. Frederic C. Howe, a leading authority on German city planning, praised him for presenting "a vision of a city like Munich, Dresden, or Düsseldorf, a city in which the state shall cooperate with the municipality to develop a center of the life of the commonwealth; a center to which the Middle West will come for education, music, and art; a city in which the university will be a democratic adjunct to the state."[76] In addition to the physical plan, the foresight to have the state, municipality, and university acquire hundreds of acres of land for forests, arboreta, and shoreline parks was a model of intergovernmental cooperation.

After Madison, Nolen earned a string of important commissions. To meet his burgeoning workload, he moved into a larger office on Harvard Square and hired the talented designer Philip W. Foster. Fifteen years Nolen's junior, Foster began his career as an office boy with Olmsted Brothers. Although he never attended college, he had a natural talent and worked diligently to become a skilled technician. In the Cambridge office, Foster oversaw day-to-day operations and collaborated with Nolen on plan design. This division of labor freed Nolen to develop expertise in the fields of transportation, town planning, housing, and land subdivision.[77]

Boston-1915 prompted an international interest in planning, one that Nolen would profit from personally and professionally. Chambers of commerce in Europe and the United States began making reciprocal trips to evaluate innovations in urban reform. Europeans were particularly fascinated by Boston's cultural milieu and its parks. The scale and diversity of the Metropolitan Park System impressed Werner Hegemann so much that he elevated Olmsted Sr. and Charles Eliot to almost mythical status in his homeland.[78] For their part, Americans studied British and German innovations in town planning, worker housing, and social services. Edward Filene and the Boston Chamber of Commerce sponsored the first major tour to Europe in June 1911. The Boston Metropolitan Planning Commission appointed Nolen and Mayor John Fitzgerald, John F. Kennedy's grandfather, as its representatives, and in June 1911, sixty businessmen, city officials, and urban experts set sail for England.

The voyage opened a new avenue in the cultural exchange that had been set in motion when young American scholars headed to Germany a generation before.[79] Frederic Howe chaired the program committee, and the tour had a decidedly German orientation, with stops in Düsseldorf, Frankfurt, Hamburg, Berlin, Dresden, Prague, Nuremberg, Munich, and Vienna. Also on the itinerary were London, Paris, Brussels, Budapest, Venice, Milan, Montreux, and Geneva. Tour members and local experts delivered lectures at each port of call, where Americans were regularly wined and dined, sometimes enjoying two banquets a day.[80] Nolen roomed with Frank B. Williams, a Harvard-trained New York attorney who specialized in city planning law. Williams had a keen interest in German building regulations, and he later joined Edward M. Bassett in drafting New York City's landmark zoning resolution of 1916.[81] Williams and Nolen went on to collaborate on a series of commissions, including drafting the first city plan and planning legislation for the state of Florida. Nolen enjoyed the group's camaraderie. Howe and Lincoln Steffens, who roomed together, were "very sanguine" companions, while Fitzgerald, a notorious imbiber, was a "lively addition" to the group. "The Mayor is quite chummy with me and consults me on many points," Nolen happily noted.[82]

In England during the first week of the tour, Nolen met Ebenezer Howard and Raymond Unwin. Walking Letchworth's streets with Unwin, Nolen studied the subtle alignments of public space and the interplay of sight lines in the picturesque neighborhoods. The lessons in town planning continued when the group proceeded to Hampstead Garden Suburb on the northern fringe of London. (Fig. 5.14) Designed by Unwin and Barry Parker in 1907, the development featured a variety of housing configurations ranging from single homes to quadraplexes and octaplexes. The pedestrian routes, intimate greens, and small parks were crafted in a fashion that left a lasting impression on Nolen. Later he enjoyed a gathering at the home of Thomas Adams, where

Fig. 5.14. Touring Hampstead Garden Suburb. Photograph by B. A. Haldeman, 1911. Courtesy Division of Rare and Manuscript Collections, Cornell University Library.

Fig. 5.15. Home of Thomas Adams (Nolen standing at far right), 1911. Courtesy Division of Rare and Manuscript Collections, Cornell University Library.

Fig. 5.16. Düsseldorf public waterfront. Photograph by B. A. Haldeman, 1911. Courtesy Division of Rare and Manuscript Collections, Cornell University Library.

he became acquainted with the leaders of England's garden city movement. (Fig. 5.15) Nolen would return to Hampstead Garden Suburb the next year to join Unwin in delivering a lecture at the University of London's town planning program. Close in age and temperament, the two men became steadfast friends. They corresponded regularly, exchanging social views, planning expertise, and their visions for constructing a more equitable urban civilization. Their families vacationed together, and once the children grew to young adulthood, each visited their "foster families" in England and America.[83]

In July Nolen celebrated his forty-second birthday in Munich. "I have a sort of thrill in Germany that I do not have elsewhere," he wrote home. He delivered a lecture in the Bavarian capital assessing Camillo Sitte's influence in drafting the city's plan.[84] He enjoyed Frankfurt but found Düsseldorf most interesting, describing the city as "a highly socialized municipality ruled by businessmen who do not believe in socialism." Since his visit a decade before, Nolen saw significant progress; the suburbs, parks, playgrounds, river esplanades, promenades, zoo, urban forests, music gardens, and even beer halls were worthy of study.[85] (Fig. 5.16) Inspired, he began writing an article on city planning in Düsseldorf during the voyage home.

Nolen's experiences in Europe raised his awareness of the advances taking place on both sides of the Atlantic, and he became a central figure in an international dialogue that would determine the future of the planning profession.[86] Since his days at Harvard, he had kept abreast of innovations in the field by subscribing to European and American journals, including *Der Städtebau, Landscape Architecture, American City,* and *Recreation.* He joined a number of organizations, including the American Society of Landscape Architects, the National Conference on City Planning, the American Civic Association, the National Housing Association, the Municipal League, the Garden Cities and Town Planning Association of England, and, later, the International Garden City Association.[87] Nolen's experience as an administrator of adult education programs was invaluable to these groups. He kept meticulous records, corresponded regularly, disseminated information effectively, and was adept in setting up lectures and conference meetings. After the European tour, Nolen was quick to reengage his new acquaintances. Under the auspices of the Boston Metropolitan Planning Commission, he sent out a questionnaire to European planners, including Thomas Adams, Raymond Unwin, Patrick Geddes, Josef Stübben of Germany, and Georges Benoît-Lévy of France, asking them to identify priorities for comprehensive planning.[88]

In 1912 Nolen solidified his rank among his international peers with the publication of "The Basis of German City Planning Procedure: An Example from Düsseldorf," which appeared in *Landscape Architecture.* As he reviewed the city's 1911 plan, he noticed that German planners had a predilection for data compilation. Contained within were twenty-four studies, including assessments of public lands, homes with gardens, urban forests, population densities, building values, housing size, average rents, food sources, and prevailing wind directions. From this information, planners were able to project the transportation and housing infrastructure for 1930 and future growth patterns for 1950. Such extrapolation of data was foreign to American planners, but the Germans had, with meticulous detail, turned their craft into a science.

Nolen's German counterparts were especially adept at transportation planning, producing studies delineating journey times, the cost and benefit of tramway expenditures, and public transit ridership. Transportation plans featured boulevards that integrated streetcar lines with right-of-ways reserved for fast trains and underground railways. Promenades linked formal gardens, public plazas, and athletic fields, while parks and forest preserves separated industrial zones from residential areas. Street widths, building setbacks, and the height and bulk of structures were regulated. Neighborhoods integrated parks and green spaces with a variety of housing types: detached homes, terrace houses, and garden apartments. Civic buildings were the focal points for neighborhood and town centers, and schools were sited by function; young children could walk to elementary schools, and secondary schools served as communal centers.[89]

In Germany, planning was arguably a generation ahead of the United States, a product of the nation's governing institutions and its inclination for bureaucratic order.[90] After writing "The Basis of German City Planning Procedure," Nolen adapted German methods to his practice. His planning reports came to contain less propaganda and more analysis. Detailed examinations of local environments were based on increasingly sophisticated studies of natural conditions, and a rudimentary social science was used to assess future land use, the demand for housing, and the delineation of zoning districts, which separated uses into a system of hierarchical urban cells. Nolen also became an advocate of city planning education, which until then had made only modest inroads in the United States.[91] Nolen expected an increased level of specialization "so that in time there will be a profession using men trained as landscape architects," he wrote to Thomas Adams. They would have an appropriate introduction to architecture but "specialize in the preparation of town and city plans."[92] Adams, a founding member of the British Town Planning Institute, had similar thoughts, and the two men began plotting a course for city planning education, an undertaking that would occupy them well into the 1930s.

Adams and his English colleagues were an inspiration to Nolen and his cohorts. Yet in 1911, when Adams and Unwin spoke at the National Conference on City Planning, they were perplexed that the Americans had yet to employ the garden city to address the demand for suburban housing.[93] In fact, the Russell Sage Homes Foundation had purchased land in 1909 for the development of Forest Hills Gardens in Queens, New York, and was about to unveil its achievement. The new community based on Howard's garden city prototype was designed by Olmsted Jr. and architect Grosvenor Atterbury as a model for future American suburbs. Located on 142 acres near a stop on the Long Island Railway, Forest Hills Gardens featured a mix of housing types set within a graceful system of parks and urban spaces. The architecture resembled the style Unwin had used at Hampstead and Letchworth.[94]

When the Forest Hills Gardens sales office opened in 1911, John Nolen was in Charlotte, North Carolina, at the behest of George Stephens. The two men had reunited on a new project, Myers Park, a suburb they envisioned as a model for cities in the southern Piedmont region. Inspired by his client and his colleagues, Nolen was determined to reframe the concept of the American suburb.

Fig. 6.1. Montclair town center, rendering, 1909. Courtesy Division of Rare and Manuscript Collections, Cornell University Library.

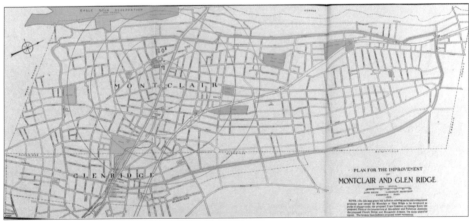

Fig. 6.2. Montclair town plan, 1909. Courtesy Division of Rare and Manuscript Collections, Cornell University Library.

6

MODEL SUBURBS AND INDUSTRIAL VILLAGES, 1909–1918

John Nolen moved to the forefront of the city planning profession on the strength of his comprehensive city plans, but as his practice expanded his interest turned to the planning of towns. The Myers Park commission offered the possibility of creating a unified civic design on a more intimate scale than a city plan. For the design of Myers Park, Nolen drew on his experience developing his first town plan for Montclair, New Jersey. In 1906, Nolen had introduced the concept of town planning to a sizable local audience at an event sponsored by the Montclair Municipal Art Commission. Two years later, he signed a $2,000 contract with the town, and in 1909 he sent the commission a 109-page report and plan presenting "a new and more appropriate type of town development."[1]

Establishing an urban center for Montclair, a New York suburb of 20,000, was Nolen's first priority. Montclair retained the "charm of the country town" but had no gathering space for residents and no public buildings other than a library and a small post office.[2] Nolen proposed constructing a civic district on an underutilized block, which could be acquired by bonding the town's collateral (valued at $27 million). Inspired by the work of Camillo Sitte, he hoped to amplify Montclair's "picturesque" quality.[3] His new plan featured a town green in front of two existing churches and the library; a city hall, two schools, a theater, and a small hotel surrounded the remainder of the green. (Fig. 6.1) By restructuring a six-corner intersection, he would create a quarter-acre plaza and improve traffic flow and pedestrian access to local businesses. The new plaza and green were integrated into a park system designed to link Montclair to its sister town, Glen Ridge. (Fig. 6.2)

Montclair's most perplexing issue was worker housing. The real estate market's "haphazard and wasteful method" had produced dilapidated neighborhoods that were similar to, Nolen wrote, "the slums of a great city."[4] He recommended that Montclair officials establish a limited-dividend housing corporation based on the English model. The corporation would purchase land, ideally inexpensive property on the town's periphery, and oversee the construction of a village of "group homes." Photographs of the model towns of Letchworth and Port Sunlight illustrated how neighborhoods could be built for the comfort and good health of the working class. Based on Nolen's recommendations over the next two years, Montclair's city commission adopted a new building code, established a park commission, and acquired park sites. However, the town center and the housing authority never moved beyond the discussion stage. Despite its limited success, Montclair gave Nolen a framework to build on.

The Montclair plan's civic aesthetic, formula for municipal investment, and housing initiative illustrated the comprehensive nature of Nolen's method of town planning. He began to refine his skills in the discipline, primarily by studying European examples and stepping up his advocacy. In 1910 he delivered the keynote address, "Comprehensive Planning for Small Towns and Villages," at the American Civic Association conference in Washington, D.C. The American Unitarian Association published the speech in a pamphlet series that included *The Individual and the Social Order in Religion*, *The Social Conscience and the Religious Life*, and *Popular Recreation and Public Morality*. Nolen's call "to establish a better social order" echoed the message of the Social Gospel, the early twentieth century moral crusade led by Protestant clergy and theologians in northern cities to secure just and decent living conditions.[5] The prevention of urban ills, not just their cure, lay at the genesis of modern planning, and rational analysis and artistic design could unveil "the divine voice of the future," Nolen proclaimed. The best prospects were in smaller, less encumbered urban areas, where expansion could be planned on a practiced set of principles. In 1900 there were 1,700 U.S. towns with populations between 2,500 and 25,000, an aggregate population of ten million, or two million more than the combined population of the nation's six largest cities. The field was open, but no matter the size of the town, municipal politics and professional expertise could run at cross-purposes. To prevent passion and greed from resolving issues of private property and public land, Nolen recommended that citizens become "masters employing servants more skillful than themselves."[6]

Having disinterested experts direct urban expansion underpinned the philosophy of progressivism. In 1909 the movement's leader, Herbert Croly, argued in his seminal work, *The Promise of American Life*, that planning was essential to procure the new republic reformers had envisioned for a generation. The "Jeffersonian superstitions" of limited government and absolute property rights had outlived their usefulness. University-trained experts engaged in "increasingly constructive experiments" were setting the course of the future city, systematically aligning parks, transit, industry, and housing by placing, Croly wrote, "fruitful limitations on certain individual freedoms."[7] The influential journalist had attended that year's National Conference on City Planning, and his support for planning was not lost on Nolen. In a series of speeches, the latter declared that "the promise of American life is bright" because the "new civic spirit" was being translated into concrete plans. Like Croly, Nolen labored to modernize Jeffersonian ideals, especially "the pursuit of happiness," which was associated with ownership of private property. A city plan procured "modern happiness" by arranging private property to secure profits and opportunities for community well-being.[8]

City planning had gained acceptance, but as a profession it had a tenuous hold on legitimacy. Practitioners faced a stream of challenges, and none more frustrating than building model communities. The list of examples in America resembled "the renowned chapter on snakes in Ireland," wrote Grosvenor Atterbury, the Forest Hills Gardens architect: "there are none."[9] American planning texts were equally rare. In 1912 Nolen contracted with American publisher B. W. Huebsch to publish his first book, *Replanning Small Cities: Six Typical Studies,* a compilation of his plans. His addresses to the National Conference on City Planning and the American Civic Association made up most of the introduction; the rest of the text consisted of reprints of his plans for Roanoke, San Diego, Montclair, Madison, Reading (Pennsylvania), and Glen Ridge (New Jersey). A civic body had sponsored each work, and its task was to turn vision into reality. The key was to educate municipal officials on the value "of the new methods of planning," Nolen concluded.[10]

A copy of *Replanning Small Cities,* held by the Department of Urban Planning at the University of North Carolina, bears an inscription by Nolen: "To my good friend George Stephens, who has at heart the replanning of his own city of Charlotte, May 29, 1912." Charlotte, the banking center for the Carolinas, was fast transitioning from town to city (its population would reach 40,000 by 1920), and Stephens recognized that growth brought a demand for quality neighborhoods. From his father-in-law, John Myers, he acquired a thousand-acre cotton farm located on a new streetcar line. He planned to develop the property in sections, with payments due when lots were sold. This arrangement allowed Stephens to hire Nolen to make Myers Park a model of "unified suburban design."[11]

Nolen stayed with the Stephens family (whose children he came to love) and spent a week evaluating the project site.[12] Three miles long and up to a mile wide, the property was mostly cotton fields, but two creeks flowed

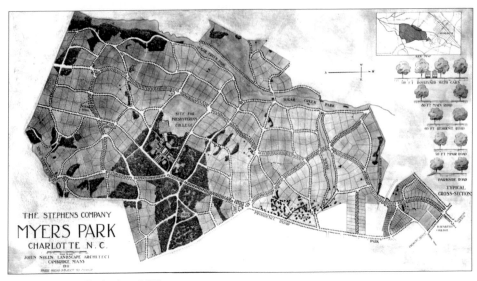

Fig. 6.3. Myers Park plan, 1911. Courtesy Division of Rare and Manuscript Collections, Cornell University Library.

Fig. 6.4. Myers Park, mature native tree canopy on public and private land. Photograph by the author, 2006.

Fig. 6.5 Edgehill Park. Photograph by the author, 2006.

through meadows and stands of oak and pine forest. Nolen joined these natural features into a plan patterned after Riverside, Illinois, Olmsted Sr.'s model Chicago suburb.[13] (Fig. 6.3) Construction commenced in 1912, and building continued at a steady pace for a decade. Following Riverside's protocol, deeds required housing setbacks, and fences and hedges were relegated to side yards. Native trees, oak, elm, and tulip poplar were planted on private properties and bordered the curvilinear streets. (Fig. 6.4) A hierarchy of street types was laid out along topographical lines. Residential streets were narrow and little more than country lanes, whereas Queens Boulevard, the principal throughway, had a 110-foot right-of-way to accommodate a streetcar line and hardwood trees planted in perpendicular rows. Access to transit was at most a two-block walk for residents, and parks were equally close at hand.

Edgehill Park, the most significant section of the park system's connective tissue, ran along both sides of the Sugar Creek floodplain, which flowed in an east–west direction through the center of the community. (Fig. 6.5) The linear park extended to a small green on the eastern edge of the community that served as a streetcar stop and the community's gateway. Granite entranceways bordered it, with openings for both pedestrians and streetcars to pass through. Inside Myers Park, the winding roadways slowed traffic, and the circuitous paths enhanced the pedestrian experience. (Fig. 6.6)

Stephens wanted a prominent civic institution to be the centerpiece of

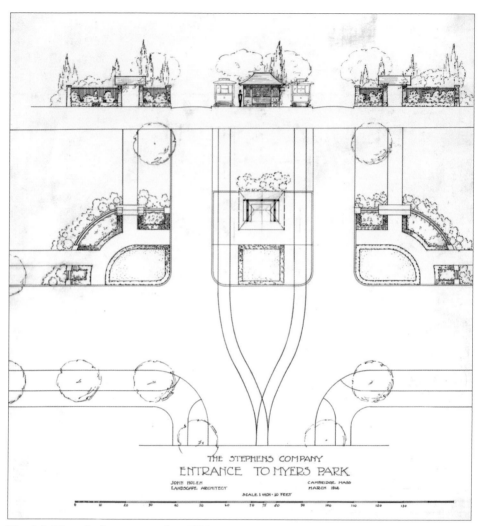

THE STEPHENS COMPANY
ENTRANCE TO MYERS PARK
JOHN NOLEN   CAMBRIDGE, MASS.
LANDSCAPE ARCHITECT   MARCH 1912

SCALE 1 INCH = 10 FEET

Fig. 6.6. Myers Park, entrance plan, 1912. Courtesy Division of Rare and Manuscript Collections, Cornell University Library.

Myers Park, and when he discovered that the Presbyterian College for Women hoped to relocate from its downtown location, he put together a deal. He purchased the college campus for $100,000 and deeded the Board of Trustees title to eighty-five acres in Myers Park. The board joined Stephens in a real estate partnership to develop fifty-five of the college's acres; the school's profits funded the endowment and building projects on the new thirty-acre campus. Presbyterian College for Women was renamed Queens College in honor of Charlotte's namesake, Queen Charlotte of Mecklenburg, and because of its new location on Queens Boulevard.

The contract Stephens signed with the Board of Trustees stipulated that Nolen would plan the campus. (Fig. 6.7) Although he had designed additions

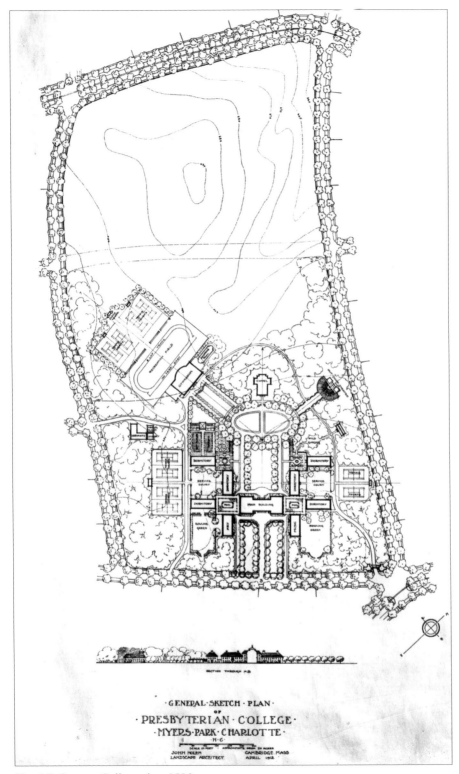

Fig. 6.7. Queens College plan, 1912. Courtesy Division of Rare and Manuscript Collections, Cornell University Library.

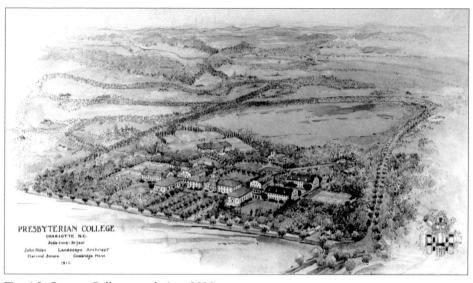

Fig. 6.8. Queens College, rendering, 1912. Courtesy Division of Rare and Manuscript Collections, Cornell University Library.

to Davidson College and the University of North Carolina, the Queens College commission offered a unique opportunity to create a model community. He sited the campus on a series of geometric grids that were enfolded into the contours of the low, rolling Piedmont hills. Buildings were arranged in an "H" pattern on two quadrangles, a concept he had employed at the University of North Carolina.[14] (Fig. 6.8) The lead architect was Charles Christian Hook, best known for his commissions at Duke University (Figs. 6.9, 6.10)

In order to handle the office's increasing workload, Nolen had assigned Earle Sumner Draper to manage the Myers Park project, which also included landscape plans for many local estates.[15] A star student at the University of Massachusetts, Draper had topped the list of sixty-five applicants for a job in the Nolen office. "I am devoted to Civic Art," he wrote to Nolen, and "I want to do more than merely get by." The young man made good on his promise and was soon the firm's principal contact in Charlotte, where he prepared landscape plans for purchasers of lots and oversaw the planting of over a thousand street trees in Myers Park.[16] Working with the legendary tobacco king James Buchanan Duke, who owned one of the community's most prominent homes, Draper arranged for native hardwoods to be transplanted from the countryside to the green strips lining Myers Park's roadways. His rapport with Charlotte's civic leadership pleased Nolen, who was enjoying the additional time spent with his family.[17]

Draper was also working on the firm's plan for Kingsport, Tennessee, and had become frustrated with the politics of managing that project. He left the

Fig. 6.9. Queens College. Photograph by James Brantley, 2012. Courtesy Division of Rare and Manuscript Collections, Cornell University Library.

Fig. 6.10. Myers Park, Colonial Revival home. Photograph by the author, 2006.

Fig. 6.11. Myers Park, residential street canopy. Photograph by the author, 2006.

Nolen office, opened his own practice in Charlotte in the spring of 1917, and, much to Nolen's chagrin, took over supervision of the Myers Park commission.[18] Nolen dashed off a letter to Stephens, recounting how he had accepted the project with "a missionary spirit."[19] Losing Myers Park would "grieve me greatly," he wrote, being the culmination "of nearly twelve years of missionary work in North Carolina." Nolen thought Draper should supervise plan implementation in North Carolina, while the Cambridge office directed park design and the planning of future neighborhoods.[20]

Stephens was finally able to resolve the issue by offering a compromise: Draper would oversee Myers Park, and Nolen would complete Charlotte's civic survey, a preliminary study to the city plan that the chamber of commerce would underwrite. The initiative would have a far-reaching effect, he wrote to Nolen, "not only in Charlotte but in other cities in North Carolina, and upper South Carolina that will follow the move that Charlotte has made."[21] Nolen accepted the proposal.[22] Later that year, Nolen completed the civic survey, the most significant feature of which was one of his long-standing visions—a park system linking city and country.[23] When the United States entered the war, the proposed city plan was shelved, and Nolen left Charlotte to devote his time to the federal housing effort.[24]

As Stephens expected, Myers Park became a model for suburbs in the Piedmont region. In 1917 the American Civic Association named the Charlotte neighborhood one of the nation's three best-planned residential communities.[25] For Nolen, Myers Park was an essential prototype, and he was ready to design garden suburbs for a range of incomes. (Fig. 6.11)[26]

Myers Park was far removed from another commission Nolen took up in March 1911—a campus plan for Tuskegee Institute in Alabama. Nolen had spent six years building a practice in the South, but he had had little direct contact with African Americans. At Tuskegee, he encountered an unfamiliar dimension of American life. "My first impression was in the great hall of the Chapel—1,700 negroes and I the only member of the white race," he wrote to his wife.[27] "It was an impressive spectacle to look out upon this sea of black faces." Mechanical problems with the slide projector impaired his lecture, but the message of civic renewal, spiritual uplift, and improved living conditions was well received.

Nolen had read the requisite literature on Booker T. Washington's experiment in higher education, but witnessing it was life-changing. "I should like to see and know the man who made all this possible," he wrote, for Washington was absent during his stay. The next day proved equally eventful, not for the knowledge Nolen imparted but for what he learned. "I have seen more or less of the students and their life. They appear a bright, earnest crowd, both boys and girls, and the merit of the work and scholarship is certainly good. I only wish that our children could have its benefits," he wrote to his wife.[28] Nolen's experience at Tuskegee deepened his belief in the innate human ability to set goals, plan, and create a meaningful and healthy common life. As he prepared to leave, he bemoaned that prejudice could bind a people's aspirations. "I cannot help feeling sorry for a race that must suffer so, simply because of the color of their skin."[29]

Housing reform had become a priority, and Nolen addressed the issue in *Report of the Boston Metropolitan Plan Commission,* one of his first projects upon returning from Europe. The success of the Boston-1915 initiative convinced Nolen and his report coauthors, Edward Filene and architect J. Randolph Coolidge Jr., of the need to harmonize development through metropolitan planning. Boston's urban core housed up to five hundred people per acre, and more than half that number slept in rooms with less than four hundred cubic feet of air space per adult, a figure below the minimum standard established in northern European cities. The cramped conditions abetted a host of problems—poor health, social disorder, and mental fatigue—that demeaned individuals and lowered productivity. "An able-bodied Negro slave in the south before the war, whose work was notoriously inefficient . . . was nevertheless worth thousands of dollars to his owner for the value of his labor. What then," the authors asked, "is the value to the community of an able-bodied freedman?"[30]

The Metropolitan Plan Commission report launched the first such planning effort in the nation and marked a new commitment to social reform.[31] Coordinating worker housing with the siting of new factories had become a major concern for government, industry, and the Social Gospel.[32] Influenced by the New York minister Walter Rauschenbusch, author of *Christianity and Crisis* (1907), Nolen set out to master the nuances of "industrial housing," as the field became known. In 1911 he was one of the 123 founding members of the National Housing Association. Lawrence Veiller, who had played a key role in passing and implementing the New York Tenement House Act of 1901, was elected president.[33] Veiller's book *Housing Reform* (1910) guided the association's effort to enlist private and public enterprise to improve housing and end the fallacy "that the poor are a different race than the rich."[34] Social workers, housing experts, and city planners attended the organization's inaugural event in New York. At the 1912 conference, Nolen gave his first presentation devoted to housing, "The Factory and the Home."[35]

According to Nolen, industry was expanding its imprint on society. To escape high taxes and organized labor, industrialists were building new factories on less expensive land at the urban edge. With the labor pool concentrated in the inner city, it became increasingly difficult for employers to secure a reliable work force. Nolen's solution was to build garden cities to house labor near factories at "low rates and in a good environment." Built at ten housing units per acre and supporting populations of 30,000, the new towns would tie into municipal park systems and rail lines. Gardens would supplement food supplies, and parks would provide opportunities for recreation. Borrowing from Ebenezer Howard, Nolen saw workers and their families enjoying the best of city and country: "the city for occasional inspiration and diversions, and the more open country on the outskirts of cities for the essentials of daily life."[36] The challenge, as Nolen framed it, was to house industrial workers in humane conditions without infringing on the rights of private landowners.[37] He encouraged the National Housing Association to champion new legislation based on Britain's 1909 Housing and Town Planning Act. Inspired by the success of Letchworth and Hampstead Garden Suburb, the British had made town planning a government function that linked public health and physical design. By using this standard in the United States, government and private industry could improve factory efficiency and provide for "well-housed and contented employees."[38]

"The Factory and the Home" set the conceptual framework for incorporating industrial housing into comprehensive planning, but, as Olmsted Jr. had noted, the profession lacked a model. As president of the National Conference on City Planning, Olmsted asked Nolen to oversee a team (made up of Boston architect George B. Ford and Philadelphia civil engineer B. A. Haldeman) to draft a prototype plan for a four-square-mile site on the edge of a generic industrial city and to present it in a special session at the 1913 conference in Boston. The team's plan combined elements of a German suburb, an English garden city, and the town of Riverside, Illinois. (Fig. 6.12) A transit line bisected a mixed-use town center, where shops and apartments were the backdrop for a prominent civic building, and a network of parkways connected neighborhoods, enclosed waterways, and buffered industrial areas. Playgrounds and ball fields abutted schools and working-class neighborhoods. A variety of housing options—apartments, duplexes, and four-unit homes— were provided, with a "Suburban Zone," reserved for more expensive duplexes and single-family homes, sited farthest from the industry. The plan sparked intense discussion at the conference. The consensus was that its physical form was adequate, but determining the details that influenced a community, such as lot prices and traffic patterns, remained a challenge.[39]

Later that year Nolen planned his first company town, or "industrial village," for Charles S. Bird Jr. of Walpole, Massachusetts. Bird, Walpole's largest employer and a reform capitalist in the mold of Edward Filene, hired Nolen after attending one of his lectures. At Nolen's urging, Ebenezer Howard's cooperative ownership model was employed at Neponset Garden Village, the first venture of its kind in the United States. Rents would be maintained at a level supported by factory wages, and increases in equity would be dispersed to benefit the community. The site was designed on the pattern of Myers Park,

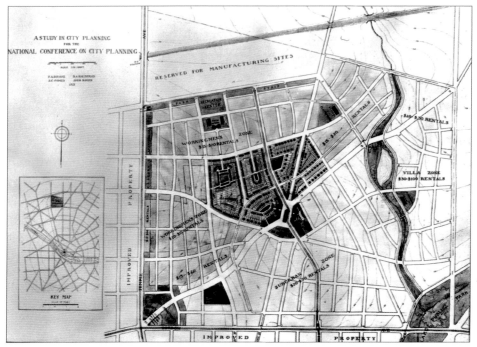

Fig. 6.12. Prototype city plan with worker housing, 1913. Courtesy Division of Rare and Manuscript Collections, Cornell University Library.

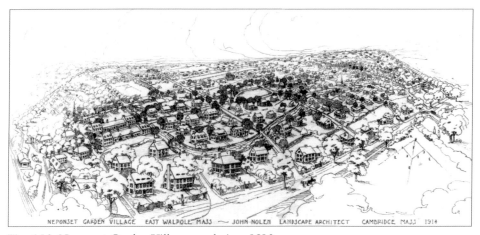

Fig. 6.13. Neponset Garden Village, rendering, 1913. Courtesy Division of Rare and Manuscript Collections, Cornell University Library.

Fig. 6.14. Francis William Park, c. 1940. Courtesy Division of Rare and Manuscript Collections, Cornell University Library.

with a curvilinear plan that lacked the garden city's defining civic orientation. (Fig. 6.13) Progress was halted by the untimely death of Bird's brother Francis William Bird, and although work resumed, the inflationary rise in construction costs eventually ended the project. Still, designing Neponset Garden Village gave Nolen experience in confronting the difficulties of adapting the garden city to American conditions and new confidence in his ability to partner with architects.[40] After World War I, Nolen replanned the town site as Francis William Park. (Fig. 6.14)

Nolen's practice brought him recognition among his peers and in academic circles. In 1913 he earned an honorary doctorate from Hobart College in Geneva, New York. The degree was bestowed during the inauguration of Hobart's new president, Lyman Pierson Powell, an Episcopal clergyman and the editor of *American Historic Towns* (1902). Powell, a graduate of the University of Wisconsin, was set to institute his version of the Wisconsin Idea at Hobart. Granting Nolen an honorary doctorate, Powell voiced "the gratitude of every trainer of youth" for a man "whose name is in a special sense is enshrined in the homes of his countrymen."[41]

    After the Hobart graduation, "Dr. Nolen" became the boss's new moniker in the Cambridge office. As a University of Pennsylvania undergraduate he had contemplated an academic career, and now in middle age he took on a professorial air. He often dressed in tweed, and with his close-cropped moustache, slightly balding pate, and tortoise-shell reading classes, he appeared to the young men in his office to be leading a graduate seminar.[42] In his correspondence with other professionals, including Thomas Adams, Raymond Unwin, Patrick Geddes, Werner Hegemann, Olmsted Jr., Charles H. Cheney, and George Ford, Nolen engaged in a give-and-take that was not unlike the rapport of tenured faculty. He often paired his project visits with lectures, and by 1915 he had spoken at a dozen colleges and universities, including Columbia, Davidson, Princeton, Harvard, the University of Wisconsin, and the University of California.[43]

City planning's academic bent led some critics to write off the urban planner as a "long-haired, dreary-eyed visionary who never had to 'meet a payroll,'" as one leading practitioner noted.[44] This criticism can be traced to the City Beautiful movement, which had been disparaged for its aesthetic pretensions and failure to meet the demands of the Progressive Era.[45] Plans needed to illustrate practical recommendations "for the permanent betterment of city life," Nolen wrote to Patrick Geddes, and after a decade of practice, Nolen had made inroads on this front.[46] In its review of *Replanning Small Cities,* the *New York Sun* noted that "the proposition upon which Mr. Nolen insists is winning yearly a wider acceptance, namely, that the primary object of improvements in town planning is not cosmetic, that the controlling considerations are safety . . . sanitization, convenience and recreation, and that beauty is a 'by-product.'"[47] The *Springfield (Mass.) Republican* voiced similar thoughts, finding Nolen's plans distinguished by their "very practical nature" and their distance from the City Beautiful movement, which had "too little practical intelligence behind it." Perhaps most important, Nolen earned consistent praise for trying to improve housing for "the average wage earner."[48]

Nolen headed one of the nation's top planning firms, but a decade of constant travel had drained his energy. In addition to regular trips across the Northeast, he journeyed to Ireland in 1914 (to judge a planning competition with Patrick Geddes) and to California, the Midwest, and the South. The trips had taken an emotional toll on the forty-five-year-old father of four. "Here I wish thee were," he wrote to his wife, Barbara, after missing their eighteenth anniversary that year.[49] Letters home lamented the time lost with his children—John Jr. was in high school, Barbara and Ted were about to enter their teens, and Humphrey was a rambunctious three-year-old. In May the family moved into a spacious home next to the Harvard College Observatory and across the street from the Harvard Botanic Garden. Building the new residence on Garden Terrace renewed Nolen's commitment to his family, and the ensuing years were marked by stability and personal growth for the children. Nolen spent more time in Cambridge and settled into a pleasant routine, walking (he would not own a car until 1919) the mile of tree-lined streets before crossing Cambridge Commons to reach his office in Harvard Square. Returning home most days for lunch, he would take a short nap before walking back to the office.[50]

In 1915, Philip Foster managed the expanded office, which included three to four planning assistants, two draftsmen, and a full-time secretary, Charlotte Parsons. Although he traveled less frequently, Nolen continued to analyze project sites and draw preliminary plans. Foster oversaw the detailed drafting of the plans while Nolen marketed the firm, consulted with clients, and presented finalized plans. In the past three years, the Nolen firm had completed projects in New England, Wisconsin, Iowa, New York, New Jersey, Pennsylvania, Tennessee, Missouri, North Carolina, Arkansas, California, and Canada. The scope of work varied: city plans for Schenectady, Chattanooga, and Sacramento; a street and park plan for Little Rock; and subdivisions for Toronto and St. John, New Brunswick.[51]

That spring Nolen drafted a preliminary plan for Country Club Plaza, the model suburban neighborhood developed by J. C. Nichols in Kansas City (Mo.). There Nolen helped introduce a new approach to residential planning that ingeniously incorporated the automobile. The fifty-five-acre site lay at the terminus of Ward Parkway, which provided an elegant entry into the plaza. (Fig. 6.15) Parking was hidden behind buildings and on rooftops, and thirty statues, murals, tile mosaics, and fountains embellished the pedestrian-scaled

Fig. 6.15. Ward Parkway, c. 1925. Courtesy Division of Rare and Manuscript Collections, Cornell University Library.

environment and Spanish-inspired architecture. The plaza and attendant neighborhoods prospered, providing the prototype for such upscale developments as Beverly Hills, California. Nichols, who was Harvard educated, continued to meet and correspond with Nolen into the 1930s.[52]

The Nolen office soon began pursuing the new contracts for company towns that were being generated by the war in Europe. As demand for military equipment increased, factory owners were forced to place a premium on securing a stable labor force.[53] Teams of experts were hired to plan industrial villages. In 1916 Nolen made his first significant contribution in the field: Kistler Industrial Village, a community he designed for the Mount Union Refractories Company.[54]

Located northeast of Mount Union, Pennsylvania, Kistler Village was sited on sixty acres across the Juniata River from the company's new brick-making plant. The low-lying property was prone to flooding, which Nolen remedied by incorporating the floodplain into the park system. (Fig. 6.16) Typically industrial villages devoted a little over fifteen percent of their land to parks, but Nolen designated almost one-third of the Kistler site to parkland. A planned 220 homes were aligned on twenty-four acres, most on 40-by-100-foot lots bordered by sidewalks and street trees. The small front yards

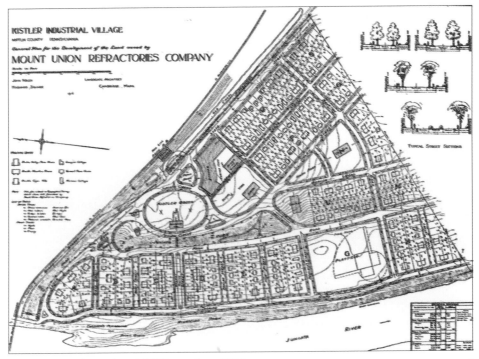

Fig. 6.16. Kistler Industrial Village plan, 1916. Courtesy Division of Rare and Manuscript Collections, Cornell University Library.

Fig. 6.17. Kistler Village, c. 1920. Courtesy Division of Rare and Manuscript Collections, Cornell University Library.

would be planted with maple trees, and these, coupled with the street trees, would create a green canopy over the tight grid of homes. An abandoned barn was retrofitted into a community center, and land was set aside for a small retail center and a train station.[55]

As at Neponset, Nolen engaged the New York firm of Mann and Mac-Neille to design the affordable 1,200-square-foot homes. The well-constructed wood buildings had durable roofs, functional front porches, and up to three bedrooms. (Fig. 6.17) They were also equipped with electricity, running water, and steel furnaces. The company deducted between twenty and twenty-five percent of worker pay for rent to subsidize an elementary school, a playground supervisor, a nurse for the school, and allotment gardens.[56] Many residents were recent immigrants from eastern Europe, whom Nolen sought to "Americanize." He was not interested in instituting a system of enforced patriotism or behavior patterns but wanted to provide "something tangible, in the form of good living conditions."[57] In 1916 the movement to provide a quality living environment was in its infancy, and Nolen wanted to humanize industrial society by giving meaning to abstractions, such as liberty and the pursuit of happiness. If Kistler had a patriarchal structure, it was designed to further democratic ends. The factory worker was expected to be a productive "citizen," Nolen wrote, "a man surrounded by his family with the refinements and conveniences which make for civilization."[58]

The construction of Kistler Village proceeded until the inflationary pressures of the war-driven economy drove building costs beyond sustainable levels. In 1917 the company consolidated its plans, constructing just half of the expected 220 homes. Neither the rail station nor the retail shops were built, but the company continued to provide services and maintain the town's infrastructure. Over the next twenty-five years rents were never raised, and at the beginning of World War II homes were sold to workers, many of whom stayed with the company until retirement. Nolen's design had introduced low-income immigrant workers to what he called "modern happiness," a concept their personal investment made real. Over fifty industrial villages were built before World War I, but Kistler was one of the few for unskilled workers.[59]

By 1916 Nolen was devoting his energies almost exclusively to industrial housing. He delivered lectures and detailed reports to the National Housing Association, the National Association of Manufacturers, the National Contractors Association, the American Civic Association, and the National Conference on City Planning. Of the issues he addressed, financing was the most daunting. More than half of the nation's labor force earned less than $800 a year—the minimum to house a family of four and pay for construction and maintenance costs. The options were limited. Either construction and land costs had to be reduced, housing standards lowered, or wages raised. Unregulated speculation had created a "house famine," Nolen wrote, as neither "private philanthropy nor the public treasure" could meet the demands of the "great masses of wage-workers."[60] Now that factory owners recognized the relationship between living conditions and labor productivity, Nolen encouraged them to invest in housing as a cost of business. They already employed a business model, dividing factories into zones to improve labor efficiency that paralleled the city planner's scheme to zone land for its highest and best use. Factories were also built with long-term loans, an apt model for financing industrial villages. Over a forty-year period, the capital invested to construct a worker community would yield a net profit of five percent.[61] Nolen's formula, essentially the Mount Union Refractories Company business plan writ large, set rents to yield a profit and meet the costs accrued from construction, land acquisition, and the establishment of a sinking fund to pay for taxes, maintenance, and property management. Between 1911 and 1916, Nolen sharpened his expertise in housing to the point that it became the cornerstone of a prospering practice.[62]

By 1917 Nolen's firm had prepared industrial village plans for American Cast Iron Pipe Company (Birmingham, Alabama), American Metal Company (Langeloth, Pennsylvania), General Electric (Erie, Pennsylvania), and General Chemical Company (Marcus Hook, Pennsylvania). In addition, the manufacturing cities of Kenosha, Wisconsin, and Waterbury and Bridgeport, Connecticut, had hired him to develop housing plans for skilled and unskilled workers.[63] Enlightened industrial policy generated some of the commissions, but most were products of the disastrous turn of events in Europe.

The Great War had reached a point in which military victory was tied to industrial output. In England it was understood that a well-housed worker was a better worker, and industrial housing became integral to the war effort. Raymond Unwin played a lead role in the British government's initiative to house labor, and he kept Nolen abreast of his activities.[64] In November 1914, Nolen received an early insight into the conflict from a German engineer he befriended on a train in California. The war would produce no winners, he was told, and the horror of the battlefield was "beyond words." That a nation that had done so much to raise the standard of urban life could engage in such bloodshed was disheartening, and Nolen's discontent grew with the escalating human loss.[65] While journeying to Charlotte in March 1916, he stopped in Wilmington, North Carolina, where he saw two interned German ships. "I pray to God that we may keep from war," he wrote. "The President may be right but it doesn't look to me so now."[66] With the nation poised to enter the conflict in early April 1917, Nolen and Hamilton Holt, the editor of the reform journal *The Independent,* led a delegation to the White House to dissuade President Woodrow Wilson from declaring war. Fifteen years later Nolen wrote to Holt, then the president of Rollins College, "What a different world it might have been if we succeeded."[67]

In the months leading up to the declaration of war, Nolen was drafting plans for the teeming Connecticut cities of Waterbury and Bridgeport, which contained factory complexes central to the U.S. munitions industry. Despite record profits and rising wages in the country, conflict between labor and capital had intensified. The European war machine was insatiable, and the laborers streaming into Connecticut were unable to find adequate housing. To complicate matters, overcrowding had pushed sanitary and social conditions to the breaking point, especially in Bridgeport, which was home to Remington Industries, the nation's leading supplier of small guns and ammunition. (Fig. 6.18) In 1910 two-thirds of Bridgeport's 100,000 residents were foreign-born, and five years later the city's population had swelled to 150,000, exacerbating the housing shortage and cultural antagonism. An inflationary spike in prices fueled social unrest: strikes were frequent and the specter of class warfare loomed. Employee turnover was rising, and with the housing shortage it was impossible for management to meet hiring quotas. In response to growing unrest, the chamber of commerce, twelve leading employers, and the city utilities underwrote the formation of the Bridgeport Housing Company. The new corporation, capitalized at $1 million, hired Nolen to assemble a housing plan.[68]

Fig. 6.18. Crowded conditions in Bridgeport, c. 1916. Courtesy Division of Rare and Manuscript Collections, Cornell University Library.

Nolen had recently completed a comprehensive city plan for Bridgeport, which set the context for the housing plan. Frank Williams, a New York attorney Nolen had met on his 1911 European tour, drew up land subdivision and building codes that prohibited the construction of two-story wood-frame structures housing more than four families. Preventing fire was the rationale, but the new standards also allowed Nolen to calculate population densities and plan infrastructure improvements in a more rational fashion. The Remington Arms Company, which had not previously invested in worker housing, changed its policy after the codes were adopted. In 1916 the company built housing for three hundred families, and it had plans to construct seven dormitories for single women and five hundred row houses and apartments for families and laborers. Realizing the novelty of their approach, the firm issued the following statement:

> Every large manufacturer who may see what we are doing will want to know what the motive or incentive of these companies is in this housing development. Is it charity? Is it a gratuity or a means of paying larger wages to employees? Or is it just a big experiment and the outcome still uncertain? The development is in no way a philanthropic or gratuitous movement but is based primarily on common sense; con-

tributed to by the ability to purchase materials and erect in quantity and to bring about a development in well-planned order.[69]

More Houses for Bridgeport, Nolen's report to the Bridgeport Housing Company, presented a three-tiered development scheme based on the prototype plan of the National Conference on City Planning. (Fig. 6.19) Single-family homes and duplexes were located on the urban periphery, worker housing for families was sited close to the city center, and rental apartments for single men and women were placed near factories. Construction was prioritized, with the highest ranking given to rental apartments and row homes for the families of unskilled laborers (who accounted for half the city's workforce). Development of the suburban zones would follow, with the stipulation that

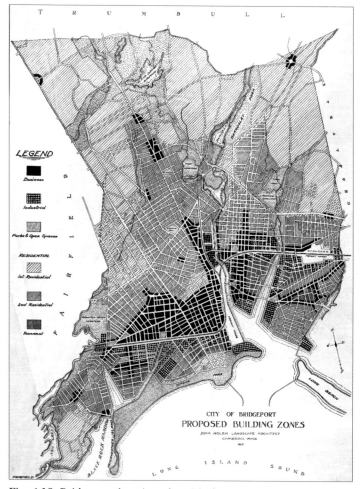

Fig. 6.19. Bridgeport housing plan, 1915. Courtesy Division of Rare and Manuscript Collections, Cornell University Library.

Fig. 6.20. Bridgeport working-class housing. Rendering by Franz Herring, 1916. Courtesy Division of Rare and Manuscript Collections, Cornell University Library.

homes should be sold on "easy terms." New development would be coordinated with the outlay of infrastructure (e.g., park and transportation systems) to supply housing in an efficient, sequential manner.[70] (Fig. 6.20)

Once America's involvement in the war appeared imminent, the federal government took a keen interest in Nolen's plans. The National Council of Defense consulted *More Houses for Bridgeport* to draw up a response to the housing shortage, which it said constituted a "war emergency."[71] In February 1917, *More Houses for Bridgeport* informed the Senate Agriculture and Forestry subcommittee hearing on "The Garden City Movement." The hearing was called to discuss the relationship between housing reform and military industrial production; with the nation prepared to encounter unimagined brutality, Richard B. Watrous, the American Civic Association's executive secretary, testified that the garden city would ensure humanity moved to a higher plane. The "present horrors" constituted "a logical indictment of civilization," he noted, and society must move "from the semi-barbarism of the present and step forth into the higher and possibly into the highest final, perfect evolution of which man is capable. This world war, and the terror of it, is preparing the minds of men for the acceptance of this new radical basis for a better civilization."[72] Watrous added that garden cities produced young men more fit for military service, an issue in a nation where twenty-five percent of city dwellers were unfit for service. The same problem plagued Great Britain during the Boer War, and reforms were instituted there, at least in part, to procure a robust defense force. Watrous cited statistics (weight, height, and general health) to document the superior fitness of children in garden cities.

"Surely the great problem of preparedness demands the building up of men as well as the creation of munitions, war machines, and factories," he concluded.[73] The congressional committee asked Watrous for examples of garden city projects in the United States, and he quoted the project list Nolen had prepared for *More Houses for Bridgeport.* Nolen's pamphlet, *A Good Home for Every Wage-Earner,* also appeared in an appendix to the committee's report.[74]

By 1917 Nolen was a recognized housing expert. After President Wilson's declaration of war on April 6, Nolen, Grosvenor Atterbury, and Lawrence Veiller formed the National Housing Association's Committee on Wartime Housing. They immediately lobbied the Wilson administration, prodding the Department of Labor to create a federal housing program.[75] Frederick L. Ackerman, the vocal spokesman for the American Institute of Architects, made the same appeal to Congress.[76] The government took action after industrial interests demanded government support for housing workers. Congress responded by establishing the United States Housing Corporation and the United States Shipping Board's Emergency Fleet Corporation to construct communities for workers in the munitions and shipbuilding industries, under the auspices of the Department of Labor. The federal government employed over forty architects and planners, including Nolen, Ackerman, Olmsted Jr., Veiller, Hubbard, and Mann and MacNeille. Nolen took on six of the eighty-two plans for new communities, the most of any practitioner.[77]

Finally in a position to improve the quality of industrial housing, Nolen was flummoxed by the ineptitude of federal bureaucracy. "One cannot tell just what will happen with regard to the demand here for housing for workers connected to war industries," he wrote to Thomas Adams in January 1918. "Something must be done. Our government is apt to move slovenly and reluctantly in the matter."[78] To break the impasse, Nolen convinced Veiller to convene a symposium on war housing, and later that month federal consultants gathered in Philadelphia.[79] Most of the participants were members of the American City Planning Institute, the professional division established by the National Conference on City Planning the previous year "to study the science and advance the art of city planning."[80] Nolen enlisted Adams, the institute's respected vice president, to give the keynote address. Adams had left England in 1914 to head Canada's Commission of Conservation, where he had been wrestling with issues of wartime housing and "social reconstruction."[81] In his speech, he proclaimed that "life preceded liberty" in the rights ascribed to American citizens. If planners failed to advance "the life of the community," they would "undermine the Constitution and the liberty it gives." Adams's fiery rhetoric set the tone as the symposium grappled with the central overarching question: would the new federal housing agencies produce meaningful change or were they merely a ploy to control labor and prevent a drift toward socialism?

Nolen believed that just as it was folly to build warships on the cheap, it "made no more sense to do it with housing." If the federal government wanted to reduce discontent and costly turnover in the workforce, it must provide decent living conditions. Building temporary housing with barely functional utilities only exacerbated labor difficulties. Industrial housing needed to be "built for permanence," he proclaimed.[82] Building for permanence became the symposium's consensus, and the government heard the message. Veiller's manual, *Standards Recommended for Permanent Industrial Housing Developments*, was adopted for federal projects and the consultants moved ahead with a renewed sense of urgency.[83]

In early 1918 Germany was gearing up for an offensive, and as Nolen observed, "America was straining every nerve to match her forces effectively against the enemy across the seas."[84] John Nolen Jr. had enlisted in the Marine Corps Reserve, and his father poured himself into his work, eager

Fig. 6.21. Protest for better housing, Wilmington. Photograph by John Nolen, 1917. Courtesy Division of Rare and Manuscript Collections, Cornell University Library.

to help win "the war to end all wars."[85] At the time, he was focused on what became one of his most important commissions, Union Park Gardens in Wilmington, Delaware. The garden city was the model for the federal housing corporations, with the stipulation that communities be built for market demand and not look "like parts of an artistic or sociological experiment."[86] Skilled design and quality construction secured the first objective, but the new communities remained experimental, testing the proposition that government could partner with planners and architects to provide quality industrial housing.

Union Park Gardens was a challenge. Wilmington was one of the nation's most densely populated cities, and its housing market was in chaos. Just as in Bridgeport, labor unrest was widespread. "All ordinary facilities had broken down; no new houses were erected to fill the breach." Nolen reported. "The emergency demanded everywhere a complete community cooperation." (Fig. 6.21) Before the war his office had designed another community near Wilmington, Overlook Colony, an industrial village built by the General Chemical Company. It was a quality project and influenced the decision by Wilmington's chamber of commerce to hire Nolen to prepare a housing plan. Following the protocol he established in Bridgeport, the Wilmington Housing Company, a public–private corporation, was formed. The company purchased a 58-acre parcel on the southwest edge of the city that was donated to the Emergency Fleet Corporation after the declaration of war. Nolen was assigned to house 553 skilled workers and their families in a "self-contained garden suburb."[87] In partnership with the architectural firm of Walter F. Ballinger and Emile G. Perrot, he completed the plan in April 1918. (Fig. 6.22)

At Union Park Gardens homes were grouped on the most level land,

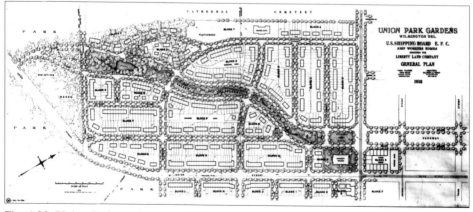

Fig. 6.22. Union Park Gardens plan, 1918. Courtesy Division of Rare and Manuscript Collections, Cornell University Library.

Fig. 6.23. Construction of Union Park Gardens, 1918. Courtesy Division of Rare and Manuscript Collections, Cornell University Library.

Fig. 6.24. Union Park Gardens parkway. Photograph by the author, 2001.

and the curving roads and meandering parkway reflected the site's varied topography. Street trees and sidewalks added to the community's pleasant appearance, while the curvilinear streets economized road construction and allowed a measure of traffic control. (Fig. 6.23) A creek was enclosed within the parkway, which ran from a wooded park on the property's northwestern edge to a village green on the southeast. Seventy-five percent of housing stock was devoted to four-unit homes that were sited within a ten-minute walk of streetcar stops. (Fig. 6.24) Building for permanence, Ballinger and Perrot used quality materials: slate roofs, brick and stucco exteriors, and pine interiors. Housing units were between 1,200 and 1,300 square feet and contained three bedrooms, a kitchen, dining room, living room, bathroom, full basement, and a porch.[88] Rents were not cheap, but they were set to the wages of the workmen.[89] Union Park Garden's utilitarian design embodied the artistic principles and efficiency that Nolen prized. (Figs. 6.25, 6.26)

Union Park Gardens appealed to the workers and their families and the development never lost value. However, the historic community is not without its critics. Some historians contend that Nolen tried to curtail labor turmoil by instilling the community with the mythic tranquillity of early industrial America.[90] However, Nolen's solution to worker discord was more nuanced. At Union Park Gardens, he proposed establishing a copartnership financing scheme to help residents purchase their units, thus freeing them

Fig. 6.25. Union Park Gardens group homes. Rendering by Ballinger and Perot, 1918. Courtesy Division of Rare and Manuscript Collections, Cornell University Library.

Fig. 6.26. Union Park Gardens, c. 1920. Courtesy Division of Rare and Manuscript Collections, Cornell University Library.

Fig. 6.27. Union Park Gardens, model neighborhood, 2010. Courtesy Delaware State Office of Planning.

"from any taint of paternalism or embarrassing relation."[91] Investment in home and community, Nolen believed, was the best way to improve labor relations. (Fig. 6.27)

Union Park Gardens advanced Nolen's vision for building a more equitable postwar society and influenced the writing of his second book, *New Ideals in the Planning of Cities, Towns, and Villages* (1919). Nolen was now a leading spokesman for the planning profession; he had written one book, edited two more, and wrote articles for the proceedings of the National Conference on City Planning, American Civic Association, and National Housing Association as well as many journals, including *The City, Landscape Architecture,* and *Annals of the American Academy of Political and Social Science.* In early 1918 the Department of Citizenship, a branch of the Army Education Commission, enlisted him to write *New Ideals,* a text for servicemen to study "fundamental principles" and "the problems of citizenship." The "relatively brief handbook," as Nolen called it, was commissioned in response to the sudden turn of events in 1918, when the Allies went from retreat to victory in a few short months.[92] (Fig. 6.28)

The war had forced innovation, and not just in town planning. Rudimentary regional plans had coordinated the federal housing programs, and Nolen was convinced that new towns could be built in logical progression from city centers. The first National Conference on City Planning after the war was held in Niagara Falls, New York, where significant federal housing had been built. "The subject of regional surveys and regional planning came to the fore," Nolen wrote to Patrick Geddes.[93] *New Ideals* set guidelines for regional planning. The analysis of soil types, topography, and natural conditions delineated the land best suited for preservation and least suited for development: floodplains, hilltops, ravines, and steep slopes. This exercise also made it possible to route transportation corridors to link the region's components: village, towns, and cites. The regional plan set the context for the city plan. With its hierarchy of road types, from major thoroughfares to residential streets, the city plan delineated the boundaries and the scale of the neighborhood, the elementary component of town planning.[94] A coordinated approach to urban planning was "not a panacea," Nolen wrote, but "it offers one safe and sure way out of our many municipal difficulties."[95]

New Ideals had a utopian edge, but experience had tempered its author's expectations. The problems of the American city were confounding, and replanning required a piecemeal approach. With peace, the most imaginative far-reaching projects would be on the urban periphery. Yet "visions, dreams," and "paper plans" would count for little without the legal basis to control the layout and character of suburban neighborhoods.[96] Nolen had helped draft Wisconsin's City Planning Act, but a decade of trial and error

Fig. 6.28. Brochure. Army Oversea Education Program, 1918. Courtesy Division of Rare and Manuscript Collections, Cornell University Library.

in implementing plans had convinced him of the need for federal legislation.[97] With the creation of the United States Housing Corporation, the
stage was set to enact laws and build new towns to "promote the general
welfare and secure the blessings of liberty to ourselves and our posterity."[98]
After November 11, 1918, this was John Nolen's mission.

7

KINGSPORT AND MARIEMONT,
1919–1926

New Ideals was written for the nearly three American million soldiers stationed in Europe, but with the turn to resolution of the global conflict in late 1918, it was issued to a different audience. The author's "gift of terse expression will serve quite as well for the civilian and the student," J. Horace McFarland wrote in a review.[1] The exigencies of World War I had turned the garden city into federal policy, and like Nolen, McFarland expected the investment in working-class housing to live on as a dividend of peace. A month after the armistice, the two men attended a meeting in Philadelphia arranged by Frederick Law Olmsted Jr. and labor leader Samuel Gompers to discuss the future of industrial housing. Nolen remained confident that planning would direct urban expansion after Felix Frankfurter, the assistant secretary of labor, wrote to him in early 1919 requesting contacts in cities with comprehensive city plans. Federal agencies were funding public works projects to employ returning troops, and Frankfurter needed to expend funds in a visible and efficient manner.[2] With a sense of optimism about future federal contracts, Nolen turned to a project that had been delayed during the war—the plan for Kingsport, Tennessee, the first comprehensively planned garden city in the United States.

Kingsport was founded in 1822 on the western edge of the Smoky Mountains and served as a station for a major road connecting the Tennessee frontier to Philadelphia and Baltimore.[3] In 1859, the region's first major railroad bypassed the hamlet and trade declined. When George L. Carter brought the Carolina, Clinchfield, and Ohio Railway to the Holston Valley in 1906, he planned to establish Kingsport as an industrial hub at a new rail spur near the

Holston River. The region was rich in natural resources, but progress came slowly to Appalachia. In 1914 financial difficulties forced Carter to sell his interests to Blair and Company, a Wall Street securities firm headed by John Dennis. A year later, Dennis formed the Kingsport Improvement Corporation and hired J. Fred Johnson, George Carter's brother-in-law, to promote the town and oversee its development.[4] Nolen learned about the commission through Harold Sears, a publisher at D. Appleton and Company who had worked with him on *City Planning* (1916).[5] Sears gave Nolen a strong endorsement, and Dennis hired him.[6]

In January 1916, Nolen made his initial assessment of Kingsport. He found that the town benefited from a prime location, but recommended a new layout for the lackluster downtown.[7] After taking notes and making some preliminary drawings, he returned to Cambridge with a concept for a garden city. Planning a new town would be an experiment, and much like "the processes of modern chemistry," he expected it to yield new solutions and unintended by-products.[8] After a series of brainstorming sessions in Cambridge, Philip Foster, the firm's lead associate, directed the drafting of a master plan delineating land uses, parks, street patterns, and transit systems. The Nolen office was overwhelmed with work that spring. Because Nolen and Foster were occupied with industrial housing commissions, management of the Kingsport project was handed down to Earle Draper. He completed a site plan before beginning work on a preliminary plan for the downtown. As the firm's junior member, he needed approval for his plans from the Cambridge office and was required to coordinate with Fred Johnson in the field.[9] Within the year, work had stalled and Nolen was forced to intervene. He sent Foster, who was more experienced in handling construction documents, to work with Johnson, but the two were soon at loggerheads over measures to realign the downtown.[10] When the United States entered World War I, the downtown plan was still unfinished.[11] The Nolen office made federal contracts a priority, essentially shelving the Kingsport project.

By the spring of 1919, support for the Charlotte city plan had withered, and federal and corporate commissions were scarce. Fortunately, the Kingsport Improvement Corporation still needed Nolen's services.[12] During the war, factories producing leather, pulp, lime, cement, brick, sewer pipe, nitric acid, sulfuric acid, and wood alcohol had filled with workers, making Kingsport the leading industrial employer in northeastern Tennessee. Its population jumped from 900 in 1916 to 5,000 by the end of the war, and demand for housing was heavy. John Dennis's brother, Ray, who had left his job as a Wall Street executive to coordinate Kingsport's development, contracted with Nolen's office for a master plan, zone study, civic center plan, park plan,

"Negro village" plan, and downtown plan. The workload was pressing, and Nolen convinced Dennis to hire Grosvenor Atterbury, the architect of Forest Hills Gardens. Before the war, Atterbury had designed the houses in a nearby company town for the Carolina, Clinchfield, and Ohio Railway, and the New Yorker was an important addition to the consultant team. In partnership with Clinton McKenzie, the chief architect, Atterbury would design a range of quality housing.

The immediate concern in Kingsport was the layout of the downtown, which had troubled Nolen since his first visit. Realigning Church Circle, where four diagonal streets intersected just north of the downtown, solved the problem. (Fig. 7.1) Sites were provided for a city hall, library, and inn next

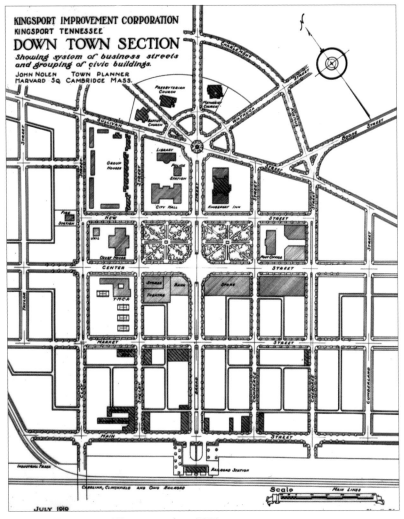

Fig. 7.1. Downtown Kingsport plan, 1919. Courtesy Division of Rare and Manuscript Collections, Cornell University Library.

to two existing churches. Two formal greens were positioned to enhance the perspective of the buildings that would front Church Circle. The circle was also set on axis with Union Station via Broad Street, a tree-lined boulevard, to form a terminating vista for the downtown. (Fig. 7.2) With the central core of Kingsport established, the master plan had its underpinning.

Fig. 7.2. Axial boulevard terminating at Kingsport Union Station, c. 1922. Courtesy Division of Rare and Manuscript Collections, Cornell University Library.

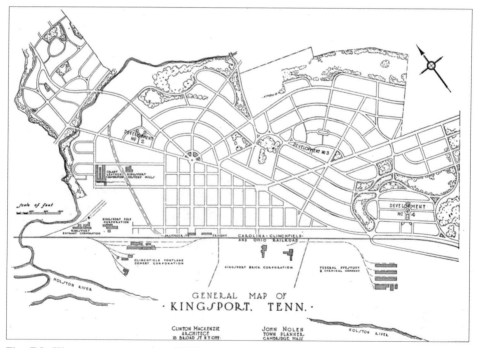

Fig. 7.3. Kingsport master plan, 1919. Courtesy Division of Rare and Manuscript Collections, Cornell University Library.

Fig. 7.4. Kingsport, larger lot homes, c. 1922. Courtesy Division of Rare and Manuscript Collections, Cornell University Library.

The plan incorporated 1,100 acres between the Holston River and the rolling hills north of town. (Fig. 7.3) To make the transition from the level, low-lying downtown to the new neighborhoods sited on higher ground, the consultants replicated Church Circle's half-crescent form. In addition to its classical elegance, the elliptical layout made it possible to align streets according to the topography and account for the rise in elevation. (Fig. 7.4) Neighborhood parks and school sites were evenly spaced, and nature preserves along the edge of town formed a greenbelt of hills and riverfront parkland.

Kingsport included neighborhoods for both labor and management. The downtown Shelby Street group houses resembled those of Union Park Gardens in Delaware. (Fig. 7.5) Clinton McKenzie, a veteran of the World War I federal housing initiative, designed the four- and five-unit, two-story structures for working families. The homes were very popular and either rented or sold based on a formula to recover the cost of construction and the price of the lots.[13] The other working-class districts were mostly bungalows located within walking distance of the factory complex. (Fig. 7.6) Atterbury was the architect for Orchard Park, an exclusive residential area with Colonial Revival homes sited on lots with panoramic views of the Holston Valley.[14] (Fig. 7.7)

The Kingsport Improvement Corporation was quick to approve and implement the neighborhood plans, but it balked at building the "Negro village." In *Remodeling Roanoke,* Nolen had deplored the housing afforded to African Americans but offered no substantial solution. A decade later, he expected that Kingsport's black enclave would be a key component in the town's success. Improved living conditions would boost morale and productivity and,

Fig. 7.5. Shelby Street group houses, c. 1922. Courtesy Division of Rare and Manuscript Collections, Cornell University Library.

Fig. 7.6. Kingsport, working-class housing, c. 1922. Courtesy Division of Rare and Manuscript Collections, Cornell University Library.

Fig. 7.7. Orchard Park, c. 1922. Courtesy Division of Rare and Manuscript Collections, Cornell University Library.

Nolen believed, create the sense of community he had observed at Tuskegee Institute.[15] McKenzie was equally enthusiastic, believing construction of the village would be an impetus to reform industrial operations in the South.[16] Finding the right property proved contentious, but eventually Armstrong Village, as the project came to be called, was sited on gently sloping land with an oak grove, a winding creek, and a riparian buffer, all of which provided a wealth of open space. A small commercial center and a public school fronted the village green. Housing followed the model of Kistler Village in Mount Union, Pennsylvania, with four-room homes set on small lots in two neighborhoods to accommodate a population of one thousand.[17] Nolen was eager to start construction, but Dennis and Johnson hesitated at committing the high-quality property to a social experiment. They felt it was a waste "to give the colored people such a fine piece of land," according to a Nolen office memo.[18] The project was terminated, and African Americans were confined to living in a blighted neighborhood near a dye plant.[19]

The Kingsport Improvement Corporation did make significant investments to improve the lives of white industrial workers, providing them with quality housing, free group health insurance, and life insurance. Kingsport also established Tennessee's first city-manager form of government to improve the coordination of municipal services, a reform that appealed to the Dennis brothers' concern with the bottom line.[20] The city taking form in the Appalachian foothills was no small accomplishment, and it began to draw notice. In 1919 the *Saturday Evening Post* declared Kingsport the "laboratory experiment for the people of America."[21] The new town offered a model, Nolen wrote, for "communities similarly destined to spring *de novo* out of the new economic conditions of the South."[22]

In June 1920, the corporation's investment in comprehensive planning earned its first major return when George Eastman, president of Eastman Kodak, purchased 277 acres to build a plant to provide an independent supply of chemicals for his photographic processes. Touring Kingsport, he had been especially impressed with the Shelby Street development and the access of factories to rail lines. The city's industrial base, which had struggled after the war, gained new credibility from the Tennessee Eastman Company's presence. (Fig. 7.8) The national economy rebounded in 1921, and factories were operated at full bore in Tennessee's fastest-growing city. It took five years for the company to earn a profit, but once its system of interlocking industries took hold, other firms followed its lead and earnings accelerated. The real

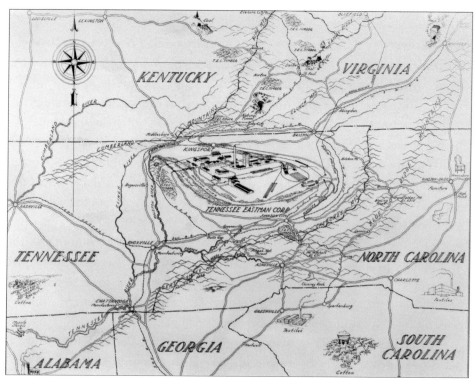

Fig. 7.8. Kingsport, a planned industrial city, c. 1922. Courtesy Division of Rare and Manuscript Collections, Cornell University Library.

JOHN NOLEN, LANDSCAPE ARCHITECT AND CITY PLANNER

estate market proved equally lucrative. The Kingsport Improvement Corporation prospered as labor and capital flowed into the town. By 1927 it employed 3,383 workers; just three years later its population had risen to 11,914.[23]

In the 1920s, the national press was keeping tabs on developments there, and a score of articles expressed a common theme: Kingsport was not a company town but a modern industrial community driven by profit and leavened by enlightened management.[24] Health care, health insurance, and quality housing benefited the working class, while corporate investment in planning had improved civic life and industrial production. Nolen remained a tireless advocate, but he worried about Kingsport's future. Neither the city hall nor the library was sited according to his design, which hinted at a fundamental problem: no planning commission or zoning code existed to implement the plan. Frank Williams had drawn a zoning code, but it had been tabled. As long as the Kingsport Improvement Corporation approved new development projects, there was little concern; but once it sold its holdings, Nolen feared the worst.[25]

The zoning code was not adopted, and Nolen completed his contractual agreement in 1922. Shortly thereafter, the Kingsport Improvement Corporation cashed in and sold three hundred acres to speculators, causing the first fissures in the plan.[26] Without significant municipal oversight, land slated for parks was replatted for commercial use; the new subdivisions lacked the quality of the Shelby Street group homes. The greenbelt was never fully established, and without a legal means to control suburban expansion, development occurred randomly. In the 1930s, experts found Kingsport to be both instructional and problematic. Still, Lewis Mumford thought it came closest to reaching Ebenezer Howard's ideal of a self-contained garden city.[27]

The Kingsport project sustained Nolen's firm during the years after the war, but as the Red Scare led Congress to eviscerate programs hinting of socialism or European reform, support for industrial housing was terminated. Union Park Gardens and related projects were later sold to private interests.[28] The federal government's shift to "normalcy" forced Nolen to rethink his practice. In December 1920 he presented the Russell Sage Foundation with a proposal to build a new town based on the specifications outlined in *New Ideals*. A heavy demand for suburban building was anticipated, and the "wartime communities," Nolen noted, were superior to the typical tract development on the urban fringe. A garden city would illustrate the social and economic benefits of planning as well as promote the foundation's mission.[29] The proposal was rejected.[30]

Later that month, Nolen wrote to Raymond Unwin describing his frustration at the lack of interest in urban reform projects. "I am quite at sea myself as to what to do, or even what to recommend about housing here," he confided to Unwin. "The way out appears increasingly difficult. Apparently our problem and yours are quite different."[31] Unwin had been named Britain's deputy director of housing, and during the 1920s he oversaw the construction of 600,000 dwelling units for industrial workers, much of it on suburban lands formerly the province of the upper and middle classes. The two men corresponded regularly, sharing the details of their projects, favorite books, and personal lives.[32] Their friendship deepened, and Unwin, more than anyone else, steeled Nolen's resolve to plan for the new forms of democracy they both saw arising from the devastation of the Great War.[33] Although the progressive movement had lost momentum, Nolen adapted to the times.

In the 1920s, the Nolen office would complete over one hundred projects and become one of the nation's most influential planning firms.[34] But in his first fifteen years in practice, only about a quarter of Nolen's city and town plans were adopted and an even smaller number implemented. City planning carried a set of assumptions different from those of many business ventures. Contracts did not dictate that a plan must be followed, and carefully elaborated schemes were often shelved. Nolen grew disheartened at times, but prosperity and a revived real estate market raised his hopes.[35] World War I had accelerated breakthroughs in communications, transportation, and industrial production, and by 1921 mass-marketed and mass-produced goods were generating the world's first full-fledged consumer economy. Per capita income increased by fifty percent during the twenties. Rather than build company towns, industry made concessions to unions and paid higher wages to stabilize the labor market. Enforcement of building and health codes improved inner-city housing conditions and lessened overcrowding. While worker housing remained problematic, a booming market helped alleviate the situation. Between 1900 and 1917 approximately 450,000 housing units were built per year; by 1922 that number reached 716,000.[36] For the first time, a majority of Americans were living in cities, and with urban expansion in full swing, Nolen encountered a new set of opportunities.

Nolen was especially gifted at discerning beauty and integrating it into his plans. His early commissions—Roanoke, San Diego, and Madison—demonstrated this proficiency, and his work at Mariemont would confirm it. Over time, he developed a sophisticated regimen for designing plans on artistic principles. "The Place of the Beautiful in the City Plan," a paper delivered at the National Conference on City Planning in 1922, articulated his goals as an artist and planner: "It is true that the beautiful in cities comes actually through the works of landscape architecture, architecture, sculpture, and engineering, but the point of greatest interest to note is that the city plan provides the location and arrangement, the elevation or gradient, the foreground and background, the vistas, balance and symmetry, the street scenes; it provides a proper sense of scale, the broad relationships, the environment and the opportunity for grouping, assembling, and composition of such works under conditions that make them truly and permanently beautiful."[37]

According to the journalist Harold Cary, Nolen was "an artist at heart, and a businessman by addition." Although broad in scope, planning included the details of aligning sight lines, integrating public uses, and spacing and orienting buildings. The goal was to produce settings that delighted the eye, offered a variety of experiences, and added value to the community. Nolen was a master of translating the aesthetics of design into the language of business and everyday life. Presenting his firm's plans to a public audience, he was part evangelist, art instructor, and investment counselor and was apt to quote the New Testament, Leonard da Vinci, and the U.S. Census. He considered planning to be "art in its broader sense," an extension of a civic vision that suffused "the Athens of Pericles, the Florence of Leonardo and the Oxford, England of today."[38] It was the planner's job, he believed, to make a city a work of art.[39]

The atmosphere of Nolen's office reflected both his passionate desire to create beautiful places and his keen awareness of how to achieve this goal. He ran his office on a disciplined schedule, but also maintained a sense of humor. The bulletin board was laden with quotations Nolen copied from the novels of Sinclair Lewis, the nation's first Nobel Prize winner in literature. Lewis's insightful and cutting portrayal of America's love of modern gadgets and quick profits amused the mostly Ivy League staff. Lampooning the George Babbitts of the world offered a respite from the business of pleasing a clientele that, Nolen bemoaned, too often lacked the imagination to complete a project.[40]

In 1924 Nolen was elected president of the American City Planning Institute, assuming the role of spokesman that Olmsted Jr. had largely abandoned.[41] Nolen's leadership was especially evident in his relationship with the young core of the profession. He tutored Justin Hartzog, Tracy Augur, Arthur Comey, Hale Walker, Russell Black, Jacob Crane Jr., and Irving Root before they went on to distinguished careers of their own. Other firms may have paid more, but Nolen's far-reaching interests at home and abroad offered opportunities not found elsewhere. The appeal of the Cambridge office was also due, Black believed, "to Mr. Nolen's kindly and generous interest in aspiring younger people."[42] A sense of camaraderie infused the workplace, and "Each

Fig. 7.9. Nolen firm motto, 1922. Courtesy Division of Rare and Manuscript Collections, Cornell University Library.

for All and for Each" was the motto chosen by the staff to adorn the office seal. (Fig. 7.9)

In these years, Nolen took a serious interest in the work of Lewis Mumford. The brilliant young intellectual had distinguished himself as a provocative critic of suburban growth with first book, *The Story of Utopias* (1922). Hailing the ideals of Emerson and Thoreau as the guiding lights for modern America, Mumford eviscerated engineers who "laid out our towns with no thought for anything but sewers and paving contracts." This myopic development pattern was set to exceed the limits of nature, and cities cut off from the source of life would degenerate into "nothing or rather nothingness."[43] On January 11, 1923, Nolen wrote to Mumford, "I am enjoying and profiting by *The Story of Utopias*."[44] The book had reenergized the middle-aged planner's fading hopes. Nolen had come to believe the American city was fraught with unsolvable political and social problems, and to replan existing municipalities offered limited returns. As the suburban migration intensified, he advocated building regional systems of interconnected new towns to capture the "flood" of human population streaming from the city.[45] The strategy was largely untested, and given the problems at Kingsport, he feared his efforts might dissipate into a quixotic crusade. Mumford helped quell Nolen's apprehension. The young writer's belief that city planning could yet lay the groundwork for a civilization based on Ebenezer Howard's vision and Thoreau's organic principles paralleled the approach set out in *New Ideals*. The day after writing to Mumford, Nolen wrote to Patrick Geddes, who had mentored Mumford: "I am in the beginning of a much more hopeful chapter in the planning of new communities."[46] A new town had stirred Nolen's ambition: Mariemont, Ohio.

Mary Muhlenberg Emery, the wealthiest woman in Cincinnati, had long contemplated building a model community for industrial workers, and after World War I, doing so became her mission.[47] Known as "Lady Bountiful," Emery became the city's leading patron of the arts and social philanthropy after the death of her husband, an influential developer, in 1906. Her determination to build a new town grew out of an enlightened concept of capitalism to which others in the decade also subscribed.[48] On the advice of her real estate adviser, Harvard graduate Charles J. Livingood, Emery hired Nolen in 1921. The reform-minded Nolen and the conservative Emery (her attorney was the Republican senator Robert A. Taft, son of the president) agreed that capital, if properly invested and nurtured, could produce a more humane and civic-centered life. A productive partnership ensued as the plan for Mariemont, named after Emery's estate in Rhode Island, took form.

Mariemont's plan was unveiled at the Cincinnati Commercial Club on April 23, 1922. The new town illustrated the application of "the constructive imagination in business," Nolen announced, to produce "widespread public welfare." In his presentation, slides of Letchworth and Hampstead Garden Suburb hinted at the character of the town to be built on a 365-acre site ten miles east of downtown "for the workingmen of Cincinnati."[49] In 1922 and 1923 references to Mariemont filled Nolen's correspondence with Raymond Unwin, who had designed Letchworth two decades earlier. At Nolen's suggestion, Livingood traveled to Letchworth and Hampstead; both men thought Mariemont could become their equivalent, a "national exemplar," a model of modern "happiness," with new "opportunities for community well being."[50]

Nolen drew the Mariemont plan with "a reverence for site," analyzing topography and existing natural conditions to determine the community's scale and form.[51] (Fig. 7.10) The lands least suited for development—floodplains, ravines, and steep slopes—were preserved in a broad swath of green. A variety of parks promoted the "joy of living" and prevented the "dreary isolation" of the suburb.[52] Dogwood Park, the largest green space, ran in serpentine fashion across the site. (Fig. 7.11) Near the entrance, a small lagoon mimicked the grotto of an Italian Renaissance garden. Trails led down to a half-mile stretch of creek at the bottom of a steeply sloped and forested ravine, a *bosco sacro* offering a passage of wildness. (Fig. 7.12) On higher ground, athletic fields and playgrounds were located near schools and within an easy walk of residences. Neighborhoods were laid out on gentle contours except for the town center, where, at the property's highest point,

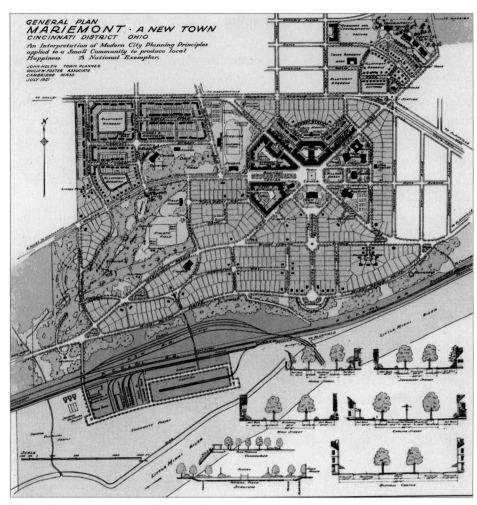

Fig. 7.10. Mariemont town plan, 1921. Courtesy Division of Rare and Manuscript Collections, Cornell University Library.

an urban square marked the confluence of four radial avenues. The town hall was on axis with the town square and a sublime natural feature, the Concourse, a scenic overlook of the Little Miami River. With its view to the distant hills, the Concourse would make Mariemont "one of the show places in the United States," in the words of Livingood.[53] (Fig. 7.13)

On April 23, 1923, Mary Emery hosted a groundbreaking ceremony attended by one hundred Cincinnati dignitaries. The Mariemont Company had been formed to oversee construction, manage rental properties, and supervise the sale of real estate; Nolen urged his client to create a cooperative investment company, modeled on Letchworth, but the idea was rejected.[54] Because Emery underwrote the company, construction moved ahead without the typical impediments. The smooth progress was noted by John Nolen

Fig. 7.11. Dogwood Park, c. 1923. Courtesy Division of Rare and Manuscript Collections, Cornell University Library.

Fig. 7.12. Dogwood Park. Photograph by James Brantley, 2011.

Fig. 7.13. The Concourse, c. 1925. Courtesy Division of Rare and Manuscript Collections, Cornell University Library.

Jr., then an engineer who was working that summer for the company: "I've just had two of the busiest days yet," he wrote to his father. "I now have six machines and two hand gangs to keep busy."[55] The $7 million that Emery invested was expected to be recouped through rents, lot sales, and trading of company stock. Construction accounted for nearly sixty percent of the monies spent at Mariemont, and it was Livingood, not Nolen, who controlled all the architectural decisions.[56] On this issue, tension simmered between the two men.

In theory the town plan was the architects' guide, but too often they embellished their own buildings at the expense of the community. Nolen wanted to check this tendency, and he enlisted Raymond Unwin to help. In the fall of 1922, Unwin had visited Cambridge and the two men assessed the Mariemont plan. The Englishman's "only fear is on the architectural line," Nolen wrote to Livingood.[57] Livingood had no such concerns, reporting that he would select the architects and review their plans.[58] Presiding over a score of architects soon tried his patience, however, and conflicting egos resulted in terminated contracts and lost time. Yet enough common ground was found to synchronize the variety of English revival styles that Livingood favored— Elizabethan, Jacobean, and Georgian—in accordance with the town plan.[59]

By 1924 Mariemont's infrastructure was in place. Trees and sidewalks lined streets and parkways, a small plant provided steam heat, and power lines were buried. A seventy-acre parcel located on the riverfront below the town was set to incorporate a sewage treatment system, community farm, and industry.[60] Residential lots ranged in size from 50 feet by 120 feet to 80 feet by 120 feet. The largest lots lined the parkway south of the town center and the road following the linear park overlooking the Little Miami River. (Fig. 7.14) In the construction sequencing, single-family homes were a secondary concern. Livingood was determined to re-create the setting of a traditional English village, and he made building the mixed-use Dale Park neighborhood the first priority.[61]

Located close to streetcar and bus lines, Dale Park offered apartments, group homes, and townhouses as rental properties. The lots for group homes (20 feet by 100 feet) and townhouses (30 feet by 100 feet) were Mariemont's smallest, and with 325 units built at eleven units per acre, it was the town's most densely developed area.[62] The Boston firm of Hubert G. Ripley and Addison B. LeBoutillier designed the neighborhood center, a pair of three-story mixed-use buildings fronting a small green. The structure's ground floors were dedicated to businesses, with standards for lighting and signage. Stone trim, proportioned gables, and window fenestration were the only decoration on the second- and third-story apartments. These simple adornments ensured

Fig. 7.14. Linear park, Mariemont. Photograph by James Brantley, 2011.

Fig. 7.15. Dale Park green and Memorial Church. Photograph by James Brantley, 2011.

that the building did not distract attention from the Mariemont Memorial Church, an elegant gray stone structure sited across the green and still under construction in 1925. (Fig. 7.15) The architect Louis Eugene Jallade designed the nondenominational community church, inspired by the Anglo-Norman parish churches of the twelfth and thirteenth centuries.[63]

The two-story group homes adjoining the Dale Park Neighborhood Center, also designed by Ripley and LeBoutillier, were built six to a section, with detailed stonework and half-timber-faced exteriors adorning the brickwork pattern used in the neighborhood center. (Figs. 7.16, 7.17, 7.18) The attached units shared walls, and allotment gardens were located on the interior of the block. Clinton McKenzie, the Kingsport architect, designed the counterweight to the neighborhood center, a three-story Tudor-style apartment building located on the opposite end of the block. Its stucco facing and exposed timbers set the standard for the adjacent two-story group homes that filled out the block. Steep roofs and rounded door arches gave character to McKenzie's units, but they lacked the creative mix of stone and brick used by Ripley and LeBoutillier.

One block away, the Maple Street development's Georgian Revival architecture added further interest and variety to the neighborhood. Cincinnati architects Edward H. Kruckemeyer and Charles R. Strong designed the "Honeymoon Cottage" over the entrance of Maple Street to frame a charming terminating vista. To accentuate the view, front-yard setbacks were gradu-

Fig. 7.16. Dale Park, group homes. Rendering by Ripley and LeBoutillier, 1924. Courtesy Division of Rare and Manuscript Collections, Cornell University Library.

Fig. 7.17. Dale Park, c. 1926. Courtesy Division of Rare and Manuscript Collections, Cornell University Library.

ally reduced until they lost six feet in depth by the street's end. Over time, the growth of the deciduous street trees refined the picturesque setting, and Maple Street resembled the neighborhoods of Letchworth and Hampstead Garden Suburb in its clarity and simple elegance.[64] (Fig. 7.19)

The Mariemont School, a two-story Georgian-style building sited on the

Fig. 7.18. Dale Park Historic District. Photograph by the author, 2001.

Fig. 7.19. Maple Street, c. 1926. Courtesy Division of Rare and Manuscript Collections, Cornell University Library.

JOHN NOLEN, LANDSCAPE ARCHITECT AND CITY PLANNER

edge of Dale Park, was completed in 1924. Young families were expected to populate the neighborhood, and the Mariemont Company paid staff to operate the school for its first three years. It was a hub of activity, offering play areas and serving as a meeting place for residents. By 1925 three hundred children were enrolled in the new school, and three hundred units were either occupied or under construction in Dale Park.[65] That June, the first single-family home subdivision, Sheldon Close, was constructed just south of the town center.[66] The "new order of the average man" that Nolen had outlined in *New Ideals* was coming to life, nurtured by gardens, quality housing, parks, public institutions, and safe, accessible streets.

The Dale Park neighborhood was on axis with the town center, an area of about ten square blocks with a central square mediating the intersection of two major streets and Wooster Pike, the principal east–west thoroughfare. A second linear expanse of green, a north–south parkway, put the center square on axis with the concourse. Mariemont's public spaces had an intimacy and intent that surpassed Nolen's previous commissions. (Fig. 7.20) Points of repose were placed throughout the community, offering views of carefully crafted greens, picturesque groupings of buildings, and expanses of nature. The village green was left in its forested state so that its deciduous trees matched the height of the surrounding two-story buildings. But it was a park on the edge of the Dale Park neighborhood that best illustrated the aspirations of Mary Emery. There, three statues designed by the French sculptor Lucien Charles Alliot depicted the role that children play in communal life.

Fig. 7.20. The Concourse. Photograph by James Brantley, 2011.

Fig. 7.21. "To Childhood," Lucien Charles Alliot, 1929. Photograph by James Brantley, 2011.

(Fig. 7.21) Ultimately, the test of Mariemont's claim to be a "national exemplar" rested on Nolen's ability to create an environment in which children could comfortably find their way to parks, playgrounds, and schools.

By late 1925 Mariemont was well established. Its population had reached five hundred, businesses were moving in, lot sales were brisk, and residents were turning an experiment into a community. Marketing Mariemont as an ideal town, Livingood gained an audience well beyond Ohio, and Nolen presented the new town as a planning model to professional organizations in Europe and the United States.[67] With the plan in place and construction in full swing, Nolen's contract was terminated in late 1926.[68] It was a mostly amicable parting. Since the previous July, when Philip Foster opened a branch office in Jacksonville, Florida, Nolen had struggled to keep up with client demands. Mariemont had been a challenge for both Nolen and Livingood, but upon reflection, both men realized they had accomplished something special. Livingood appreciated Nolen's dedication and the talent he had assembled. "At evening one feels as if . . . [the residents] were in an English village already," he wrote to Nolen. "We oriented [it] just right. Frankly I am wondering if there will be anything as beautiful as Dale Park where you took every advantage of nature."[69]

Mariemont marked the apex of Nolen's career. Unlike Union Park Gardens, where the civic buildings were never constructed, the flourishing Ohio community demonstrated the success of Nolen's most cherished ideals. It was the template for the new towns being planned in Florida and a model that Nolen shared with other urban experts. In 1923, at the International Cities and Town Planning Conference in Gothenburg, Sweden, he explained that Mariemont was not just an endeavor to improve conditions "in Cincinnati, but to do it on terms and conditions that can be duplicated wherever initiative, capital and sound planning can be combined to support an enterprise of great public importance, namely, the building of news towns and suburbs."[70] Mariemont's success also prompted him to take up a tabled project, writing his third and best-received book, *New Towns for Old*.

Nolen had started the book in 1921 with help from Sylvester Baxter, who was seventy-one at the time. Baxter wrote the introductory section and collaborated with Nolen on chapters devoted to Myers Park, Kistler, Kingsport, Union Park Gardens, and East Walpole. The manuscript was rejected, but the response to Mariemont convinced Nolen to write a revision.[71] He reworked Baxter's text, dedicated a chapter to the new Ohio town, and added a concluding chapter devoted to regional planning and his Florida commissions. Published in 1927 by the Boston firm Marshall Jones, *New Towns for Old* received positive reviews in the *New York Times, American City, Review of Reviews,* and *Survey*.[72]

Mariemont was mentioned in the introductory chapters and the conclusion, and the plan for Dale Park neighborhood was Nolen's most refined presentation. Nolen wrote about Mariemont as an "anticipatory example" of what awaited once the suburban countryside was transformed into "smiling garden cities and towns."[73] *New Towns for Old* presented the concept of an organic regional city of integrated satellite communities limited in size and built to sustain nature "rather than to overtax the rigid outlines of our present cities."[74] Nolen had reason to be optimistic. He had corresponded with President Calvin Coolidge and Secretary of Commerce Herbert Hoover on issues related to planning, which had become a recognized instrument of government.[75]

But on the eve of the Great Depression, Mariemont's potential was fading. Rising inflation impeded construction of additional working-class housing, and the promise of providing homes for a range of incomes in a garden suburb was broken.[76] Despite its best intentions, the Mariemont Company exposed the limitations of large-scale private planning.[77] Nevertheless, in 1936 a federal study assessing planned communities looked favorably on Mariemont, especially the Dale Park neighborhood and the variety and quality of the parks.[78] It was only after World War II, when automobile traffic increased exponentially, that the new town's first significant problems arose. Nolen thought he had designed a community for the "motor age," but he failed to fully gauge the car's impact. As in Union Park Gardens, space allocated for community gardens was paved for parking, and commuter traffic overwhelmed the principal throughway.[79]

Despite the automobile, however, the town's basic structure endured. Its walkable streets and the alignment of neighborhoods, parks, and schools made it easy for children to traverse their surroundings, and the town has drawn praise for the opportunities it affords to children.[80] The integration of apartments, townhouses, single-family homes, businesses, and civic buildings makes it a "model too important to ignore," in the estimation of the architect and urban planner Andrés Duany.[81] Mariemont was placed on the National Historic Register in 1979, and in 2008 the American Planning Association honored Marimont as "a prized artifact, and a vital, living embodiment of the value and benefits that sound planning principles return to multiple generations and lifetimes."[82] In 2011, Nolen's skill in adapting the English garden city was recongnized when Hampstead Garden Suburb and Mariemont became sister cities.

Certainly, something as complex as city planning offers few simple standards. But Mary Emery, shortly before her death in 1926, offered this measure: "The children? Do you feel safer about them? Are their faces a bit ruddier? Are their legs a little sturdier? Do they laugh and play a lot louder in Mariemont? Then I am content."[83]

8

FLORIDA, 1922–1931

At a city planning conference in Jacksonville, John Nolen declared that the "story of Florida is a story of adventure romance written through a long history—four centuries. . . . The early search was for the Fountain of Youth and for gold, and the modern one is not essentially different."[1] The lure of leisure and lucrative real estate made Florida, according to Lewis Mumford, "the desire of the heart and the end of human aspirations."[2] During the 1920s Americans yearned to escape the routine of industrial life and experience paradise—if only for a brief time—and Florida was the destination.[3]

In St. Petersburg, taxpayers funded advertising to entice tourists south. As a local realtor admitted, the city had no industry, and so citizens had to take "wealth and tribute from all the world to make our city grow."[4] In 1921 $8,000 was allocated to the chamber of commerce for "boosting," a subsidy that reached $270,000 by 1926.[5] In 1922 lot sales, construction, and property values were growing at an accelerated rate. Over the next three years, property values increased tenfold, and the *St. Petersburg Times* sold more real estate advertising than any newspaper in the nation except the *Miami Herald*.[6] The frenetic real estate market raised expectations and concerns. Unless plans were drawn to direct the city's speculative development schemes, "we may perish by our own ostrich-like ignorance," warned William Straub, editor of the *St. Petersburg Times*.[7]

Originally from North Dakota, Straub was one of Florida's preeminent reformers. In 1899 poor health had forced the young journalist to leave his home state and a job at the *Grand Forks Daily Herald*. After settling in St.

Petersburg, the mild seaside climate aided his recovery from lung ailments. Having gained new life from "the flowering peninsula of Pinellas," Straub became the self-appointed guardian of a sanctuary drawn from "the master plan of divine dreams."[8] He purchased the *Times* in 1902 and initiated a four-decade crusade to create an unmatched tourist metropolis.[9] After orchestrating the creation of a public waterfront on Tampa Bay, an immediate tourist attraction, he convinced the Pinellas County Chamber of Commerce to hire the Olmsted Brothers to design Florida's first park plan. The county commission refused to implement it, but the setback was brief. After World War I, Straub rallied the St. Petersburg city council to establish Florida's first city planning board. He chaired the new organization, whose first order of business was to sign John Nolen to a $6,500 contract.[10]

Nolen traveled to Florida in March 1922 to find a city in bloom. Azaleas, hibiscus, and bougainvillea brightened the landscape of pine and palms, and orange blossoms scented the air. The public waterfront and gulf beaches reminded him of southern France. Flying over the Pinellas Peninsula in a two-seat airplane, he was astounded by what he saw: miles of waterfront, unspoiled tracts of subtropical jungle, and large sections of developable land. He now understood why there were "so many realtors," he told a reporter.[11] The city was subdividing land on a largely speculative basis, and the results reminded him of the havoc wrought in San Diego. In a meeting with the Pinellas County commission, he proposed that his firm draft a countywide plan to coordinate public investments with St. Petersburg. Although no agreement was reached, Nolen returned to Cambridge intent on drawing a plan for "St. Petersburg and Its Environs."[12]

Nolen envisioned the Florida city and its region as a single unit. "This seems to be an opportunity to do rather more than we have ever been given the chance to do before," he wrote to attorney Frank Williams.[13] St. Petersburg was a bellwether propelled by a vibrant tourist economy and modern technology. Improvements in the transmission of electricity and the automobile had quickened the pace of urbanization, and the gap that once separated city and country was closing. "Where the country was once an agricultural region producing food for cities, it has now become, through the use of motor transportation, part of the city," Nolen wrote.[14] Given this trend, regional planning was essential in St. Petersburg. Not only was the city growing haphazardly, but the municipal government had yet to find a reliable source of potable water. Incorporated in 1892, St. Petersburg jumped from 1,575 residents in 1900 to 14,237 in 1920. By 1923 the city had a population of 20,000, with an estimated 100,000 seasonal visitors.[15] Yet vast tracts of undeveloped land remained. With an open canvas for his aspirations, Nolen plotted to set a new precedent with Williams, who was contracted to draft the requisite legal documents.

After helping Alfred Bettman draw up New York City's zoning code, Williams had become a leading authority in the nascent field of city planning law. His 1922 book, *The Law of City Planning and Zoning*, was "a veritable encyclopedia of city planning subject matter, precedents, practices and references," Bettman wrote.[16] For the new plan to have legal standing, Williams knew that St. Petersburg first had to obtain a special city planning bill from the state legislature. Nolen wanted him to draft the legislation based on the British Housing and Town Planning Act of 1909. In England, planners prepared a master plan and then followed up with more detailed town and neighborhood plans.[17] Nolen felt that American planners needed such a system because zoning had proven to be an ineffectual tool. It was "a *negative measure*," Nolen wrote; "it simply tells what private property owners cannot do with their own property." In a free-market society, city plans needed to be laden with incentives for private developers to make "constructive expenditures."[18] Nolen's holistic approach embedded value in a range of properties, which allowed investors to assess a property rationally and estimate its future worth.[19]

Williams liked Nolen's idea for drafting planning legislation, but he was hardly confident about its implementation. In England the Ministry of Health ratified general plans, and local governments completed the more detailed town plans. Without a similar planning authority in Florida, the legal reform Nolen envisioned would fail. Williams thought it best to employ the Department of Commerce's *Standard State Zoning Enabling Act* of 1922.[20] In 1921 Herbert Hoover, then commerce department secretary, had appointed an advisory committee (Bettman and Williams were members) to draw up guidelines for local governments to establish and amend zoning laws. Hoover was an advocate for city planning. An engineer by training, he believed establishing a system of consistent standards to guide development would improve government efficiency, especially in addressing housing and infrastructure investment. The new enabling legislation satisfied Williams, who was sure it would receive the support of the state legislature. Nolen followed William's counsel, and the attorney prepared Florida's first city planning bill based on the federal law.[21]

The new legislation granted the city council the power to regulate private development and facilitate the expenditure of public dollars. It also empowered the municipality to plan and zone land to protect, as the U.S. Constitution set forth, the "health, safety, morals, and general welfare of the community." The planning board, in its advisory role to the city commission, oversaw the platting of subdivisions, utility expansion, the preservation of natural lands, and the administration of the zoning ordinance.[22]

Florida's first comprehensive city plan, *St. Petersburg Today, St. Petersburg Tomorrow*, cast a grand vision for the small city of ten square miles.[23] A regional plan established the boundaries for a 130-square-mile tourist metropolis encompassing the lower third of the Pinellas Peninsula (the city's current boundary). It delineated the routes of major thoroughfares, with the future regional city encircled by a greenbelt made up mostly of coastal salt marshes and the largely undeveloped barrier islands. The city proper was bounded by small farms and a park system that connected to the ring of nature preserves. Because a recent hurricane had destroyed the only bridge to the barrier islands, the strand of fragile landforms set to be the city's premier nature preserve, Nolen proposed a tram running from the mainland for easy access to the gulf shore.

Nolen planned a tourist district along Boca Ciega Bay at the tram's terminus. It was one of six zoning categories, along with industry, business, neighborhood business, apartments, and residential (duplex and single-family homes). (Fig. 8.1) Building heights were limited to four stories, with hotels and apartments set within walking distance of the tram and the streetcar line on Central Avenue, St. Petersburg's main east–west thoroughfare. Central Avenue marked the eastern boundary of the tourist district and its compact business center. A parkway ran along the edge of the bay and linked into a second tourist district to the south. Central Avenue was dotted with neighborhood centers sited at streetcar stops; these clusters of stores, churches, public buildings, parks, and apartments were expected to facilitate social cohesion, limit the spread of unsightly commercial uses, and mitigate traffic problems. Additional centers would anchor the new residential neighborhoods in the outlying areas and were also placed within walking distance of all homes.[24]

With the peninsula's mild climate, the city would be oriented to active recreation and the outdoors, with parks sited within a half mile of all residences. Suburban neighborhoods were laid out along topographical contours and bounded by either nature preserves formed around creeks, lakes, and bays or parkways encapsulating creeks and wetlands. The parkways were designed to store and channel floodwaters, an essential function in a hurricane-plagued region.

The parkway's fingers of green ran through black as well as white neighborhoods. Straub claimed friendship with African Americans. He knew St.

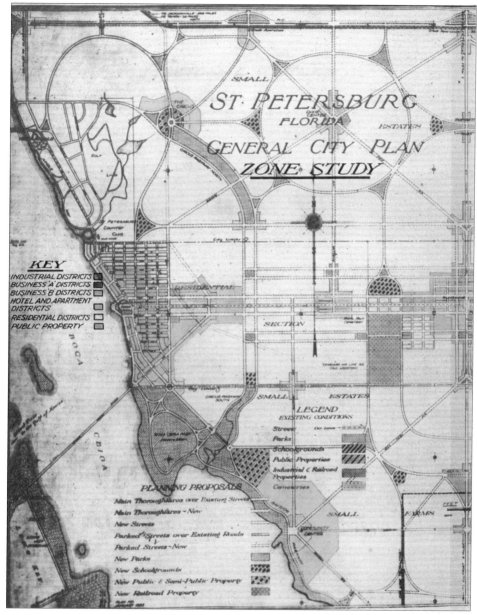

Fig. 8.1. St. Petersburg city plan and zoning study, 1923. Courtesy Division of Rare and Manuscript Collections, Cornell University Library.

Petersburg could never become the centerpiece of an American Riviera with eighteen percent of the population living in underserved conditions. Most blacks inhabited substandard residences owned by white landlords in the city's cramped south side ghetto. Streets were generally unpaved, and access to gas, electricity, sewers, and drainage was negligible.[25] To help his cause Straub engaged C. M. Roser, an influential builder. Roser recommended creating a corporation of businessmen to secure additional land and supervise the building of "a colored section with schools, churches, theaters, good roads, and easy transportation to the business section."[26]

In late December 1922, Straub learned that the West Palm Beach city commission had taken measures to segregate African Americans within a restrictive zone. He wrote to Nolen, wondering if St. Petersburg should do the same. Since Nolen, at the time, was under contract with the newly organized planning board of Palm Beach, this issue was of special interest, and he dashed off a letter to Frank Williams asking his advice.[27] The attorney thought it best to be on record against racial zoning. The Supreme Court had ruled against it 1917, although some southern cities refused to follow the decision. Nevertheless, discrimination was slowly receding, and St. Petersburg needed "a broader basis" for its planning law.[28] When Nolen informed Straub he could not endorse racial zoning, the latter agreed, but segregation remained an unstated policy.[29] The city plan extended industrial zones along the railroad to maintain a physical barrier between the races. Yet even if Nolen did not directly attack Jim Crow restrictions, he did envision a better life for African Americans. Three parks and two neighborhood centers were planned in the black community, and the expectation was that road paving and utilities would be extended into the area.

Elected officials in West Palm Beach were eager to relocate African Americans, however, and they employed city planning to this end.[30] In Nolen's discussions with the planning board, racial zoning had not been a priority; directing urban expansion was the primary goal.[31] But Mayor L. Garland Biggers had a different idea. After reviewing Nolen's preliminary plan in December 1922, he recommended redrafting it to create "concentrated zones" of blacks on land between the railroad and the Everglades, an impenetrable wilderness at the time. "If we designate an area for the colored population tonight, we have accomplished a rather important step," an official asserted at a joint meeting of the city council and planning board. It was decided to relocate African Americans, who constituted forty percent of the population, to three zones: two for local blacks and the third for "Nassau Negroes," the term employed to define blacks of Caribbean heritage. Each area would be connected to the city by a single avenue. "Looking twenty-five years ahead," Biggers declared, "we are now designating the places where the Negro occupancy will be encouraged. . . . We are trying to put them in such locations as they will most congenitally be situated to their places of labor and fulfill the needs of the white people."[32]

Karl Riddle, the city engineer of St. Petersburg, informed Nolen that his plan did not "clearly define white and colored sections." Moreover, the proposed relocation of the railroad would remove the physical barrier between the races. Removing "a principal thoroughfare bordered on one side by colored people and on the other side by white people is an unnecessary hazard in the South," Riddle noted. "In fact, such a condition should be avoided in any part of the country." The message was clear: Nolen was to draft a zoning code that defined racial divisions before making any revisions to the plan.[33]

Riddle's letter sparked a seventeen-page response from Cambridge. "*No plan should be limited to zoning*," Nolen wrote to Orrin Randolph, the chairman of the planning commission, especially when it enforced "the suppression rather than the exercise of imagination."[34] His firm adhered to a set of principles, he wrote, "whether it pays financially or not."[35] Nolen refused Riddle's request, and in April 1923 he presented a regional plan and a master plan to the city council. (Fig. 8.2) The land the council wanted populated with concentrated zones of African Americans was instead designated for parkways, nature preserves, and farm plots. Racial zoning was unconstitutional, the text stated: "It is not possible legally to set aside such districts and restrict them to any one race or color."[36]

Nolen's attempt to inject an element of equality into African American life in St. Petersburg confronted a strain of racism as virulent as anywhere in the South. In 1920 Florida had the highest lynching rate in the nation relative to its population.[37] After the state's justice system failed to secure convictions in the lynching of two African Americans in 1919, Dr. William A. Byrd, an official with the National Association for the Advancement of Colored People, claimed that the "Anglo-Saxon ability to rule the South has

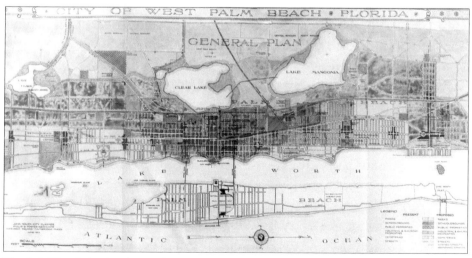

Fig. 8.2. West Palm Beach city plan, 1923. Courtesy Division of Rare and Manuscript Collections, Cornell University Library.

been tested and found an ignominious failure. Civilization in Florida has broken down."[38] In January 1923, civilization vanished altogether after an organized band of armed whites laid siege to the African American village of Rosewood, located ninety miles north of St. Petersburg. After a pitched battle, Rosewood was burned to the ground and at least thirty residents died; the rest fled, never to return.[39] St. Petersburg was the destination for many of the one hundred or so survivors because it was considered one of the safest places in Florida for blacks. But even in this tranquil resort community, violence was a fact of life.[40]

Lynching marked the darkest edge of life in St. Petersburg, while beatings, petty abuse, and insults were the norm for African Americans, and harassment from law enforcement officials was common, especially during the tourist season. Except when caring for white children, black nannies could not visit city parks or beaches or occupy the green benches spaced throughout the downtown. Blacks risked fines or imprisonment if they crossed north over Central Avenue after dark. The Ku Klux Klan also staged regular torchlight marches with the approval, and often participation, of elected officials.[41] A black exodus ensued in the spring of 1923 as some of the city's hundreds of African American laborers, brought in mainly from Alabama and Georgia, headed north to pursue promises of better pay and equality. Fearing that the loss of manpower would impede the road-building projects opening up land for development, city officials ordered police chief E. J. Bideman to arrest anyone transporting workers from the city. It also became a misdemeanor for black laborers to disavow work agreements.[42]

Florida's first city planning election was held in this atmosphere of social unrest. In March 1923 Straub led a delegation to Tallahassee that procured the St. Petersburg Planning Law; a referendum would be held that August. The election proved to be a divisive affair. According to Straub, it "was as abusive as any ever held in St. Petersburg, and that is saying a great deal."[43] The anti-planning forces were championed by Lew Brown, editor of the *St. Petersburg Independent,* who questioned the soundness of an initiative drawn by a Cambridge consultant and a New York lawyer. In the midst of an unsurpassed real estate boom, the plan's lofty notion of city building impinged on pecuniary pursuits and sacred rights. Brown warned citizens that they should "get busy and protect your home and liberty." With government oversight of private property, he noted, "What red-blooded American citizen would want to buy real estate in St. Petersburg and submit to such dictation?"[44]

The idea of investing in the African American community was even more contentious. In 1916 Brown had earned the title "father of the white primary." He regularly penned racist tirades, and a month before the referendum he stated that the "majority of Negroes are of the low order of intelligence, are not physically clean, and lacking in moral perception." Rather than improve their living conditions, he wanted to replace "lazy and shiftless" black laborers with immigrants from the agricultural sections of England. "It will be a happy day in the South," he said, "when white men take the place of Negroes."[45] Racism and speculative desires undermined the planning law, and it received just thirteen percent of the vote in the referendum. Straub initiated a new city planning campaign, but vital momentum had been lost. Nolen was shocked that hostility toward African Americans had derailed the plan. This was only the beginning of his confrontation with racism in Florida.

In September 1923, the West Palm Beach planning initiative collapsed. After learning the results of the referendum in St. Petersburg, a third of the nine-member planning board resigned. Especially damaging was the loss of Alfred Wagg and Orrin Randolph.[46] Wagg had arranged Nolen's hiring and, with Randolph, tried to steer municipal officials away from racial zoning. After the city council began granting permits that effectively voided major provisions of the city plan, Randolph informed Nolen that "we thought to remain on the board [was] a waste of time."[47] No new members were appointed, and the city plan was shelved. Nolen was dumbfounded by the local government's indifference. "If there were faults on our side we need to know," he wrote to Riddle, because "the action of the city council seems incomprehensible."[48]

Nolen moved on from the political imbroglios in St. Petersburg and West Palm Beach and began pursuing private commissions where race was not the overriding issue. After returning from Scandinavia in September 1923, he refused an offer from Riddle to draft a zoning code. What he had seen in Norway and Sweden stirred him to gauge the market for new towns, especially in Florida.[49] By the fall of 1924 Nolen had contracted for twenty projects in Florida, including commissions in Clearwater, Tampa, St. Petersburg, Sarasota, St. Augustine, and Clewiston, a new town project in the heart of the Everglades. To meet the growing demand for his services, he began contemplating a full-time presence in the state.[50] Like many, he had developed an affinity for the climate, having fallen under the "spell of the tropics" when he first visited in 1922. Florida was also, he noted, a "great laboratory of city and town planning."[51]

John Nolen Jr. had accompanied his father on the 1922 trip. A civil engineer trained at the Massachusetts Institute of Technology, the younger Nolen learned the family business from the ground up. Like his father, he loved the outdoors. He took summer jobs in Glacier National Park and the Maine wilds to gain proficiency in surveying and site analysis. He was employed as a hydrogeographer in the Panama Canal Zone before returning to the United States in 1923 to take a job as an engineer at Mariemont. Through the liaison between the Mariemont Company and the Nolen office, he gained valuable experience helping coordinate implementation of his father's town plan.[52]

In early 1925 Nolen hired his son to manage the burgeoning roster of Florida commissions and to evaluate the prospects of opening an office there. (Fig. 8.3) Writing to his father in June, Nolen Jr. doubted that such an opportunity would reappear in the near future. "Every edition of the paper carries some new projects that have planning possibilities," he reported. "A little energy and push would bring in all the work we could do." The jobs varied. City plans tended to be time consuming and not well paid, but they were essential if the firm was to build a presence in the state. Residential subdivisions commanded higher fees and required a quick turnaround. He

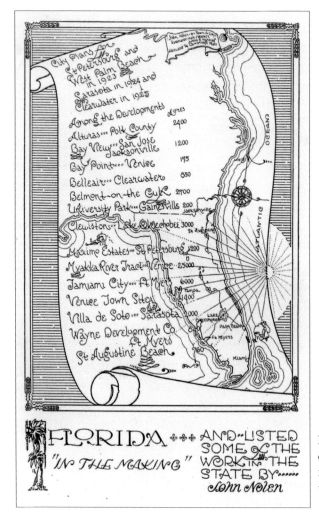

Fig. 8.3. Nolen's Florida commissions. Courtesy Division of Rare and Manuscript Collections, Cornell University Library.

recommended setting up an office with a staff of three: two planners and a secretary. In addition, Hale Walker and Justin Hartzog, talented new hires in the Cambridge office, would need to visit Florida regularly.[53] Nolen acted quickly on the report. Within a month, Philip Foster was running an office in Jacksonville, assisted by landscape architect Francis Mulvihill, Nolen Jr., and a secretary. Clewiston was Foster's immediate focus.

Founded in 1920, Clewiston was at the midpoint of the highway and railroad running between West Palm Beach and Fort Myers, the southernmost transportation routes crossing Florida. It was located on the southern shore of Lake Okeechobee and appeared destined to reap the agricultural cornucopia that the "reclaimed" lands of the Everglades portended. In the 1880s private entrepreneurs had launched a massive drainage project between Fort Myers and the southwestern section of the lake. Results were slow in coming until 1905, when the state stepped in to oversee and fund reclamation efforts. By 1920 three hundred miles of canals threaded the Everglades, and water levels had dropped to expose rich underlying deposits of peat or muck soil. In 1921 the federal government opened an experimental agricultural station near the lake. Scientists found the drained wetland soil ideal for growing sugar cane, a valuable discovery in resource-poor Florida, and soon investors from Chicago and New York were pouring money into a frontier region expected to rival Cuba as a source of sugar.[54]

In 1922 Alfred Wagg, the West Palm Beach banker and planning board member, introduced Nolen to Marian Horwitz O'Brien and John O'Brien, Philadelphia investors interested in sugar production. Marian O'Brien was instrumental in hiring Nolen, and her husband brought in Alonzo Clewis, a Tampa banker, as the final stockholder in the project.[55] Only fifty people inhabited the hamlet when Nolen first visited, but the opening of the new rail terminus raised expectations. John O'Brien, Clewiston's founder, ran a farming operation that began packaging and exporting produce. O'Brien was also eager to invest in sugar cane, and Nolen was directed to plan a modern agro-industrial complex. The project stalled and was not revived until 1925, when Bror Dahlberg, president of the newly formed Southern Sugar Company, bought the deed to the 2,500-acre property. An astute Chicago businessman, Dahlberg acquired an additional 15,000 acres of land to grow, harvest, and refine sugar. He also had a scheme to manufacture Celotex, a building material derived from sugar cane. Dahlberg had Nolen draft a new plan, but Dahlberg would have the final say.[56]

Clewiston was built on reclaimed lakefront land. During the rainy season (July to October), Lake Okeechobee overflowed its banks, and the water ran into a series of streams that converged into the vast "river of grass" that flowed south down the center of the peninsula for one hundred miles. Several miles wide and often only a few inches deep, the river's slow meandering allowed the underlying organic soils to absorb considerable amounts of water; the deepest deposits of the rich underlying peat bordered Lake Okeechobee.[57] Engineering and planning this watery landscape to human ends was highly experimental. Clewiston may have been surrounded by nature, but the town site had been dredged, leaving a stark landscape without vegetation.

Dahlberg envisioned Clewiston as the "Capital of the Everglades," and Philip Foster obliged, drafting a plan patterned on Washington, D.C. (Fig. 8.4) The cross-state highway bisected the town, running between the civic center and a twelve-square-block business district. An outdoor amphitheater framed by a lawn and palm grove was the point of emphasis in the civic center, which included sites for a library, theater, hotel, and city hall. Two radiating boulevards connected the civic center to the retail–hotel districts on Lake Okeechobee. The train station anchored the business district and a hundred-acre industrial zone bounded by a 120-foot-wide canal. The rail and canal would facilitate the movement of goods, but it was the state highway that was fast becoming the prime transportation route.

Nolen realized automobile traffic would intensify in the coming years.[58] To slow speeds and provide for pedestrian safety, a hundred-foot-wide "natural reservation" fronted the state highway with medians and buffers planted with palms. (Fig. 8.5) Dahlberg also anticipated the automobile's popularity, and after reviewing the consultants' proposal, he asked that the reservation be removed to provide more commercial space.[59] Nolen had wanted to concentrate development in the town center, but the automobile was redefining development patterns. Mass production had made car ownership increasingly affordable, and between 1925 and 1929, the number of registered vehicles in the United States jumped from 20.1 million to 26.7 million.[60] Tourists were driving to Florida in record numbers, and outlying regions like the Everglades were being opened for development. In 1930 Florida was the first state in the South to have a majority of its population classified as urban.[61]

The demand for outdoor recreation also shaped Florida. In Clewiston, a golf course and a lakefront beach broke the town grid, becoming the backdrop for its most expensive neighborhoods. Foster located nurseries in each neighborhood and wanted a greenhouse built on axis with the amphitheater in the civic center.[62] His efforts were soon recognized. In September 1925 the *Miami Herald* reported that a "garden city" was taking form in Clewiston, noting its mix of housing, a park system, and "a logical transportation system," with plans to build a bank and hotel.[63] Worker cottages were under construction, and the streets and parks were being integrated into the existing

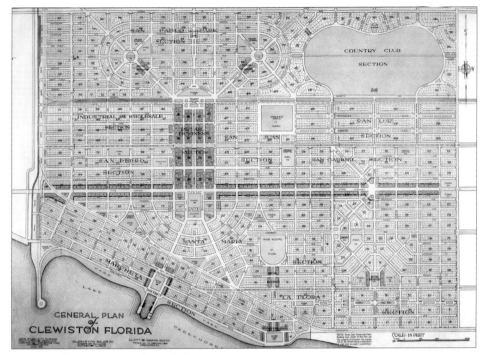

Fig. 8.4. Clewiston town plan, 1925. Courtesy Division of Rare and Manuscript Collections, Cornell University Library.

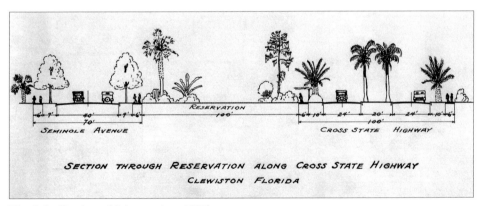

Fig. 8.5. Clewiston highway plan, 1925. Courtesy Division of Rare and Manuscript Collections, Cornell University Library.

network of drainage canals. (Fig. 8.6) Royal Palm Avenue was the first street to be paved and planted with royal palms to create a promenade between the civic center and the lakefront. (Fig. 8.7) In March 1926 the lakefront bathing area was reduced to a two-hundred-foot-wide section after Hale Walker and Nolen Jr. found only a thin overlay of sand covering the limestone.[64]

On September 17, 1926, a major hurricane blew across south Florida, and torrential rains flooded the 750-square-mile lake. Driven by tremendous winds, a wall of water rushed over the ten-foot ridge protecting Clewiston, leaving behind two to five feet of standing water. The town was fortunate that there were no deaths and the buildings were left mostly intact. A group of Celotex structures and commercial establishments were lost, but the new Clewiston Inn escaped harm. Within a week the water and electricity systems

Fig. 8.6. Clewiston worker cottages, c. 1930. Courtesy Clewiston Historical Society.

Fig. 8.7. Royal Palm Avenue, Clewiston, c. 1940. Courtesy Clewiston Historical Society.

were operating, storm waters were being pumped out, and streets and homes repaired. With the shelter of its protective ridge, the town had braved the storm reasonably well, especially compared to nearby Moore Haven, eighteen miles to the west, where over three hundred people lost their lives.[65]

Nolen's Florida commissions, which were located primarily on the Gulf Coast and near Jacksonville, escaped major damage. However, the Nolen office was shaken by a different storm—a clash of wills between Nolen Jr. and Philip Foster. The latter had struggled to keep the busy Jacksonville office in working order, and Nolen Jr. thought the older man was shirking his responsibilities, caught up in the contagious buying and selling of real estate. The situation deteriorated when the young consultants Justin Hartzog and Hale Walker sided with their peer, and Nolen Sr. had to intercede. In October 1925, after a month of back-and-forth letters, he offered Foster the choice of returning to Cambridge or resigning.[66] "It would be an utter impossibility to again assume the relationship of the old days," Foster replied.[67] The separation was not cordial, and dividing up clients proved problematic. The two men did not resolve their differences until January, when Nolen instructed the office accountant to give Foster "the benefit of the doubt of every uncertain item and to be on the generous side." Nolen tried again to reconcile with his longtime associate, but Foster claimed "so much friction and disharmony" had passed that he would not enter into any arrangement. Foster stayed in Jacksonville and oversaw a small practice that specialized in residential subdivisions. The hard feelings lasted until 1932, when the two men reestablished their relationship after a conciliatory letter sent by Nolen.[68]

In early 1926, Hartzog and Walker opened an office for the firm in St. Petersburg, where William Straub had succeeded in choreographing a renewed interest in city planning.[69] He also created a statewide advocacy group that helped Sarasota and Clearwater secure planning acts.[70] With other cities adopting plans, the new St. Petersburg city commission hired Nolen to a $6,500 contract. Population had surged to 60,000, and Straub reported that more and more subdivisions were being opened on a purely speculative basis and with questionable financing.[71] Special assessment bonds were issued to pay for municipal improvements (roads, water, and sewer) on the assumption that development would follow, property values would increase, and the bolstered tax rolls would retire the bonds. The platting and sale of lots proceeded rapidly as municipalities extended infrastructure. The Florida real estate market

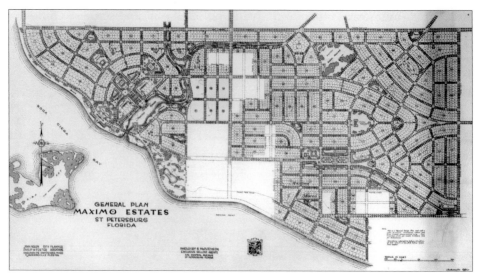

Fig. 8.8. Maximo Estates plan, 1925. Courtesy Division of Rare and Manuscript Collections, Cornell University Library.

hit new highs, and the banks handling the bond sales set records for deposits. By 1926 municipal officials, bankers, and investors conspired to subdivide enough land to house the entire population of the United States.[72] Regulating the real estate market was taboo among a populace immersed in land speculation. In St. Petersburg, Hartzog was directed to scale back the ambitions that filled the firm's first plan. Nolen had decided the office's public commissions would be more conservative, for he had learned how politics could compromise a visionary proposal.

Hartzog's new plan for St. Petersburg established a framework to guide development, but without a greenbelt, neighborhood centers, or tourist districts, it lacked the scope and scale of the 1923 plan.[73] Nevertheless, it was an important document. Investments in the city's infrastructure now had a logical sequencing and special care was taken to protect bayfronts and the lower peninsula's interconnected system of waterways. Straub wanted St. Petersburg to employ a full-time city planner to implement the plan. City officials would then be privy, he wrote, to the "good business judgment" guiding "several subdivision owners."[74] One of the Nolen office's most innovative commissions was Maximo Estates, which was prepared for a St. Petersburg developer. (Fig. 8.8) The quality of this project was not unusual, as the office's plans for new towns and neighborhoods, such as University Park in Gainesville and San Jose Estates in Jacksonville, documented the skills of a firm at the height of its influence. (Figs. 8.9, 8.10, 8.11)

During this time, Nolen also devoted himself to the new Florida towns of Belleair and Venice, projects he featured in *New Towns for Old*. In 1923

Fig. 8.9. San Jose Estates plan, 1925. Courtesy Division of Rare and Manuscript Collections, Cornell University Library.

Fig. 8.10. San Jose Estates, new homes, c. 1926. Courtesy Division of Rare and Manuscript Collections, Cornell University Library.

Fig. 8.11. San Jose Estates, town center, c. 1926. Courtesy Division of Rare and Manuscript Collections, Cornell University Library.

a group of Boston investors had formed the Belleair Development Company and hired him to design an upscale resort suburb on a four-hundred-acre site of high, dry land next to Clearwater Bay.[75] Clearwater, the Pinellas County seat located twenty-five miles north of St. Petersburg, bordered the property to the north and the Belleview Hotel lay to the south. Constructed in 1897, the Belleview was the crown jewel of the hotels established by railroad magnate Henry Plant between Sanford and Fort Myers.[76]

In the 1920s the resort suburb replaced the development model Plant and Henry Flagler had employed, and Coral Gables set a new standard. George Merrick's Venetian masterpiece near Miami was home to the grand Biltmore Hotel, an upscale shopping district, the University of Miami, and a range of residential neighborhoods.[77] By 1924, the Belleair Development Company was prepared to build a resort suburb that would rival Coral Gables.[78]

Nolen's plan for Belleair resembled that of Mariemont, the new town he had recently designed near Cincinnati. (Fig. 8.12) The plan featured a linear park along a bluff with panoramic views of Clearwater Bay. A boulevard connected the park with a small business district and a golf course. Belleair's cultural aspirations were exemplified by an arts building and amphitheater within a formal park at the midpoint of the main boulevard. The plan was ambitious, and given his previous experience in Florida, Nolen feared his Boston clients might lack the resources to implement it. He encouraged them to follow the example of Palos Verdes, an Olmsted Brothers project on the southwest edge of Los Angeles. "Florida is in a turmoil of real estate speculation, in a wilder

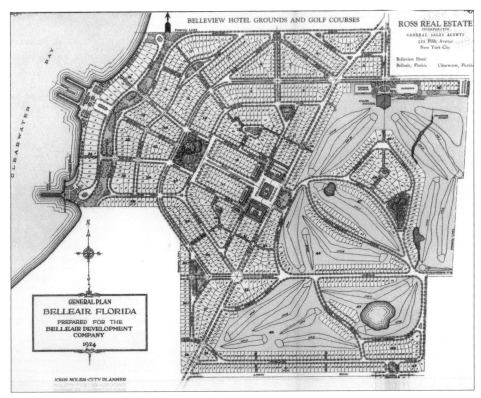

Fig. 8.12. Belleair town plan, 1924. Courtesy Division of Rare and Manuscript Collections, Cornell University Library.

sense than California, and I am not sure what I can persuade them to do," he wrote to the architect Charles Henry Cheney in early 1924.[79]

Cheney was an important contact for Nolen. Working as a consultant for Olmsted Brothers, he had designed the master plan for Palos Verdes, the firm's most significant town planning project in the 1920s.[80] Cheney transformed the 3,200-acre property located on a hilly peninsula into an idyllic residential landscape that accommodated both automobiles and active recreation. Twenty-eight percent of the site was devoted to parks, and ninety percent of the residential units were single-family homes.[81] The Palos Verdes Art Jury, composed of prominent local architects, was created to ensure that new buildings harmonized with the plan. Mediterranean Revival architecture was the preferred style, and a building's color, material, and roof pitch had to meet designated specifications. Restrictive deeds ensured that residents complied with regulations establishing setbacks and height restrictions; deed covenants also barred the sale of property to blacks, Asians, and Jews. In the 1920s, and especially in new suburbs, such restrictions were commonplace, a response to racial fears that constituted what the historian Robert M. Fogelson, in his analysis of Palos Verdes, describes as the "bourgeois nightmare."[82]

Fig. 8.13. Belleair home. Photograph by the author, 2012.

In contrast to racial zoning, racial covenants in private deeds were legal and remained so into the 1950s. In Belleair the crux of the issue for Nolen was not race but finding a legal means to implement the plan. Following Cheney's lead, he pushed the Belleair Development Company to place lot restrictions in deeds and establish an art jury.[83] The appeal was ignored, but as in Kingsport, a private company ensured that development conformed to the plan.[84] Like Palos Verdes, Belleair became an upper-middle-class neighborhood where single-family homes predominated, greens dotted the landscape, waterfront parks offered stunning views, and a golf course provided a recreational landscape. Mediterranean Revival homes along palm-lined streets established the aesthetic of north Pinellas County's premier neighborhood. (Fig. 8.13) After touring Belleair, the Clearwater city commission hired Nolen to draft a comprehensive city plan. In late 1924, Nolen shared the Belleair plan with Dr. Fred Albee and won the commission for Venice, a new town being planned twenty miles south of Sarasota.[85]

Fred H. Albee, a renowned Harvard-educated orthopedic surgeon who had wintered in Florida since 1917, dreamed of building a city around a modern medical center. In 1924 Albee hired Nolen, his classmate at Harvard, to design the Nokomis–Bay Point subdivision. After Nolen had demonstrated his practical planning skills, Albee purchased 1,400 acres of beachfront real estate south of Venice Bay and asked him to plan a new town.[86] A seasonal visitor to Florida, Albee soon learned that town building was a time-consuming and expensive business. Nolen sensed his client's apprehension and began seeking support for the project.[87] In late May the Brotherhood of Locomotive Engineers, the nation's oldest and wealthiest union, purchased the property under a contract that called for Nolen to stay on as project consultant.[88] The Brotherhood of Locomotive Engineers continued acquiring property, eventually running its holdings to more than 25,000 acres. Planning Venice became Nolen's top priority. "I have entered into an agreement with them [the BLE] to plan the whole of this property immediately," he wrote to Straub, who wanted him to focus more intently on St. Petersburg.[89] With 91,000 members and ample resources, the union was investing for the long term. Having such a large parcel under single ownership provided the opportunity to draw a full-scale regional plan and take advantage of natural features. "We are ready to do our utmost to make this plan thoroughly good and interesting," Nolen informed officials."[90]

"Nature led the way" in the design of the Venice plan.[91] The Myakka River and its floodplains were preserved, and the higher elevations in the hinterland were set aside for agriculture. Closer to the coast, eighty-two five-acre plots for growing citrus formed a greenbelt around the city. A series of parkways enfolding small creeks ran to the gulf and bounded Venice to the east and south. Venice Bay and the Gulf of Mexico framed the rest of the city planned for 12,000 residents. (Fig. 8.14) Venice Avenue ran through the center of a three-block commercial core and apartment–hotel district. Loggias were designed to line the street and provide shade. (Fig. 8.15) Where the Gulf of Mexico came into view, the avenue broadened into a parkway, and city hall was sited at this point. The parkway, to be planted with palms, live oaks, and subtropical vegetation, terminated at a beachfront scenic reservation, the centerpiece of a linear park that preserved the beach dune system. (Fig. 8.16)

In addition to Nolen's trademark layout and consideration of natural elements, Venice featured a unique aesthetic. Both the placement of buildings and the architectural style projected the image of a cultured lifestyle centered around natural beauty.[92] (Fig. 8.17) Mediterranean Revival architecture—with its open courtyards, tiled roofs, stucco exteriors, high ceilings, and arched windows and doorways—combined practicality and aesthetics to meet the challenge of the hot, humid climate. (Fig. 8.18) The Brotherhood of Locomotive Engineers hired A. Stewart Walker and Leon N. Gillette, a major New York firm, to oversee the town's construction and design the train sta-

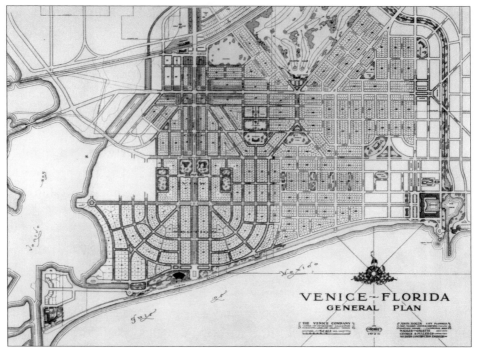

Fig. 8.14. Venice city plan, 1926. Courtesy Division of Rare and Manuscript Collections, Cornell University Library.

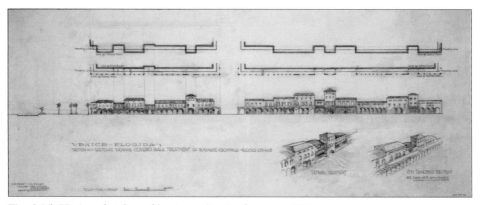

Fig. 8.15. Venice, sketches of business district frontage, 1926. Courtesy Division of Rare and Manuscript Collections, Cornell University Library.

tion and the bank. The effort was inspired by two Venetian landmarks—the campanile in the Piazza San Marco and the Palazzo Ducale. A town architect assigned to the project established a Mediterranean Revival template to review building plans, a process foreign to most property owners. (Fig. 8.19) Most residential units in Venice were single-family homes, but apartments were located in the downtown and adjacent to a three-and-a-half-acre park.[93] The largest homes fronted parkways with easy access to the beach, and parks and

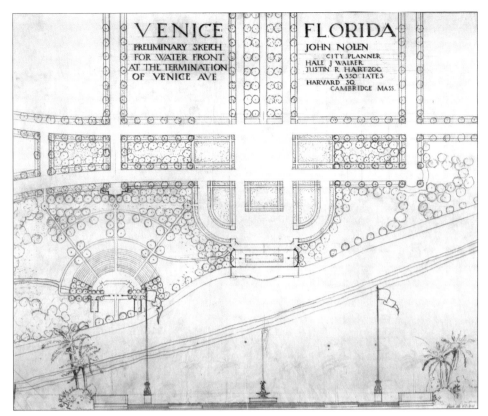

Fig. 8.16. Beach front park designed for Venice, 1926. Courtesy Division of Rare and Manuscript Collections, Cornell University Library.

Fig. 8.17. Venice Hotel, c. 1927. Courtesy Venice Historical Society.

Fig. 8.18. Venice downtown, c. 1927. Courtesy Venice Historical Society.

Fig. 8.19. Hotel and commercial building, Venice, c. 1940. Courtesy Venice Historical Society.

Fig. 8.20. Granada Apartments, c. 1930. Courtesy Venice Historical Society.

schools were placed within walking distance of neighborhoods. Venice was a new type of garden city that considered the relationship between residential growth, tourism, and industrial development.[94] (Fig. 8.20)

Because Venice was expected to be a regional agro-industrial center, an industrial zone next to the rail station was slated for agricultural processing plants and shipping facilities. The Edgewood District, a working-class neighborhood, lay to the east. A simple grid was used to create smaller, less expensive lots while still providing basic amenities and a pedestrian orientation. With jobs in agriculture, light industry, and tourism, "Venice would be a place where the ordinary man could have a chance to get all that the rich have ever been able to get out of Florida," the union announced in one of the thousands of marketing brochures.[95] (Fig. 8.21)

Fig. 8.21. Venice promotional brochure. Courtesy Division of Rare and Manuscript Collections, Cornell University Library.

The "ordinary man" certainly did have a place in Venice, provided he was white. Deed restrictions prevented the sale or rental of property to non-Caucasians.[96] Given this constraint, Nolen wanted to dedicate a section of the city to African Americans. "The provision for the negro working population is an issue of great importance" but "not well solved," he wrote to union officials. "The only satisfactory answer is planning a tract completely for Negro village life."[97] The union agreed to allocate 230 acres for Harlem Village, a name "that would be acceptable to colored people," Nolen thought.[98] Bounded by a parkway and five-acre farms owned by whites, Harlem Village had 705 residential lots with 50-foot frontages and 120 apartment units with 25-foot frontages in a business district that framed a town green. (Fig. 8.22) A formal park, a playfield, and a bathhouse on the shore of a two-acre lake constituted the civic center. The Walter Page School, a ten-acre park, sites for four churches, and three playgrounds completed the community infrastructure. Residential neighborhoods with tree-lined streets followed the same grid pattern used in the Edgewood District. Officials expected between 3,500 and 4,000 residents, which would account for approximately one-third of Venice's anticipated population.[99] In 1926 a small army of laborers, more than half of them African American, went to work implementing the Venice city plan. Nolen pleaded with the union to "speed up plans for the Negro Village," but just as in Kingsport, African American housing was a priority for the consultant, not his clients.[100] Harlem Village was never built; instead the union expended its resources on constructing the downtown and the white residential neighborhoods.

Nolen feared the Brotherhood of Locomotive Engineers would further deviate from the plan, so he persuaded union officials to hire a resident landscape architect. Prentiss French was a Harvard graduate and nephew of the famed sculptor Daniel Chester French; he was an exceptional designer and had Nolen's complete confidence.[101] Having spent three years working at Palos Verdes, he had experience in transforming a barren site into a verdant landscape. In 1926, French put Nolen's plans into action. In late spring, land was cleared for a six-acre nursery to supply plants for a series of intensive landscaping projects. By fall, French had 4,770 trees, 3,800 shrubs, and 1,450 vines in various stages of growth. He also implemented planting regimens for streets, parks, the civic center, and residences. Seventy-five percent of the trees planted were native, and French chose mostly natives when massing shrubs as well.[102] Steady progress ensued, and for once "the landscape work gets the attention it deserves," Nolen happily noted.[103] In July, he confided to Raymond Unwin that Venice was his best Florida project and the most original plan his office had produced. The union was in the midst of spending $15 million on the project—proof that city planning had taken hold in Florida.[104]

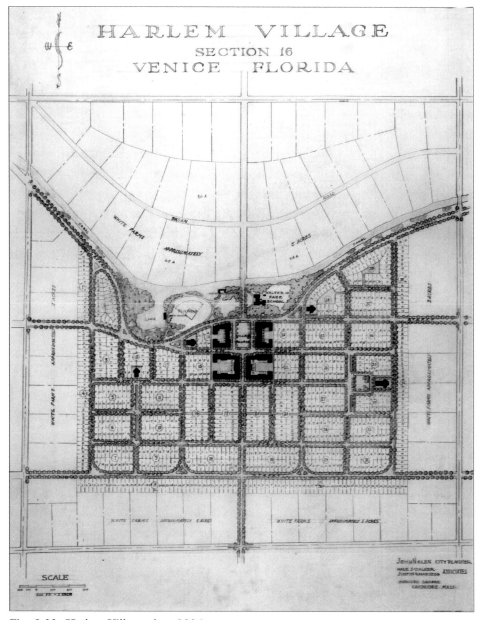

Fig. 8.22. Harlem Village plan, 1926. Courtesy Division of Rare and Manuscript Collections, Cornell University Library.

By 1926 Nolen had earned over fifty commissions in Florida and worked with a broad range of clients, the most significant being the newly formed Miami City Planning Commission. A year earlier, he had addressed the group at an event arranged by Jessica Seymour, the influential leader of the Florida Federation of Garden Clubs and a champion of city planning.[105] Seymour urged Nolen to hold the upcoming National Conference on City Planning in

Florida. As president of the American City Planning Institute, Nolen had the opportunity to focus attention on planning at a key "psychological moment." It would be an opportunity, Seymour added, that "no city planner has had in this country before."[106] The conference was indeed held in St. Petersburg in March 1926, and two hundred "erudite, aloof, exalted, campus-looking personages" traveled south to enjoy the exotic Florida milieu.[107] Included in the number was a second generation of city planners, represented by Nolen Jr. and Edwin Unwin, Raymond Unwin's son. Holding the event in Florida drew a good audience, and Nolen had an ambitious agenda. In his presidential address, he proposed the establishment of a state planning agency (as Frank Williams had suggested) and adoption of a state plan, which would provide the framework for drafting a system of interconnected regional cities and garden suburbs.[108] Almost instantly Nolen's grand vision evaporated as the real estate market spiraled into decline that spring. As Nolen observed, "Almost everything that is good and bad in the flesh is to be seen in Florida."[109]

Any hope that the market would reverse itself dissolved when a hurricane struck southern Florida in September 1926. Although Clewiston escaped largely unscathed, Miami was devastated. The city of over 100,000 was ground zero for the intense storm with sustained winds clocked at 128 miles per hour. A fifteen-foot storm surge breached Miami Beach, the barrier island made habitable by dredge and fill, and obliterated Coconut Grove, its longest-standing settlement. In Miami proper, nearly 5,000 homes were destroyed and another 9,100 needed repair. Once insurance agents completed their assessments, the city had lost sixty-four percent of its appraised real estate value.[110] The forces of nature and free enterprise exposed the speculative delusions behind the Florida real estate boom. That winter thousands left worthless investments, their dreams, and Florida behind.[111]

In 1927 Florida's jerry-built financial system collapsed when payment came due on the special-assessment bonds that had financed the infrastructure for hundreds of new subdivisions. With speculators and property values long gone, thousands of vacant lots reverted to local governments. Left holding worthless assets and a declining tax base, municipalities foundered as debts mounted. St. Petersburg epitomized Florida's sordid financial affairs. Between 1923 and 1927 the city's bonded debt jumped from $3.8 to $23.7 million, with six percent interest. In 1928 the debt reached $28 million, the first bank closed, and fraudulent dealings in other financial institutions were disclosed, saddling the city with the second highest per-capita debt in the nation. Five years earlier, Nolen had warned that the "speculative haphazard" outlay of public improvements would create "adverse conditions that residents would have to contend with for a generation."[112] The urban infrastructure would eventually cover an area capable of serving a city of 200,000, five times St. Petersburg's 1930 population. "Many improvements cost more than the reasonable value of all the properties that benefited from these investments," the city manager reported.[113] Nolen could not understand why a city plan had not been adopted. He had another concern as well: the planning board had yet to pay a list of invoices.[114]

By late 1927, Nolen's entire Florida practice was in jeopardy. Belleair, Maximo Estates, and San Jose Estates had failed, and Venice seemed destined to do the same. Payments from Clewiston were inconsistent, and public sector clients had reneged on contracts. The future looked bleak. "City after city that contemplated sound planning work during the boom days has dropped the whole thing," Nolen wrote to Jessica Seymour.[115] He closed the St. Petersburg office. Walker and Hartzog returned to Cambridge, and Nolen Jr. took a position with the Regional Planning Federation in Philadelphia. He did well there and went on to marry and become a fixture in the profession.[116] His father's fortunes remained precarious, however, as Florida had "busted."

In the wake of "the orgy of unrestrained greed," William Straub led a chorus calling for a "New Florida."[117] Across the state, similar appeals were made in favor of creating a more diversified economy invested in agriculture, industry, and tourism. The Florida legislature passed measures to regulate the issuance of assessment bonds and real estate transactions, but the economy continued to contract. The promise of a New Florida dissipated along with Nolen's commissions. Invoices to St. Petersburg and the Brotherhood of Locomotive Engineers had gone unpaid for a year. Nolen hoped to stem his losses by securing a commission in Daytona Beach, but in February 1928 city officials refused to sign a pending contract.[118] Municipalities could no longer afford the services of a city planner. The tide of prosperity that had washed over Florida receded in equally dramatic fashion. Once-prosperous cities were now entrenched in debt with no hope of relief. "The problem in Florida now is to pay the piper for the tune played during the boom," Rudolph Weaver, the director of the University of Florida's School of Architecture, wrote to Nolen.[119]

For Nolen, Venice epitomized the paradox of the boom. By 1928 the city was all but abandoned, yet its civic–commercial core and intricate system of plantings and parks, including the scenic reservation at the terminus of Venice Parkway, modeled the progress in town planning.[120] Characterized by well-apportioned spaces and varied interpretations of Mediterranean Revival architecture, Venice was a modern city built on classical proportions.[121] (Figs. 8.23, 8.24, 8.25)

Nolen's plan for Venice had always instilled high expectations. In the

Fig. 8.23. Beachfront park, Venice, c. 1950. Courtesy Venice Historical Society.

Fig. 8.24. Venice, c. 1930. Courtesy Venice Historical Society.

Fig. 8.25. Venice Historic District. Photograph by the author, 2000.

hands of the Brotherhood of Locomotive Engineers, it also incited financial ruin. In 1928 the union had fifteen pending lawsuits, and creditors, Nolen among them, demanded thousands of dollars in unpaid bills. Nolen's suit cost $700, but he considered it "one of the penalties we must pay for our Florida work."[122] In one of his last letters, Prentiss French reported that "nothing happens at Venice and when I say nothing I mean nothing." The town had effectively been evacuated, and the landscape architect had no faith in the union's management.[123] An investigative committee determined that "with only a small degree of intelligence," disaster could have been averted.[124] By April 1929 the Brotherhood of Locomotive Engineers was mired in losses, and after spending two years hounding its treasurer for payments, Nolen reconciled his loss at $4,000, thirty percent of his yearly profits. This setback, coupled with a $3,000 shortfall in St. Petersburg, sent his firm into a tailspin.[125] The Great Depression had come early to Florida and to Nolen. "I am tired! I have given up my hope for financial independence or a chance to gradually retire in old age," he wrote to his wife in December 1928.[126]

Despite all his efforts, Nolen had only one client left in Florida, Bror Dahlberg. The midwestern entrepreneur was forging ahead with his plan to build a modern industrial empire in the heart of the Everglades. There was hope that Clewiston, a village of three hundred residents, would become the

Fig. 8.26. Clewiston Hotel. Photograph by John Nolen, 1932. Courtesy Division of Rare and Manuscript Collections, Cornell University Library.

"Chicago of the Everglades," for sugar still had value.[127] (Fig. 8.26) In 1928 the Southern Sugar Company had 8,000 acres in cultivation, owned another 100,000 acres of prime muck land, and planned to invest $30 million in drainage projects. A skilled political operative, Dahlberg had also been lobbying the federal government to subsidize reclamation projects and enact a higher sugar tariff. That year he wrote a $5,000 check to the Republican National Committee hoping to end the Democratic Party's free-trade policies and its grip on the South.[128] Dahlberg's investment paid off. In his landslide victory, Herbert Hoover ended the Democratic Party's dominance in the South by carrying Florida. Three months later, the president-elect visited Clewiston.[129]

After the election, Dahlberg rehired Nolen to plan an airfield on the vacant site of the Clewiston golf course.[130] The airfield was operational in time for the "Sugar Fete," Dahlberg's grand unveiling of a new 15-million-ton-capacity sugar mill. On January 13, 1929, Dahlberg's flight from Chicago to West Palm Beach, the airport's first night landing, garnered extensive press coverage. The next morning he flew on to Clewiston to host a luncheon and ceremony for state dignitaries who arrived in a caravan of one hundred cars and buses from West Palm Beach. Dahlberg gave a commanding performance. He claimed the Southern Sugar Company was "following in the steps of early pioneers," but with the aid of "modern science." The plan to integrate the sugar industry and urban development in Clewiston was "steadfastly moving ahead."[131] Governor John W. Martin spoke next. Dahlberg's enterprise would "revolutionize this section of our state," he claimed, provided the federal government underwrote "Everglades drainage."[132] The Southern Sugar Company did more than petition elected officials. Executives regularly sent checks (for which they were reimbursed) to the Republican Party as an investment in federal land reclamation. It was money well spent.[133] Two weeks after the Sugar Fete, Herbert Hoover visited the new Clewiston sugar mill and spent the evening in the small town. A year later the Republican Congress appropriated funds for the Army Corps of Engineers to build what became the Hoover Dike, a thirty-eight-foot embankment enclosing Lake Okeechobee; in 1937 the southern half of the dike was complete. The centerpiece of the northern Everglades' drainage system, the eighty-five-mile limestone and sand barricade cost $20 million. At that point, the careers of both Herbert Hoover and Bror Dahlberg lay in tatters.[134]

The simultaneous collapse of both the stock market and the building industry forced the Southern Sugar Company into receivership in the summer of 1930, and the title to the derelict operation passed to the U.S. Sugar Corporation at a receivers' sale. By then Clewiston was mired in hardship.[135] Scrip had replaced the dollar as a means of exchange, and Nolen was struggling to be paid for services rendered. "We are not financed to wait long for payments and our margin of profit . . . is very small," he informed a Clewiston official.[136] Two years later, the $2,000 bill was finally settled. Nolen looked forward to "better times . . . when we can carry Clewiston forward to its local conclusion."[137]

Nolen's practice never recovered from its Florida entanglements. In 1931 he let Hale Walker go, leaving Justin Hartzog as the other lone principal. His practice was barely solvent. He and secretary Charlotte Parsons staffed the Cambridge office, but it was little more than a formality. Hartzog, unable to subsist on the firm's meager workload, was working as an independent contractor. Nolen was paring back every part of his business. In a letter terminating his membership with the Boston Authors Club, he noted that when employed he seldom attended meetings, but being "unemployed I do not have the funds." It proved to be just one of the "many pleasant things" he would relinquish in the ensuing years.[138]

9

THE DEAN OF AMERICAN CITY PLANNING, 1931–1937

In 1931 an unexpected trip to Germany provided Nolen with some relief from the hopeless situation in Florida. Through a grant from the Oberlaender Trust, Nolen was able to launch a six-week study of German city planning and attend the conference of the International Federation of Housing and Town Planning in Berlin.[1] Arriving in Hamburg in late May, he found that the financial catastrophe born across the Atlantic had reached European shores. President Hoover's moratorium on the acceptance of World War I reparation payments from Germany accomplished little. In June, Nolen assumed presidency of the International Federation of Housing and Town Planning, a post that acknowledged his ongoing efforts to create relationships with European planners.[2] After the collapse of the Darmstadt (national bank) that July, it became impossible to exchange the Reichsmark for foreign currency. Unemployment surged past twenty-five percent as financial crisis gripped the country.[3] Yet despite the troubles, the German center held. The Nazis and Communists, holding eighteen and thirteen percent of the Reichstag's seats, respectively, were still considered extremist parties, and the Social Democrats controlled the government. Economic worries occupied the public mind, and politics, though contentious, remained focused on solving problems through the democratic process.[4]

After the conference, Nolen traveled across Germany to assess advances in city planning. "The beautifying of riverbanks and waterfronts, harmonizing the new developments with the old, effective building controls, the widespread planting not only of trees but of shrubs—there is green everywhere," he reported. Spending most of his time outdoors, he enjoyed living with "less clothes, less apparatus for play, less spectators, and more active recreation."[5] During his last week in Germany, Nolen stayed at Sonnenland, a nudist colony near Hamburg in the Lüneburger Heide forest. His interest in nudism grew out of the logic of the garden city. Fresh air, openness, and communion with nature were keys to healthy living, and for Nolen these attributes were integral to good design. A year before, at a housing conference, Nolen had commented on the importance of creating room for enjoying the healthful rays of the sun. "The plan for the home should provide for sun porches for rest and sleeping, and a private sunny corner, what the English call a sun pocket, protected from the wind, where one can enjoy a complete sunbath without reserve. Ten minutes in the sun without clothes is said by modern authorities to be as beneficial as a whole day outdoors with clothes." He stayed in a small inexpensive dormitory room at Sonnenland and appreciated the simple healthy meals. Most of all, he enjoyed spending time outdoors unhindered by convention. "In fifteen minutes the strangeness of no clothes disappears and then there is only a sense of new freedom, and an escape from an unnecessary limitation upon the pleasure of games, swimming and social intercourse," he wrote to his wife. "It seems *so good*!" In the summer of 1931, it was still possible for Nolen to write of Germany: "I have never felt so much at home."[6]

Upon returning to the United States, Nolen wrote a *Boston Herald* editorial voicing his concern over the Weimar Republic's increasingly desperate situation. In the face of growing instability, he stated, goodwill had to be maintained between Germany and the United States. Unemployment was rife in both nations, and prewar Germany, with its tradition of planning and municipal investment, offered a model that lay between the extremes of laissez-faire capitalism and Soviet communism. Constructing decent housing for the poor and improving the living environment for all classes would put thousands to work. In addition, it was time for the federal government to curtail its "short-sighted policy of industrial exploitation." Dedicating funds for conservation projects to protect forests, beautify public waterfronts, and prevent soil erosion—areas in which German and American expertise was unsurpassed—promised to generate jobs and foster international cooperation.[7]

Nolen's proposal was little more than wishful thinking. President Hoover and Heinrich Bruning, the conservative Weimar chancellor, adamantly opposed the welfare state. Inaction plagued both men, and their conservatism was disastrous. Hoover became a lamentable political figure, while Bruning was viewed as the Weimar's most unpopular chancellor. In the teetering state, the vainglory of Prussian virtue proved deadly, accelerating Germany's descent into a maniacal and brutal dictatorship.[8]

When he returned to America, Nolen's fiscal dilemma mirrored the plight of countless Americans as the economy fell into paralysis. By the spring of 1932, housing starts had declined by five hundred percent in three years, over one hundred cities no longer provided funds for the indigent, and for the first time in the nation's history, the urban population was declining as thousands returned to the land to survive.[9] Assessing the situation, the usually upbeat Nolen questioned the moral fitness of humanity. "Modern man is destructive, rude, commercial, shortsighted, wasteful," he proclaimed at a Pennsylvania planning conference that year. "We might almost say he is a natural vandal, lacking a sense of values and a sense of proportion." There was no alternative but to plan. Investing capital for long-term returns and appropriating it in a rational, systematic manner was the only way to reconcile "the rights of property" and "the rights of the public." Moreover, if growth was not controlled, the countryside and its communities were "in danger of being gradually destroyed."[10]

The situation was bleak, but there were glimmers of hope. Since the early days of the Great Depression, Nolen had been an advocate for a federal housing program. He was part of a network of like-minded thinkers that included new acquaintances, such as the historian Bernard DeVoto and the economist David Coyle, and longtime associates like Raymond Unwin, Thomas Adams, Grosvenor Atterbury, Charles Beard, Lawrence Veiller, and Richard Ely. In the summer of 1932 Ely, the former University of Wisconsin economist, was collaborating with Nolen on a project to measure housing quality. Semiretired and in his late seventies, Ely was involved with the new Institute for Land Economics in New York. He had also taken up residence in Radburn, New Jersey, to live "in the midst of the housing laboratory."[11]

Nearly a decade before, Lewis Mumford had joined architects Henry Wright and Clarence Stein to form the Regional Planning Association of America, a small but influential group of planners and housing experts.[12] The association's goal was to direct urban growth by developing a system of interconnected regional cities and towns, much as Nolen would propose in his 1926 address at the National City Planning Conference in St. Petersburg. Mumford saw Roosevelt as a leader capable of reviving the moribund housing industry along socially progressive lines. As governor of New York, Roosevelt had created the New York State Commission on Housing and Regional Planning, the first such body in the nation. Stein chaired the group, and the association's members believed they would play a significant role in the new administration.[13]

Established by the City Housing Corporation in 1929, Radburn was the planning association's blueprint for reconstructing the American city. Wright and Stein, veterans of the World War I federal housing initiative, reconfigured the garden city on "superblocks" to keep automobile traffic on the periphery of neighborhoods. Homes were clustered around common greens, while underpasses ensured the safe movement of bicyclists and pedestrians. Twenty-five percent less space was allocated to utilities and streets than in a typical subdivision, a savings the developer invested in supporting recreation, landscaping, and park maintenance.[14] As a board member of the City Housing Corporation, Nolen was particularly impressed by the opportunities Radburn offered children, who could play on the common greens outside their homes and traverse the community on its system of bike and walking trails.[15] Though the depression halted construction, Radburn remained at the forefront of the city planning profession, a model the federal government was expected to use after the stunning electoral victory of Franklin Roosevelt.

The town represented "a finger exercise preparing for the symphonies yet to come," Mumford declared after the election.[16] Nolen had similar hopes. After a generation of struggle, government was poised to employ planning to rehabilitate the failed economy and social structure.[17] A month before the inauguration, Nolen anticipated that "David Coyle, George Soule, Charles Beard, and Stuart Chase" would "endorse city and regional planning . . . as part of the big 'Planning Idea.'"[18] Once Roosevelt laid out the New Deal at his inaugural, the possibilities seemed endless. "These are great days to be alive," he wrote to Howard Strong, a Minneapolis civic leader.[19]

Nolen's optimistic letter came the month before Robert Luce, the Republican congressman representing Cambridge, solicited his advice on a new federal agency, the Tennessee Valley Authority. Nolen sent him a copy of *New Towns for Old,* with the chapter on Kingsport highlighted. The TVA might consider Kingsport's example, Nolen noted, which proved what industrialists could accomplish if they did not "exploit the real estate situation or their own employees."[20] In addition, the consultant's last significant commission was a regional plan, drawn in 1931 for Dubuque, Iowa. (Fig. 9.1) The corporation was charged with delivering electricity, managing natural resources, developing model towns, and instituting land use planning; its authority extended over most of Tennessee and into parts of Alabama, Georgia, Kentucky, Mississippi, North Carolina, and Virginia.[21]

In late June 1933, Nolen contacted Earle Draper, the TVA planning director, asking if he might secure "at some point in time regional planning or

CITY OF DUBUQUE IOWA REGIONAL PLAN

Fig. 9.1. Dubuque regional plan, 1931. Courtesy Division of Rare and Manuscript Collections, Cornell University Library.

consulting work in the Tennessee Valley."[22] Having drawn plans for Kingsport and Johnson City, he was arguably the nation's leading expert on planning in the Tennessee Valley. Felix Frankfurter sent a note to director David Lilienthal encouraging him to consider Nolen, whom he called a noted housing reformer and "a grad of our own [Harvard] landscape architecture school."[23] George Marston, the San Diego civic leader, also weighed in on Nolen's behalf, writing to Arthur E. Morgan, chairman of the TVA board, that "in San Diego the Nolen Plan is a civic slogan."[24] Lawrence Veiller sent a telegram to Morgan describing Nolen as "easily one of the country's leading town planners, an experienced, intelligent, sane, and practical person and yet with vision and imagination."[25] And George Stephens sent a recommendation to Morgan recounting how Draper had learned his craft at Myers Park under Nolen's direction; since establishing his own practice, Draper's approach to "community planning followed along the lines of Dr. Nolen's methods and policies."[26]

Nolen did not get the job.[27] By the end of 1933, he had not yet landed a new planning commission. Although he had worked on state park projects in Vermont and Florida as a consultant for the Department of the Interior, younger men were taking the lead in the planning field. Justin Hartzog, Hale Walker, Jacob Crane, and Tracy Augur, all of whom started their careers in the Nolen office, were employed in the Greenbelt Program, the New Deal's most progressive planning initiative and a division of the Resettlement Administration. The program's director, Rexford Guy Tugwell, a former Simon Patten student, originally expected to build one hundred new towns, but intense opposition from real estate interests and neighboring communities forced him to scale back his ambitions. Ultimately, only three Greenbelt town projects were built, but two of Nolen's protégés earned significant commissions: Hartzog directed the planning of the town of Greenhills in Ohio, and Walker helped design Greenbelt, Maryland.[28]

The Greenbelt towns had an informal layout that lacked the crisp geometry of Mariemont and Venice. Stein, a consultant to the Resettlement Administration, believed that civic-center-based plans limited spontaneous social interactions. Residences in the new towns were aligned on mews and along linear greens to encourage the development of meaningful relationships between neighbors.[29] At the same time, the Greenbelt architectural style, Weimar modernism, inspired the belief that housing the working class with factory-like precision promoted democracy. Informed by the German Bauhaus, the architecture's spare functionalism rejected the picturesque building style that defined the garden city. Modernist architecture also announced a new approach to city planning, the development of a hygienic urban environment in which technology ordered life and served the needs of all classes.[30]

Nolen kept abreast of the progress in the Greenbelt communities through Hartzog and Walker. He still met regularly with Hartzog to discuss potential commissions, the state of the profession, and the lectures they presented to students at Harvard. In 1934 the two planners were hired by the National Resources Board to develop an operating framework for the New Hampshire state planning board. Though the pay of $25 a day was a quarter of what Nolen had earned in the 1920s, it was a job, his first planning commission in two years.[31] The work was mostly mundane, but contributing to a grand scheme—establishing state planning boards across the nation—was reward-ing.[32] Nolen's experience in the South proved especially valuable to the agency, and he began working on a semi-regular basis, writing reports for agencies in Alabama, Georgia, and Florida to "discreetly promote urban and local forms of regional planning."[33]

Nolen's chief at the National Resources Board was Charles W. Eliot II, grandson of the Harvard president who had helped secure Nolen's first public commission.[34] Eliot, a landscape architect who had earned one of the first city planning concentrations offered at Harvard, was made director of the National Planning Board in 1933.[35] The board set goals to guide the preparation of regional and city plans, which provided the framework for allocating funds to the Public Works Administration (PWA) and Works Progress Administration (WPA). Local city planning boards administered the projects funded by these agencies, which made city planning essential for garnering federal dollars.[36]

The National Resources Board formula for disbursing federal funds put a premium on comprehensive planning. After the St. Petersburg city coun-cil finally adopted Nolen's second plan for the city in 1933, the WPA and PWA began investing in improving the city's infrastructure, especially its sub-standard water supply system.[37] Meanwhile, in San Diego the federal gov-ernment funded harbor improvements, highway connections, and two major parks in conformance with Nolen's 1926 city plan. The WPA also under-wrote the construction of city and county buildings on the civic center site that Nolen identified in both his 1908 and 1926 plans. (Fig. 9.2) "Today the dream of the Boston city planner is coming true," the *Christian Science Monitor* reported after the first building opened in 1937.[38] Three years later, the National Resources Board designated San Diego as one of five prototype cities for programming and financing of public works projects.[39] The New Deal had successfully institutionalized planning, but Eliot's desire to create the "habitation for a new social order," a challenge also facing the Tennes-see Valley Authority, the Resettlement Administration, and the Subsistence Homesteads Division, proved more daunting.[40]

The Subsistence Homesteads Division, established in conjunction with

Fig. 9.2. San Diego County Administration Building, 1937. Courtesy San Diego Historical Society.

the National Resources Board, exemplified the bedeviling inconsistencies that plagued New Deal planning. The agency was created to help poor tenant farmers raise their standard of living by combining subsistence agriculture with part-time industrial work. In 1934 Nolen earned one of the agency's first commissions, the "farm city" of Penderlea in southeastern North Carolina.[41] The plan for Penderlea placed 150 ten-acre truck farms in a horseshoe design around a civic core, which had sites for a school, civic and commercial buildings, and a central marketing plant. (Fig. 9.3) In 1935 the Resettlement Administration acquired the Penderlea property. It then purchased additional acreage, and Nolen's plan was redrawn to accommodate twenty-acre farm plots. By January 1937, 112 of the 147 homesteads were occupied. The opening of a hosiery factory, underwritten by the Farm Security Administration (which now oversaw the project), generated jobs. As the economy improved, Penderlea prospered but never became the model agro-industrial community

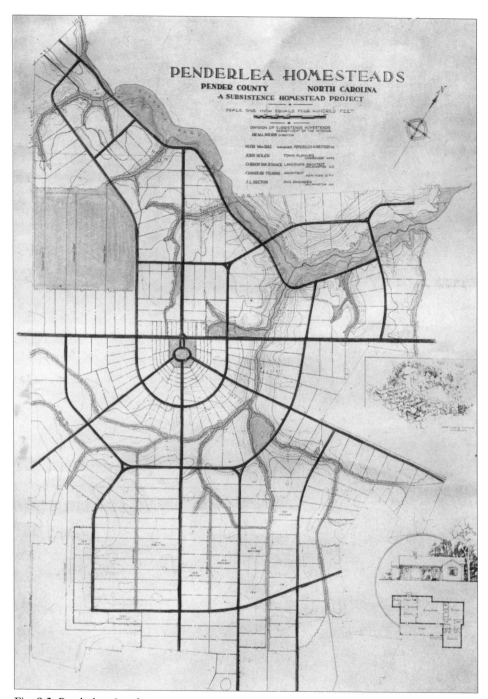

Fig. 9.3. Penderlea city plan. Courtesy Division of Rare and Manuscript Collections, Cornell University Library.

originally envisioned. In 1947 the federal government withdrew its support, and Penderlea was consolidated into 105 farms of 40 to 125 acres before being sold at public auction.[42]

Penderlea's transformation from cooperative enterprise to private property epitomized the New Deal's trial-and-error approach to community planning.[43] In a letter to Raymond Unwin, Nolen commented that "things keep moving here, but it is hard to tell what the net results are. The directions are not altogether clear." Housing, in particular was "a mystery, and no one seems to know the first spot toward the way out."[44] The Tennessee Valley Authority bore the brunt of Lewis Mumford's criticism. Its "sporadic patchwork" of plans typified the New Deal's "total indifference to guiding principles or definite goals."[45]

In the early 1930s, however, once Nolen became invested in the federal agencies, his frustrations faded. Although the reports he wrote for the National Resources Board were not his best work, he took satisfaction in instituting a rational decision-making process to replace the ill-formed speculative actions of the past. Progress was slow and correcting earlier mistakes onerous given

Fig. 9.4. John Nolen, c. 1932.
Courtesy Division of Rare and Manuscript
Collections, Cornell University Library.

the collapse of "civic guidance" during the depression.[46] But the mid-1930s federal planners had reason for optimism, civic life was invigorated, and the economy had stabilized.[47] The New Deal also energized the study of city planning, which Nolen, the recognized "dean" of American city planning, wholeheartedly embraced.[48] (Fig. 9.4)

An advocate of planning education since the early 1910s, Nolen had continued to pursue academic work as he managed his professional practice. In 1927, he partnered with Thomas Adams on an initiative sponsored by the American City Planning Institute to educate practitioners systematically. Then serving as the institute's president, Nolen had high expectations, but without a full-time staff little headway was made. The next year Adams, as chair of the New York Regional Plan Association, hosted the Conference on a Project for Research and Instruction in City and Regional Planning at Columbia University. An exhaustive discussion between academics and professionals ensued, and the conference provided the impetus for the Rockefeller Foundation to fund the nation's first School of City Planning.[49]

In 1929 Harvard received a $240,000 grant to establish a graduate school dedicated to the "trained guidance of city growth" and the "development of the planning profession."[50] Since 1924 the Department of Landscape Architecture had offered a master's focused on city planning, and by 1928 twenty-eight students had earned such degrees, including Charles Eliot II.[51] Henry Hubbard, chair of the landscape architecture department, was named director of the university's School of City Planning. Hubbard, editor of *City Planning,* the journal of the American City Planning Institute, organized a twenty-course curriculum, drawn primarily from the departments of architecture and landscape architecture. Emphasis was placed on land analysis, physical planning, and applied research. Hubbard employed Nolen and Adams, both part-time instructors at the Massachusetts Institute of Technology, to teach the technical aspects of the discipline.[52]

The school's opening was announced on October 21, 1929, the day before the stock market crashed. Establishing a professional degree in academia was difficult enough, but the national fiscal crisis intensified the challenge. The Rockefeller grant and the camaraderie of Hubbard, Adams, and Nolen, who were longtime associates, stemmed the crisis.[53] The new school reinvigorated Nolen. An acknowledged "lifelong student," he was soon invested in teaching and developing a new avenue of research grounded in social science.[54]

The Harvard City Planning Studies series was also launched 1929, suggesting that Harvard University Press would take on contemporary urban issues by publishing books with a more analytical bent than previous works in the field. Federal funding formulas and traffic engineering demanded quantitative analysis, which challenged the assumptions of a profession that originated from the "art" of landscape architecture. In the early 1930s classical traditions in art and design were giving way to a modernist vision that venerated efficiency and the machine. Following in the wake of the European modernists, the "mechanical city" challenged the "organic city" as the model for city planners. Rather than a means to identify the natural limits of growth, modernists saw technology as a tool to overcome nature's constraints.[55] Aligning urban components with formulaic precision and quantifying the human experience became the new modus operandi. Among academics, economics and sociology were considered sciences and the means to rejuvenate society and end the depression.[56]

The first book in the series, Henry and Theodora Kimball Hubbard's *Our Cities Today and Tomorrow* (1929), revealed just how difficult it was to mold an art into a social science. In his review, Nolen voiced his concern that natural conditions were being ignored in the rush to quantify the urban environment.[57] Mumford had similar concerns, warning that a "mechanized armature" was set to spread over the landscape and sever humanity's connection to nature. Cities would devolve into places for consuming, not living. The desire to consume would eventually lead humans to defile "their own nest, reaching into the sky after the moon" for "more paper profits" and "more vicarious substitutes for life."[58] Efficiency might be procured, but at what cost?

Harland Bartholomew's contribution to the Harvard series, *Urban Land Uses* (1932), epitomized city planning's utilitarian shift. The book was devoted almost exclusively to quantitative analysis and included over one hundred charts documenting ratios of population to the acreage of a particular land use, such as parks, single-family homes, and industry, to aid in developing a "more scientific zoning practice."[59] A civil engineer by training, Bartholomew was the top transportation expert in the planning profession and its lead advocate for building freeways. He disdained both European convention and the notion that city planning was an art. Tables of charts and projections steeped in statistics and analysis made it easier to defend a plan on the public dais, in court, and on the engineer's drafting table. In a world demanding calculation and efficiency, Bartholomew saw beauty as irrelevant.[60]

Despite the increasing focus on statistical analysis in the profession, Nolen continued to teach city planning as a mix of art and science. In his estimation, "civic development, not numbers," lay at the heart of city planning.[61] His Harvard lectures displayed an intellectual dexterity not found in the measured reports he compiled for New Deal agencies. Students in his town planning course were challenged to envision a new social order that would provide "a way out of the Depression."[62] Early in the semester, Nolen presented the "Great Idea," the notion of considering "the city as an Organism."[63] In this scheme, cities were best perceived as biological organisms designed to reproduce life. Students learned to analyze natural conditions to determine the limits of urban expansion and identify which lands were best suited for agriculture, forests, parks, and development. Nolen encouraged students to glean knowledge from the historical city. Classical Athens, Renaissance Florence, and republican Geneva were repositories of civic design and spiritual value that offered essential insight into the "well-ordered organic city."[64]

For Nolen, city planning was a cooperative enterprise. Practitioners gathered relevant contributions from the fields of sociology, law, economics, public administration, engineering, landscape architecture, and architecture. In order to be successful, a planner needed "the wisdom of Solomon, the heart of a prophet, the patience of Job and the hide of a rhinoceros."[65] In teaching the art of town design, Nolen focused on the garden city. Before drawing their own plans, students analyzed Letchworth, Hampstead Garden Suburb, Forest Hills Gardens, Mariemont, and Radburn. Park systems and neighborhoods were integrated into a civic framework, and housing densities were capped at twelve units per acre. While this rule could bend, any calibration made the pedestrian environment a focal point of street design in a transportation system.[66] In the 1930s, approximately two-thirds of urban commuters in the United States were pedestrians, bicyclists, or transit riders.[67] Nolen, who had walked to his Harvard Square office for thirty years, also had students examine Cambridge to find and measure the attributes of a walkable urban environment. As his students struggled to determine the role of the automobile in the post-depression city, Nolen reminded them that humans were biological organisms, not machines. Their task was to ensure that technology was used to advance both the standard of living and the art of life.

The instructor concluded the course with a plea for students to tour Europe, the same directive he had given to young planners in his office a decade earlier. America's problems could be worked out by observation and study overseas, but that "does not mean copying," he had assured Russell Black.[68] Nolen recounted to his class how Patrick Geddes encouraged his students to visit Paris to indulge in the pleasures of urban life before they ever studied the city. Visiting Europe enlivened the senses as well as the mind. At the same time, Nolen reminded his students that Paris had been designed and built by men of inordinate personal ambition. The despotic powers of Napoleon III created the City of Light, and dictators in Italy and Germany were not reluctant to plan. In a world wracked by uncertainty, the challenge to democracy was "to make and carry out large-scale, far-seeing land planning."[69]

Nolen returned to Europe in 1935 to preside over the International Federation of Housing and Town Planning conference in London, where the organization was headquartered. By then the garden city had largely run its course, with critics claiming its organic design and picturesque architecture constituted a romantic nostalgia the modern world could ill afford.[70] The organization had split in 1928, when Dutch and German modernists formed the International Housing Association to focus on housing in the central city rather than the suburban periphery. As the depression deepened, urban housing projects appealed to municipal governments desperate to provide work and shelter.[71] Nolen was not doctrinaire when it came to architecture. He thought it folly to adhere to traditional styles; architecture with a "modern distinctive beauty" had an important role, provided that buildings were sited and grouped in conformance with a city or town plan.[72] Nolen's advocacy for the primacy of land analysis and civic design found little play among the Europeans, who were increasingly eager to promote an "International" style of architecture where form followed function and the city was described as "a machine to live in."[73] He stepped down from the organization's presidency in 1935, saddened by his inability to find common ground.[74] In 1937 the International Federation of Housing and Town Planning merged with the International Housing Association, and in a symbolic gesture the new group moved its offices from London to Brussels. The continental aspirations of the modernists now defined city planning.[75]

After his experience with the federation, Nolen focused on assessing the role of landscape architecture in planning. In a 1935 article in *Landscape Architecture,* he asserted that Frederick Law Olmsted Sr. was a pioneer of city planning and "always a *land planner.*" Olmsted had set the basis for the evolution of the profession, as practitioners moved "from the planning of estates to public parks, parkways, and boulevards; from boulevards to suburban development and land subdivision; from land subdivision to neighborhood unit development and new towns; and from new towns to the orderly improvement of whole states and regions."[76] He initiated a new book with Henry Hubbard to determine the value of parkways, part of an effort to keep environmental analysis as a point of focus in a rapidly changing field. New schemes were being touted to transform the city into a hygienic machine, but Nolen was drawn to a novel experiment at the arboretum of the University of Wisconsin, a "monument to conservation," the *Christian Science Monitor* reported.[77]

Over two decades earlier in *Madison: A Model City,* Nolen had recommended that the university create an arboretum to capture "the scientific value" of "open air laboratories," with the goal of making it a central component of the Madison park system.[78] In the early 1920s, Michael B. Olbrich, an attorney and president of the Madison Parks Foundation, initiated a campaign to implement the park system as laid out in the plan. By 1927 four new parks had been created, and Olbrich convinced the University of Wisconsin Board of Regents to establish an arboretum along Lake Wingra. He secured donations to purchase 250 acres, but the project lost momentum after his suicide in 1929.[79]

In the early 1930s, Joseph W. Jackson, president of the Madison and Wisconsin Foundation, made the arboretum his priority. He badgered municipal officials to hire Nolen and convinced the Civilian Conservation Corps to improve the arboretum. Jackson had considerable influence at the University of Wisconsin, where he had lined up donors to fund a "chair of conservation" for his acquaintance Aldo Leopold.[80] Although an accomplished forester and naturalist, Leopold lacked a doctoral degree, and in 1933 land conservation and wildlife management barely qualified as fields of science. Jackson was convinced that Leopold's field experience, pioneering studies in game management, and philosophical insight matched the qualifications of the university's top faculty. The Wisconsin Idea still held sway in Madison, and university president Glenn Frank met Jackson's demand that Leopold be hired and "set up with an outdoor lab" at the new arboretum.[81] In July 1933 university officials named Leopold to the positions of professor of wildlife management and research director for the arboretum.

In his first semester, Leopold was released from teaching duties to join four colleagues on the Arboretum Committee. Their goal was to reconstruct a remnant of the native Wisconsin landscape. The committee's roundtable approach generated a spirit of collaboration.[82] Leopold gained valuable insight form Norman C. Fassett, a botany professor known for his experiments using fire to regenerate prairie grasses. For the Yale-trained forester, prescribed burning was a radical departure from protocol; but after collaborating with Fassett, Leopold led students in setting fires on the arboretum's derelict pastureland to regenerate the native seed stock. Analyzing the varied natural processes that played into land restoration, Leopold delved deeper into the study of ecology and laid the foundation for his academic career.[83]

As plans for the arboretum took shape, Jackson continued hounding city officials to hire Nolen. In the meantime, several hundred men were working on creating the parks Nolen had identified in 1911, with the arboretum the most promising project. The Civilian Conservation Corps was set to improve the site based on plans drawn by the university team.[84] The arboretum's opening ceremony was set for June, and Jackson and Frank arranged for Nolen to

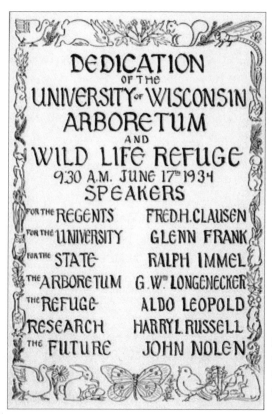

DEDICATION
OF THE
UNIVERSITY OF WISCONSIN
ARBORETUM
AND
WILD LIFE REFUGE
9:30 A.M. JUNE 17TH 1934
SPEAKERS

FOR THE REGENTS   FRED. H. CLAUSEN
FOR THE UNIVERSITY   GLENN FRANK
FOR THE STATE   RALPH IMMEL
THE ARBORETUM   G. WM. LONGENECKER
THE REFUGE   ALDO LEOPOLD
RESEARCH   HARRY L. RUSSELL
THE FUTURE   JOHN NOLEN

Fig. 9.5. Announcement, University
of Wisconsin Arboretum dedication.

Courtesy Division of Rare and Manuscript Collections,
Cornell University Library.

be the featured speaker. (Fig. 9.5) In his talk, "The Future of the Arboretum," the sixty-four-year-old reformer reminded the crowd that land restoration was a fledgling but timely enterprise. Just a month before, a dust storm had blanketed southern Wisconsin, an apocalyptic reminder of the nation's unprecedented environmental problems. For Nolen, the arboretum represented the kind of partnership necessary "to repair the physical, biological, and aesthetic wastes of the three centuries since our stern Puritan forbears landed at Plymouth and began to subdue nature to their needs for liberty." Nolen noted that the arboretum scientists' experimental methods of improving reforestation techniques, protecting water supplies, and abating soil erosion surpassed anything he could have imagined a quarter century before. The arboretum was set to redefine land conservation, but it needed "an interpreter" to ensure that its "great scientific ideas and public services" reached a wide audience.[85]

Leopold was the interpreter, and in his speech he presented a new concept—an arboretum dedicated to reclaiming nature. Traveling back in time to 1840, he told the audience, "you would not only fail to recognize the place; but you might fail to realize you were in Wisconsin." The site once held "orchard-like stands of oaks, interspersed with copses of shrubs, and the profusion of prairie grasses and flowers." Fires set by Native Americans to improve hunting had sculpted the landscape, preventing the overgrowth of oak and providing nutrients for the prairie's grasses, many of which were now extinct. Madison's pioneers suppressed fire and engineered the land along new lines by channeling irregular sloughs into ditches. After decades of intensive farming, the fertility of the former prairie had vanished. The soil had either washed away or played out, leaving a tangled vegetative cover of brush and thistle. The Dust Bowl had exposed the consequences of poor land management, and repairing the damage required ecological understanding. Scientists who had been "busy building machines" must become "busy" with "the earth itself." The university's arboretum would be a "living exhibit," Leopold announced, a model of "an environment fit to support citizens."[86] (Fig. 9.6) Within the year, he transferred the research initiated at the arboretum to an abandoned homestead he purchased on the Wisconsin River.[87] The insights he gained through restoring the damaged land were recorded in what became a revered text, *The Sand County Almanac* (1949).[88]

After the opening of the arboretum, Nolen returned to Cambridge to celebrate his sixty-fifth birthday. He had no thoughts of retiring. Like Leopold, he was intent on securing humanity's tie to nature in a society that venerated the machine. This notion was at the center of one of his last public speeches, the commencement address at the 1936 Girard College graduation.

Fig. 9.6. Darrel Morrison, Native Plant Garden, University of Wisconsin Arboretum. Photograph by Darrel Morrison.

In his speech, Nolen celebrated Stephen Girard's philosophy of educational reform, noting that his emphasis on citizenship, service, and a well-ordered physical environment led to individual and societal advancement. "Life becomes an art when work and play, labor and leisure, mind and body, education and recreation are guided by a single vision," he told the graduates. Influenced by such Enlightenment thinkers as Jean-Jacques Rousseau and Johann Heinrich Pestalozzi, Girard championed the holistic training of children. But it was the influence of Romanticism, the love of nature and children, that put him on par with "the Concord philosophers." When Nolen arrived at Girard's school, the insights of Emerson, Thoreau, and Alcott informed his education. In his will, Girard stipulated that the curriculum should be periodically updated, and it was time, Nolen announced, to initiate "training in the conservation of land and other natural resources." A commitment to outdoor field studies would elevate scholastic aptitude, character development, and the memory of the school's founder.[89]

The address was delivered with "a lyrical quality of rather exquisite beauty which suited perfectly the parts of his speech which dealt with the beauties of nature and effects of nature upon the child," noted Cheesman Herrick, Girard's president.[90] Many years before, Nolen had embraced the poetics of nature in Girard's woods and gardens, and it colored his ambition. He had labored so that children could live closer to nature, a mission Herrick honored by giving Nolen the Distinguished Alumnus Award. "I shall treasure the award always," the surprised recipient told Herrick. At the alumni meeting that followed, Nolen reunited with classmates he had not seen in fifty years and shared a photograph of his own graduation.[91] Nolen left Philadelphia with a renewed sense of purpose. He had spoken his mind on education reform, and he was ready to do the same in Cambridge.

Sorting through his mail in the spring of 1936, Nolen found a letter marked "confidential" from Henry Hubbard. The School of City and Regional Planning was in crisis.[92] Hubbard had given the Rockefeller Foundation a proposal to renew its funding, which was set to run out. He had written the original grant, and this updated version was "excellent" and "of great public service," according to foundation officials. The administration, however, refused to support it.[93]

Hubbard's troubles began the previous summer when Harvard president James Conant hired Joseph Hudnut, a reputable modernist architect, to be the dean of the School of Architecture. Hudnut's ambition went beyond architecture and, with Conant's blessing, he set out to reorient the design professions—architecture, landscape architecture, and city planning. In his first year he laid the groundwork for a new Graduate School of Design dedicated to modernism. He also proposed to downgrade the School of City and Regional Planning to a department and place it within the new School of Public Administration. Planning was not an art but a social science, Hudnut claimed.[94] The new dean's scheme had a glaring inconsistency, Hubbard noted. Pragmatism, design skills, and collaboration—keys to the new Graduate School of Design—were also the attributes that made Harvard's city planners more employable than its architects. Hudnut rescinded his order, and a policy of benign neglect ensued.[95] Hudnut did not secure a single donor for City and Regional Planning, and in the meeting with the Rockefeller Foundation, he refused to pledge funds for the school's continuance. To complicate matters, the administration categorically refused to allow Hubbard to raise funds. "I hope that friends of the movement will not drop their nerve even though it looks like a hard fight," he wrote to Nolen.[96]

At the same time Hudnut was planning his coup, Hubbard and Nolen were struggling to reconcile social science and landscape architecture in their new book, *Parkways and Land Values* (1937), to be published as part of the Harvard City Planning Studies series. Largely an economic exegesis, the study analyzed parkways in Boston, Kansas City, and New York to assess the benefits of incorporating natural aesthetics into road building. Besides moving traffic, parkways provided elegant settings for the wealthy (and their tax dollars), offered a range of recreational opportunities, and, with proper planning, could spur quality development. In Kansas City, Ward Parkway had been integral to J. C. Nichols's prototype project, the Country Club Plaza. Documenting a parkway's return on investment, the authors verified a long-held assumption: "Parkways were the framework for a new town-and-country community by providing a practical means for a better distribution of population."[97] It was hardly a novel concept; having parkways order the suburban hinterland dated back at least to the Olmsted Brothers' early-twentieth-century park plans. Now, however, they had a worth that had been estimated but never valued. The book received little notice, especially from the engineers designing the new high-speed freeways. That they ignored the landscape architects' formula for calculating aesthetic and recreational values was hardly surprising, especially given the turn of events at Harvard.[98]

After the meeting with the Rockefeller Foundation, Hudnut proposed closing the School of City and Regional Planning for a year; in the interim, new hires would be made to aid in reshaping it according to modernist principles. The only hope Hubbard saw was to find a donor before the administration made its final decision in mid-July. He recruited Nolen to secure a donor and "stir up anything that you think desirable." It was to be a clandestine operation, "without any communication of record," Hubbard wrote. He also advised Nolen to burn his letter after reading it.[99]

At sixty-six years old Nolen was of retiring age, yet he was actively involved in a plot to undermine the Harvard administration. He first met with Henry Sturgis Dennison, a liberal Boston businessman and recent appointee to the National Resources Board, who was engaging but noncommittal.[100] Next he contacted Edward Filene, the department store magnate and long-time supporter of city planning. The two men's relationship went back thirty years, and the situation was awkward for Nolen. He had gone to Filene for numerous favors over the years, from funding the American City Planning Institute to hiring his youngest son Humphrey for a part-time job, but this time a major gift was involved, an endowment that would yield at least $15,000 a year. In a letter marked "confidential," Nolen informed Filene it was not "money, but advice as to what, if anything, you think could be done."[101] Filene identified the John Price Jones Corporation and Tamblyn and Brown, money-raising agencies in New York, as the solution to the problem.[102] Nolen and Hubbard had hoped for more.

At the July deadline, no donor had been found and the School of City and Regional Planning was closed; it would be moved to the Graduate School of Design and reopened in a year. Hubbard found little solace in the decision other than the twenty letters, mostly from planning practitioners, questioning Conant's judgment.[103] Nolen thought the American City Planning Institute should send Conant a carefully prepared statement to force Hudnut to state his intentions.[104] In December Hudnut made his plans clear when he hired Walter Gropius to teach architecture in the Graduate School of Design.

The internationally renowned architect promised that collaboration and the study of natural laws deduced by analyzing the way machines operate would unlock a creative new vision. Then, the Graduate School of Design would unveil to the nation its plans for an open, sunlit city of measured efficiency. Working in concert with Hudnut over the next decade, Gropius waged a war for modernism with military ambition, if not strategic precision. He also ensured that city planning became, as a disheartened Henry Hubbard wrote, "the adopted child of another profession."[105] According to the architectural historian Vincent Scully, Gropius eviscerated the "the fine American planning profession . . . at its heart."[106]

After the School of City Planning closed in July 1936, Nolen journeyed to Mexico with Barbara to raise his lagging spirits. Their cruise to Havana and

Vera Cruz was followed by a five-day stay in Mexico City. Dancing, dining, and general merriment were the order of the day, interspersed by a visit to the Floating Gardens of Xochimilco and a meeting with Carlos Contreras, a local city planner.[107] On the return home, Nolen was afflicted by an intestinal ailment, but he had little time for rest. Without Harvard, he needed to find a new source of income. His health continued to wane, and he started reading a new book, *Strength through Suffering*, to help him make his way in what now constituted "the strenuous work of city planning."[108]

In October Nolen headed to a National Resources Board conference in Mississippi, where he delivered a cursory paper on the tie between regional and state planning in the Southeast.[109] George Merrick, the Coral Gables developer, saved what was an otherwise dull event. Merrick had overcome the financial collapse of Coral Gables to resurface as the chairman of the Dade County Planning Commission. Florida, Nolen knew, far surpassed other southern states when it came to planning, and in a private meeting Merrick shared some interesting news. Federal dollars were available, and metropolitan Miami needed a blueprint for the future. Merrick outlined a grand scheme to create a system of interrelated parks and tourist districts between Miami and Key West. A nationally recognized expert was needed, and Nolen fit the bill. The two men agreed to resume talks when Nolen visited Miami in November.[110]

Nolen returned to Florida on his most promising trip in years. He had a new commission in Clewiston and meetings were set in Miami with Merrick and C. H. Schaeffer, Florida's director of state parks. Yet despite ideal weather and pleasant accommodations, Nolen's energy was flagging. Struggling with acute pain, he could eat breakfast but had difficulty digesting other meals. At dinner he watched longingly as others drank the wine he had to forgo, though he did indulge in coffee to get through morning meetings. Going into the field proved to be a tonic. In Clewiston, he wrote to his wife: "Don't worry my love! I'm really feeling better and will promise to keep thee posted faithfully."[111] While there, he found the dike around the southern half of Lake Okeechobee nearing completion, and the United States Sugar Corporation was seeking to invest in its newly secured holdings. In Nolen's opinion, the mammoth thirty-eight-foot structure had severed the connection between the civic center and the lakefront, casting a pall on his original plan for the small town. He took notes for a report he later completed in Cambridge, but his real interest lay in Miami, where efforts were under way to make south Florida a national destination.[112]

The inspiration for showcasing the Miami region grew out of an initiative to establish Everglades National Park. Nolen had been involved in the project since 1929, when promoters envisioned a 25,000-square-mile preserve running between Lake Okeechobee and Cape Sable.[113] The depression forced a reappraisal, as a vast swamp, even one as unique as the Everglades, was not a typical national park. The New Deal revived expectations, and John C. Gifford, a professor of tropical forestry at the University of Miami, joined the seemingly ageless J. Horace McFarland in leading a coalition to establish an "All Florida Corridor." A parkway would connect a national park in the Everglades with a second national park to include Silver Springs, the Ocklawaha River, and a section of the Ocala National Forest in north-central Florida. A series of demonstration forests and state parks would punctuate the parkway, Gifford wrote to Nolen, to inspire "those who come after us" and who must build on "what we leave."[114]

Creating an interconnected system of national and state parks thrilled Nolen, especially after Schaffer contacted him to discuss a position.[115] Nolen had two items in his favor, the standing of the Wisconsin park system and the work he did helping design Highlands Hammock State Park (located near Sebring, Florida) for the Department of the Interior in 1933. The Civilian Conservation Corps implemented the plan, and the opening of the new park raised hopes that the federal government would fund the Everglades project.[116] In addition, Clara I. Thomas, a St. Petersburg landscape architect, and Prentiss French, both of whom worked on Highlands Hammock, had urged Schaffer to hire Nolen.[117] After his meeting with Schaffer, Nolen rushed off to meet Merrick, the local developer, but missed him and had to reschedule the meeting. Nolen would return to Miami after Christmas to discuss a full-time consultancy with the Dade County Planning Commission.[118]

In late 1936, the Florida projects were coming together for Nolen, much as the Wisconsin commissions had three decades before. At that time, of course, he was in the prime of life; now his health was more precarious. "Our news is all good," he wrote to Cheesman Herrick, "except that I am struggling to regain health in my digestive organs. It has reached the state where I am headed for the hospital this week, and an operation."[119] The noted surgeon Daniel Fiske Jones performed exploratory surgery, during which he found highly advanced stomach cancer that appeared terminal. Nolen managed a visit to his Harvard Square office, but after a return to the hospital shortly before Christmas he was confined to home.[120] "I am not easily reconciled to these deprivations, but the doctor says I must be good, so here I am, powerless," he wrote to the economist David Coyle in January 1937.[121] His family made him as comfortable as possible in an upstairs room, where he rested on an Asian recliner before an open fire. He dictated a few letters to his secretary Charlotte Parsons but saved his strength for visits from his children and four grandchildren.[122]

By early February, the concoction of Guinness and sherry Nolen sipped to soothe the constant pain was failing him and the prospects looked bleak. "I am doing all I can to keep a cheerful outlook, but there are elements of discouragement in the present situation," he wrote to a friend.[123] Yet, there was still a project to complete. Frederick "Fritz" Gutheim, a visionary Washington, D.C., planner whom John Nolen Jr. had befriended, had encouraged Nolen to prepare his papers for a book. It would not be a biography but a record of the Cambridge office that documented the evolution of the planning profession. Nolen wanted to emphasize the "facts" of his work, not the story of his life.[124] But his life was ebbing, and within a week he lay on his deathbed.

On February 11, 1937, John Nolen received his final letter, written in Raymond Unwin's hurried hand on Gramercy Park Hotel stationery. Nolen's daughter was living in New York, and she had phoned Unwin, who was teaching at Columbia, to inform him of her father's condition. "I am much distressed to find your illness is so serious," he immediately wrote to Nolen. "Had I known I should have made every effort to see you before you reached this stage." Unwin knew his friend had despaired over the situation at Harvard and the demise of his practice, and so he offered "this consolation— beyond what is true of most—that you have lived your life to some purpose." The letter continued: "The value of your work in the pioneer period of planning over here is recognized and is most highly appreciated in England and in many other lands where your leadership in the field is known, and where your genial and helpful personality have endeared you to a very wide circle. . . . I cannot tell you how much I have valued your help, your experience, and above all your personal friendship." Thoughts were also offered to the family, followed by a heartfelt entreaty. "I wish there were something more than this poor letter I could do to help you, and in some little way to repay the many kindnesses I have had from you!"[125]

One week later, Nolen died. His passing was noted in the *New York Times,* *Boston Globe,* and *Boston Herald* and in cities such as Madison, San Diego, and St. Petersburg, where his plans still informed the public agenda. William Straub could only hope a consultant of "John Nolen's caliber" would return to St. Petersburg.[126] In Madison, municipal officials were expecting Nolen to return; after years of wrangling, Joseph Jackson had finally convinced them to rehire Wisconsin's first city planner, but the letter from Madison lay unread at Nolen's death.[127]

According to his obituary in the *American Magazine of Art,* Nolen's death marked "the end of a period in the history of American City Planning." He

Fig. 9.7. John Nolen's gravestone, 2011. Courtesy Mount Auburn Cemetery.

had pursued his art with a missionary zeal, establishing a practice that produced exemplary plans for parks, towns, and cites across the nation. After devoting years of study to the profession, he established standards and procedures still followed by contemporary practitioners. He was also a renowned mentor. The most accomplished author among his peers, Nolen left behind "the only fully developed theory of city planning and its significance and principles."[128] As a young man he had imagined himself as a university dean, and at his death he was fondly known as the dean of American city planning.

Nolen was buried in a picturesque glen in Mount Auburn Cemetery, an exemplary nineteenth-century landscape. Flanked by dogwoods and laurel, his resting place is marked by a boulder, and nearby a small marble slab reads: "John Nolen: Landscape Architect and Pioneer in the Art of City Planning in America." (Fig. 9.7) It is fitting that the country's first rural cemetery also claims Charles Eliot. Where Eliot envisioned an "Emerald Metropolis" filled with green cathedrals, Nolen sought nothing less than a return to the garden. His vision of the garden city may yet be our salvation.

EPILOGUE

Providing St. Petersburg with good city planning was John Nolen's intent in 1923 when he drafted Florida's first comprehensive city plan, a vision of an American Riviera with interconnected systems of parks and preserves giving public access to beaches and bays. To prevent "an unhappy situation on the shoreline through the excessive and illogical building out into the water," Nolen instructed municipal officials to establish a bulkhead line limiting fills to areas contiguous with the coastline.[1] The recommendation went unheeded. In 1940 Harland Bartholomew, hired to update St. Petersburg's city plan, dismissed Nolen's work as the "optimistic opinion of the ideal city." His new plan was drawn on the premise that cities were like machines and should be engineered to run efficiently. The natural conditions that Nolen deemed essential were ignored.[2]

By 1970 twenty-five percent of Boca Ciega Bay had been either dredged or filled. It took a federal legal precedent, *Zabel v. Tabb,* to end the "monstrous desecration," as Florida governor Leroy Collins called it, of the coastal lagoon.[3] Forty years after Nolen recommended the policy, bulkhead lines were established to rein in dredging. In 1973 the St. Petersburg City Planning Department prepared one of the nation's first growth-management plans using Ian McHarg's ecological design method. No one knew that the new plan paralleled Nolen's 1923 work because the only copy of Florida's first regional plan was boxed in the Cornell University archives.[4]Although new plans were implemented, the problems in St. Petersburg were too severe to reverse.

Today St. Petersburg's bays are fouled, its pedestrian death rate is the nation's second highest, and a hurricane will wreck havoc on the heavily populated barrier islands.[5] Yet St. Petersburg is not without hope. In the early 2000s, Nolen's plan informed a wide-ranging civic initiative to create a more pedestrian-oriented and ecologically balanced city. Difficulties remain, but St. Petersburg is experiencing a rebirth. Billing itself as Florida's "first green city," it is struggling to take form along the lines that Nolen envisioned.

In the mid-1980s Miami architects Andrés Duany and Elizabeth Plater-Zyberk also rediscovered Nolen's work. The inspiration for their plan of Seaside, Florida, the prototype new urbanist community, came from Nolen's new towns, especially Venice.[6] As James Howard Kunstler observed in 1993, "Seaside is a modified neoclassical grid straight out of John Nolen."[7] By then Seaside was the most studied new town project in the nation. Before Duany and his firm uncovered the value of Nolen's work, the urban planner was "frequently viewed as the P. T. Barnum of early twentieth century planning, a man who used his considerable public relations and networking skills to popularize the idea of city planning."[8] By contrast, Duany saw Nolen as a skilled designer who was the equal of his more acclaimed contemporaries, the Olmsted Brothers, Clarence Stein, and Henry Wright. Nolen's ability to create walkable towns with a sophisticated mix of parks, housing types, streets, and shops appealed to Duany, who also realized that environmental protection and human-scaled town planning were inseparable. By 1989 he was calling on planners to combat the spread of "placeless" suburbs by practicing the art mastered by Nolen.[9]

In 1990 the University of Miami School of Architecture, where Plater-Zyberk was a professor, hosted a symposium on Nolen, and the university art museum displayed his plans. The event documented the relevance of John Nolen's work to current practice, as well as to the cities he had planned. The DPZ firm established an office in Myers Park headed by Tom Low, one of the nation's leading experts on Nolen.[10] The firm also allied itself with West Coast architects Peter Calthorpe, Dan Solomon, Liz Moule, and Stefanos Polyzoides to form a coalition dedicated to building walkable neighborhoods based on historical precedent. In 1993 the six architects founded the Congress of the New Urbanism, which published a charter demanding "the restoration of existing urban centers and towns within coherent metropolitan regions, the reconfiguration of sprawling suburbs into communities of real neighborhoods and diverse districts, the conservation of natural environments, and the preservation of our built legacy."[11] In 1919 Nolen had made a similar pronouncement, calling on the federal government to build systems of interconnected villages, towns, and cities that would unite regions, preserve natural systems, and support industrial democracy.[12]

The new urbanism inspired intense debate, especially among academicians. Critics claimed the "neotraditional" towns and neighborhoods, like Nolen's Union Park Gardens in Wilmington, Delaware, marked a fine line between meeting market demand and pandering to sentimental visions of a mythic community.[13] But this debate over style did not deter the movement's central message—the need to build sustainable, pedestrian-oriented communities. New urbanism quickly moved from novelty to policy, inspiring reforms in public housing, coastal zone planning, environmental protection, transportation policies, and municipal coding.[14] Duany realized that there were few precedents for implementing the new plans, in part because Nolen "could count on the competence of architects to behave in an urbanistically responsible way."[15] Moreover, as Nolen had pointed out, zoning codes remained "a *negative measure*" that "simply tells what private property owners cannot do with their own property."[16] The DPZ firm developed a new tool to guide plan implementation: the "form-based code." Rather than regulating floor area ratios and separating uses, the form-based code addressed the mass, scale, and design of the built environment. With a more detailed physical configuration of a property and its buildings, developers could visualize how a project might accrue value over time.[17]

Civic-minded developers in the mold of George Stephens and Charles Livingood also brought Nolen's legacy to fruition.[18] In 1995 developer D. R. Bryan studied Myers Park and historical neighborhoods in Winston-Salem before drafting a plan for Southern Village, a Chapel Hill suburb. Over half of the 1,175 housing units, including townhouses on John Nolen Lane, were clustered at ten units per acre and set within an interconnected park system. A school and mixed-use town center were the focal points of the plan. Getting the project built required convincing officials to reconfigure Chapel Hill's existing codes, which facilitated automobile traffic rather than pedestrian movement. Southern Village's profitable mix of residences, parks, and retail drew national attention, with features in *Time,* the *Wall Street Journal, Builder,* and *U.S. News & World Report.*[19] Studies found that residents drove less and walked more. Southern Village also performed significantly better than conventional subdivisions in safeguarding water quality and mitigating the impact of storm water runoff.[20]

After the collapse of the real estate market and the onset of the Great Recession in 2008, Venice became an important test case. The city had weathered Florida's economic maelstrom reasonably well, especially when compared to other sprawling developments in the region. For example, in 2010 Venice had sixty percent fewer foreclosures than nearby Leigh Acres, and its average sale price of $110 per square foot was three times higher. But economics was only one measure of stability. Spencer Briggs, a filmmaker who directed a PBS documentary on Nolen's enduring influence in Venice, found that the town's compact form made it not only charming but also "democratic because it's walkable."[21] A memorial had been built to honor Nolen in 1976, and citizens of Venice still discuss his "intentions with the passion of constitutional scholars seeking the thinking of the Founding Fathers."[22]

In Madison, Nolen's ideal of a model city became a local legacy. In 1995 a symposium called "Nolen in the '90s" drew three hundred participants who debated how to engage in his visionary planning. Three more such events were held in the next decade. Inspired by *Madison: A Model City,* experts and citizens collaborated to produce an agenda that moved Madison to the vanguard of the urban sustainability movement. In 2011 a local journalist proposed repurposing Nolen's plan "for the next century," writing that it is still capable of setting "a new standard of city-making."[23]

Nolen's accomplishments are also acknowledged by the planning, architecture, and environmental professions as well as by civic organizations throughout the country. In 1998 the American Planning Association honored Nolen as a national planning pioneer, and a decade later it designated Mariemont one of the "Great Places in America."[24] The Florida chapter of the Congress of the New Urbanism awards the John Nolen Medal, while the San Diego chapter of the American Institute of Architects and the University of Wisconsin Arboretum confer the John Nolen Award. The arboretum, the nation's longest ongoing ecological restoration project, represents Nolen and Leopold's effort to counter the destructive use of land, a central tenant of the sustainability movement.[25] Nolen's designs also became a source of guidance and inspiration for civic groups in Charlotte, Savannah, Madison, and Venice. The current city plans for Roanoke, Clearwater, and Sarasota are prefaced by Nolen's plans.

With the rise of the new urbanism and smart growth movements, Nolen's concept of planning has taken hold and is continuing to evolve.[26] Infill projects, form-based codes, livability indicators, transit-oriented development, and ecological restoration are now integral to the planning profession. Nolen would undoubtedly recognize the scale and intent of these initiatives and identify with the challenges facing new urbanist planners. Confronting the modernist agenda in 1930, Nolen feared "the merging of neighborhoods into a soulless urban mass." His solution was to strike a balance between nature and the city, as well as equilibrium between public and private rights. "If this could be realized," he wrote, "it would seem to be Utopia enough in this modern commercial world of ours." With Nolen's body of work as a historical precedent, today's practitioners have an invaluable aid in their struggle to achieve "Utopia enough."[27]

NOTES

INTRODUCTION

1. Lewis Mumford, "The Next Twenty Years in City Planning," *Proceedings of the Nineteenth Conference on City Planning* (Washington, DC: American Institute of City Planning, 1927), 57.
2. Nolen became president of this organization at its June 1931 conference.
3. John Nolen, *New Towns for Old: Achievements in Civic Improvement in Some American Small Towns and Neighborhoods* (1927; reprint, Amherst: University of Massachusetts Press in association with Library of American Landscape History, 2005), 9.
4. Ibid., 33.
5. Ibid., 7.
6. Nolen quoted in Robert A. M. Stern, David Fishman, Jacob Tilove, *Paradise Planned: The Garden Suburb and the Modern City* (New York: Monacelli Press, 2014), 167.
7. Nolen, *New Towns for Old*, 7.
8. Ibid., 156.
9. Justin Hartzog, "John Nolen," *Planners Journal* 9 (March/April 1937): 3, 55.

1. THE RISE OF AN URBAN REFORMER, 1869–1902

1. Dorothy G. Beers, "The Centennial City, 1865–1876," in *Philadelphia: A 300-Hundred Year History,* ed. Russell F. Weigley (New York: Norton, 1982), 436–48.
2. John Nolen Jr. and Barbara Nolen Strong, "The Nolen Family Album: A Record of Five Generations," 3–6, John Nolen Papers, Division of Rare and Manuscript Collections, Cornell University, Ithaca, NY (hereafter NP) (hereafter Nolen and Strong, "Family Album); Charles D. Warren, introduction to John Nolen, *New Towns for Old: Achievements in Civic Improvement in Some American Small Towns and Neighborhoods* (1927; reprint, Amherst: University of Massachusetts Press in association with Library of American Landscape History, 2005), xiv–x.
3. Nolen and Strong, "Family Album," 5.
4. Edgar P. Richardson, "The Athens of America, 1800–1825," in Weigley, *Philadelphia,* 215–25; Alan M. Zachary, "Social Disorder and the Philadelphia Elite before Jackson," *Pennsylvania Magazine of History and Biography* 99 (July 1975): 288–92.

5. Henry A. Ingram, *The Life and Character of Stephen Girard* . . . (Philadelphia: J. B. Lippincott, 1887), 162; *Girard College Course of Study for Eight Years* (Philadelphia: J. B. Lippincott, 1894), box 38, NP.

6. See Nolen's Girard College alumni address, "Stephen Girard: An Educational Pioneer," *Steel and Garnet* 40 (June 1936): 70.

7. *Girard College Course of Study*, 2–9; Nolen, "Stephen Girard," 70.

8. John L. Hancock, "John Nolen and the American City Planning Movement" (PhD diss., University of Pennsylvania, 1964), 8; John L. Hancock, "John Nolen: The Background of a Pioneer Planner," in *The American Planner: Biographies and Recollections*, ed. Donald Krueckeberg (New York: Methuen, 1983), 40–41.

9. Nolen and Strong, "Family Album," 5; Nolen, "Stephen Girard," 71; Nolen to Barbara Nolen, August 6, 1931, box 14, Nolen Schatte Papers, Radcliffe Institute for Advanced Study, Harvard University, Cambridge, MA (hereafter NSP).

10. Harold Cary, "John Nolen—City Planner: The Father of a Great Profession," *Success* 50 (March 1923): 18.

11. Nolen and Strong, "Family Album," 5–6.

12. "History of the Wharton School of Business," University Archives and Records Center, University of Pennsylvania, www.archives.upenn.edu; Nancy Cohen, *The Reconstruction of American Liberalism, 1865–1914* (Chapel Hill: University of North Carolina Press, 2002), 1–22.

13. Susan Jacoby, *The Age of American Unreason* (New York: Pantheon, 2007), 67–71; Daniel T. Rodgers, *Atlantic Crossings: Social Politics in a Progressive Age* (Cambridge: Belknap Press of Harvard University Press, 1998), 90–102; David F. Lindenfeld, "The Myth of the Older Historical School of Economics," *Central European History* 26 (December 1993): 405–16.

14. Stanley Buder, *Visionaries and Planners: The Garden City Movement and the Modern Community* (New York: Oxford University Press, 1990), 72–73; Paul Boyer, *Urban Masses and Moral Order in America, 1820–1920* (Cambridge: Harvard University Press, 1978), 228–30.

15. Rodgers, *Atlantic Crossings*, 1–24; Samuel Hays, *Conservation and the Gospel of Efficiency* (Cambridge: Harvard University Press, 1959).

16. Peter McCaffery, *When Bosses Ruled Philadelphia: The Emergence of the Republican Machine, 1867–1933* (University Park: Pennsylvania State University Press, 1993), 40–55; Carolyn T. Adams, *The Politics of Capital Investment: The Case of Philadelphia* (Albany, NY: SUNY Press, 1988), 143–46.

17. Simon N. Patten, *The Consumption of Wealth* (Philadelphia: Publications of the University of Pennsylvania, 1889); Daniel M. Fox, *The Discovery of Abundance: Simon N. Patten and the Transformation of Social Theory* (Ithaca, NY: Cornell University Press, 1967), 95–114.

18. "Cities," Patten declared, "do not get free parks, pleasant streets, fine public buildings, and other means of enjoyment, until their people take a pride in them, and love to make them beautiful." *Consumption of Wealth*, 40. Patten would fully articulate his thought in *The New Basis of Civilization* (1907), perhaps best known for its call for a federal income tax.

19. Simon N. Patten, *The Economic Basis of Protection* (Philadelphia: J. B. Lippincott, 1890), 60.

20. Hancock, "Pioneer Planner," 42.

21. For the New Historians, the "usable past" was an essential tool to direct the growth and ends of industrialized nations. See Kevin Mattson, "The Challenges of Democracy: James Harvey Robinson, the New History, and Adult Education for Citizenship," *Journal of the Gilded Age and Progressive Era* 2 (January 2003): 48–79; Richard Hofstadter,

Progressive Historians: Turner, Beard, Parrington (New York: Random House, 1968); and Ernst Breisach, American Progressive History: An Experiment in Modernization (Chicago: University of Chicago Press, 1993).

22. Hancock, "Pioneer Planner," 42.

23. James directed Nolen's honors thesis. Building on his mentor's work, Nolen developed a rational calculation to improve management of the gas works, laying out a procedure to minimize waste by incorporating into the city budget appropriations for the cost of manufacturing gas and the plant's future improvements. With this calculation, gas prices could be set to represent the resource's full cost and impose a fiscal restraint against politicians' underwriting the expansion of political patronage with gas works funds, standard practice when McManes headed Philadelphia's notorious "Gas Ring." Nolen's thesis was a quintessential Wharton School project, but it was more than just a research document: his indictment of the McManes machine afforded a measure of retribution for the death of his father. John Nolen, "The Philadelphia City Gas Works," in The City Government of Philadelphia, ed. Edmund James (Philadelphia: University of Pennsylvania Wharton School, 1893). See also Edmund James, "The Relation of the Modern Municipality to the Gas Supply," Publications of the American Economic Association 1 (May/July 1886), and Adams, Politics of Capital Investment, 143–46.

24. Oliver Larkin, Art and Life in America (New York: Holt, Rinehart & Wilson, 1960), 293–300.

25. Philip Schaff, The Renaissance: The Revival of Learning and Art in the Fourteenth and Fifteenth Centuries (New York: Putnam, 1891), 11.

26. Nolen and Strong, "Family Album," 6.

27. Nolen to Schatte, January 3, 1892, box 1, NSP.

28. Nolen to Schatte, August 23, 1894, box 1 NSP; University of Pennsylvania Record of the Class of '93 (Philadelphia: Avil Printing Co., 1893), box 44, NP.

29. Frank Edmonds to Nolen, October 19 and 24, 1894, box 18, NSP.

30. Hancock, "Pioneer Planner," 41.

31. Philadelphia Times, May 11, 1893, box 20, NSP.

32. Carol Halsted, "Onteora: An Ideal Summer Club," Godey's Magazine 135 (July–December 1897): 178–83; Nolen to Schatte, June 10, 1892, box 1, NSP.

33. Hugh F. McKean, The Lost Treasures of Louis Comfort Tiffany (Atglen, PA: Schiffer, 1980), 4, 103; Amelia Peck, Candace Wheeler: The Art and Enterprise of American Design, 1875–1900 (New York: Metropolitan Museum of Art, 2001); Candace Wheeler, The Annals of Onteora (New York: E. W. Whitfield, 1914), 1–8, 49–51, 55.

34. Mary Warner Blanchard, Oscar Wilde's America: Counterculture in the Gilded Age (New Haven: Yale University Press, 1998), 51.

35. Nolen and Strong, "Family Album," 10.

36. Hancock, "Pioneer Planner," 41.

37. Candace Wheeler, Content in a Garden (Boston: Houghton Mifflin, 1901), 1, 45.

38. John Nolen, introduction to Humphry Repton, The Art of Landscape Gardening, ed. John Nolen (Boston: Houghton Mifflin, 1907), xvii.

39. Nolen to Schatte, June 3, 1894, box 1, NSP; Nolen to Schatte, June 30, 1894, box 1, NSP.

40. Nolen to Schatte, August 9, 1894, box 1, NSP.

41. Nolen and Strong, "Family Album," 9–10; Nolen to Schatte, August 27, 1893, box 1, NSP.

42. Nolen to Schatte, October 22, 1894, box 2, NSP; Jon A. Peterson, The Birth of City Planning in the United States, 1840–1917 (Baltimore: Johns Hopkins University Press, 2003), 67; John Nolen, "The Art of Planning Cities: Landscape Architecture and the City Spirit," American Magazine of Art 27 (January 1934): 31.

43. William Wilson, *The City Beautiful Movement* (Baltimore: Johns Hopkins University Press, 1990), 52–63.

44. Christopher Tunnard, *The City of Man* (New York: Charles Scribner, 1970), 309.

45. Wilson, *City Beautiful Movement,* 63–65; Richard Guy Wilson, "Architecture and the Reinterpretation of the Past in the American Renaissance," *Winterthur Portfolio* (Spring 1983): 69–87; Nolen to Schatte, October 22, 1893, box 1, NSP.

46. Nolen and Strong, "Family Album," 7.

47. In the late 1850s Margaretta Forten (1806–1875) founded a grammar school for black children that was named after her father, James Forten (1766–1842). By the 1890s the James Forten School served the children of blacks and recent Jewish immigrants. See John F. Sutherland, "The Origins of Philadelphia's Octavia Hill Association," *Pennsylvania Magazine of History and Biography* 99 (January 1975): 26.

48. Nolen and Strong, "Family Album," 8; personal correspondence documenting the courtship of John Nolen and Barbara Schatte is found in box 2, NSP.

49. R. D. Roberts, *Eighteen Years of University Extension* (Cambridge, UK: Cambridge University Press, 1891), 63, 66, and 108, box 45, NP.

50. Hancock, "Pioneer Planner," 43–45.

51. American Society for the Extension of University Teaching, *Statement by Board of Directors* (Philadelphia, 1891), 1, box 45, NP.

52. Nolen to Schatte, July 17, 1894, box 20, NSP.

53. American Society for the Extension of University Teaching, *Statement by Board of Directors* (Philadelphia, 1894), box 45, NP. On Ruskin's role in the field of urban planning, see Michael Lang, *Designing Utopia: Ruskin's Urban Vision for Britain and America* (London: Black Rose Books, 1999).

54. John Nolen, *Annual Report of the Secretary,* American Society for the Extension of University Teaching (Philadelphia, 1900), 2, box 45, NP.

55. Nolen and Strong, "Family Album," 10.

56. Nolen to Schatte, October 2 and 8, 1894, box 2, NSP.

57. Nolen to Schatte, October 19, 1894, box 2, NSP.

58. Nolen and Strong, "Family Album," 11.

59. Hancock, "Pioneer Planner," 44–45; Nolen and Strong, "Family Album," 15.

60. *Philadelphia Evening Telegraph,* May 5, 1895, box 20, NSP.

61. Richard Dennis, *Cities in Modernity: Representations and Productions of Metropolitan Space, 1840–1930* (New York: Cambridge University Press, 2008), 51; Tristram Hunt, *Building Jerusalem: The Rise and Fall of the Victorian City* (London: Weidenfeld & Nicolson, 2004), 308–12.

62. James L. Machor, *Pastoral Cities: Urban Ideals and the Symbolic Landscape of America* (Madison: University of Wisconsin Press, 1986), 13–14; Sam Bass Warner and Andrew H. Whittemore, *American Urban Form: A Representative History* (Cambridge: MIT Press, 2012), 65–80.

63. Nolen and Strong, "Family Album," 11.

64. "Wedding," April 23–27, 1896, box 20, NSP.

65. Nolen and Strong, "Family Album," 12.

66. John Nolen, "A Suburban Home for Six Thousand Dollars," *Country Life in America* 8 (August 1905): 425–26.

67. Ibid.

68. Nolen and Strong, "Family Album," 12.

69. Ibid., 15.

70. Edward Griggs to Nolen, August 28, 1901, box 18, NSP.

71. "Meditations by Prof. Griggs," review of *A Book of Meditations* by Edward Howard Griggs, *New York Times,* April 4, 1903.

72. "ASEUT Syllabi," box 45, NP.
73. John Nolen, *Edward Howard Griggs: His Personality and His Work* (New York: Huebsch, n.d.), 1–2.
74. Nolen to Alan Harris, January 25, 1904, box 69, NP.
75. Edward H. Griggs, *The New Humanism: Studies in Personal and Social Development* (New York: Huebsch, 1899), 119–42.
76. Nolen, *Edward Howard Griggs*, 3; Nolen and Strong, "Family Album," 15.
77. Nolen to Barbara Nolen, June 5, 1901, box 5, NSP; Frank Edmonds to Nolen, June 19, 1901, box 18, NSP.
78. Barbara's adoptive family had migrated from the town of Gera in 1853.
79. Nolen and Strong, "Family Album," 16.
80. John Nolen, *Remodeling Roanoke* (Roanoke: Stone Printing Co., 1907), 26.
81. Nolen's analysis of Lucerne is presented in his plan for Madison, WI; John Nolen, *Madison: A Model City* (Boston, 1911), 146–48. In 1906 he returned to study Lucerne, where he got "chuck full of professional ideas"; Nolen to Barbara Nolen, August 31, 1906, box 7, NSP.
82. Warren, introduction to *New Towns for Old*, xxvi–xxvii; Rodgers, *Atlantic Crossings*, 186–207.
83. David H. Pinkney, *Napoleon III and the Rebuilding of Paris* (Princeton, NJ: Princeton University Press, 1958); Robert Fishman, *Urban Utopias in the Twentieth Century: Ebenezer Howard, Frank Lloyd Wright, Le Corbusier* (Cambridge: MIT Press, 1982), 103–33; James Kunstler, *Cities in Mind: Notes on the Urban Condition* (New York: Free Press, 2001), 1–40. Nolen to Harris, November 12, 1904, box 69, NP.
84. Ruth Hanisch, "City Planning According to Artistic Principles, Vienna 1889," in *Manifestoes and Transformations in the Early Modern City*, ed. Christian H. Cordua (Burlington, VT: Ashgate, 2010), 125–36; George R. Collins and Christiane Crasemann Collins, *Camillo Sitte and the Birth of Modern City Planning* (New York: Random House, 1965).
85. Christiane C. Collins, "Camillo Sitte across the Atlantic: Raymond Unwin, John Nolen, and Werner Hegemann," in *Sitte, Hegemann, and the Metropolis: Modern Civic Art and International Exchanges*, ed. Charles C. Bohl and Jean-François Lejeune (London: Routledge, 2009), 177–78.
86. Hancock, "Pioneer Planner," 46–47.
87. John Nolen, "The Basis of German City Planning Procedure: An Example from Düsseldorf," *Landscape Architecture* 2 (October 1911): 53.
88. Nolen and Strong, "Family Album," 16; Nolen to Barbara Nolen, September 10, 1906, box 7, NSP.
89. E. M. Forester, *A Room with a View* (1908; reprint, London: Penguin Classics, 2000), 71.
90. John Nolen, "What Is Needed in American City Planning?," in *Proceedings of the First National Conference on City Planning* (Chicago: American Society of Planning Officials, 1909), 74–75.
91. Charles W. Eliot, *Charles Eliot, Landscape Architect* (1902; reprint, Amherst: University of Massachusetts Press in association with Library of American History, 1999), title page.

2. LANDSCAPE ARCHITECT, 1902–1905

1. Nolen to Alan Harris, January 25, 1904, box 69, NP.
2. Keith N. Morgan, introduction to Charles W. Eliot, *Charles Eliot, Landscape Architect* (1902; reprint, Amherst: University of Massachusetts Press in association with Library of American Landscape History, 1999), vii.

3. Nolen to Barbara Nolen, September 17, 1902, box 5, NSP.

4. Morgan, introduction to *Charles Eliot,* x–xxiv.

5. Henry Farnham May, *The End of American Innocence: A Study of the First Years of Our Own Time, 1912–1917* (New York: Oxford University Press, 1959), 56–57.

6. Eliot, *Charles Eliot,* 33.

7. Morgan, introduction to *Charles Eliot,* xxviii–xxx.

8. Karl Haglund, *Inventing the Charles River* (Cambridge: MIT Press, 2002), xx–xi.

9. Sylvester Baxter (1850–1927), a Boston journalist and early city-planning advocate, gained acclaim by writing the introduction to *Looking Backward;* by the end of the century, only the Bible and *Uncle Tom's Cabin* had outsold Bellamy's book. Nationalist clubs across the United States (and, later, England) were formed to advance Bellamy's vision of a more just and livable city. See Charles D. Warren, introduction to John Nolen, *New Towns for Old: Achievements in Civic Improvement in Some American Small Towns and Neighborhoods* (1927; reprint, Amherst: University of Massachusetts Press in association with Library of American Landscape History, 2005), liv–lvi, and Stanley Buder, *Visionaries and Planners: The Garden City Movement and the Modern Community* (New York: Oxford University Press, 1990), 34–36. In England, *Looking Backward* inspired Ebenezer Howard's cooperative land development model. See Standish Meacham, *Regaining Paradise: Englishness and the Early Garden City Movement* (New Haven: Yale University Press, 1999), 56–58.

10. Haglund, *Inventing the Charles River,* 117.

11. Eliot, *Charles Eliot,* 680–89.

12. Eliot quoted in Haglund, *Inventing the Charles River,* 212.

13. Sonja Dümpelmann, "The Park International: Park System Planning as an International Phenomenon at the Beginning of the Twentieth Century," *German Historical Institute Bulletin* 37 (Fall 2005): 75–86.

14. Lewis Mumford, *The Culture of Cities* (New York: Harcourt, Brace, 1938), 220; Ian McHarg, *A Quest for Life: An Autobiography* (New York: Wiley, 1996), 358–61.

15. Nolen to Charles Briney, December 13, 1902, box 5, NSP; Nolen to Barbara Nolen, September 19, 1902, box 5, NSP.

16. John Nolen, "Aid from the University Extension Methods," *Library Journal* 48 (May 1903): 225–27.

17. Nolen and Strong, "Family Album," 19; John L. Hancock, "John Nolen: The Background of a Pioneer Planner," in *The American Planner: Biographies and Recollections,* ed. Donald Krueckeberg (New York: Methuen, 1983), 45.

18. Nolen to Charles Briney, November 11, 1902, box 6, NSP.

19. Edward Griggs to Nolen, July 1, 1903, box 6, NSP.

20. Cecil Lavell to Nolen, July 21, 1903, box 18, NSP.

21. Nolen and Strong, "Family Album," 20.

22. Jon A. Peterson, *The Birth of City Planning in the United States, 1840–1917* (Baltimore: Johns Hopkins University Press, 2003), 206–7.

23. Melanie Louise Simo, *Forest and Garden: Traces of Wildness in a Modernizing Land, 1897–1949* (Charlottesville: University of Virginia Press, 2003), 116–17; Anthony Alofsin, *The Struggle for Modernism: Architecture, Landscape Architecture, and City Planning at Harvard* (New York: Norton, 2002), 21–24.

24. J. Sturgis Pray, "The Department of Landscape Architecture in Harvard University," *Landscape Architecture* 1 (July 1911): 55–56.

25. Probably to avoid confusion with Flavel Shurtleff, a prominent Massachusetts city planning attorney, Arthur Shurtleff changed his last name to Shurcliff in 1930.

26. Nolen to Harris, November 12, 1904, box 69, NP.

27. A graduate of Harvard, MIT, and the École des Beaux-Arts, Guy Lowell (1870–1927) was the architect for Lowell Lecture Hall (1902) and Emerson Hall (1904) at Harvard as

well as the Museum of Fine Arts, Boston (1909). He was also an expert in Italian Renaissance gardens and had studied at the Royal Botanic Gardens in England. In Boston he gained experience in horticulture and landscape gardening working with his father-in-law, Charles Sprague Sargent, the dynamic director of the Arnold Arboretum. In 1910 Lowell helped implement the plans Charles Eliot had drawn for the Charles River Esplanade. See Kimberly A. Shilland, "Guy Lowell," in *Pioneers of American Landscape Design*, ed. Charles A. Birnbaum and Robin Karson (New York: McGraw-Hill, 2000), 230–33; Robin Karson, *A Genius for Place: American Landscapes of the Country Place Era* (Amherst: University of Massachusetts Press in association with Library of American Landscape History, 2007), xix.

28. Peter J. Schmitt, *Back to Nature: The Arcadian Myth in Urban America* (New York: Oxford University Press, 1969), 4. See also Jeffrey Sachs, *Arcadian America: The Death and Life of an Environmental Tradition* (New Haven: Yale University Press, 2012).

29. Peterson, *Birth of City Planning*, 163–64.

30. William H. Wilson, *City Beautiful Movement* (Baltimore: Johns Hopkins University Press, 1989), 80–87.

31. In his introduction to Charles W. Eliot's biography, Keith Morgan notes that "What Would Be Fair, Must First Be Fit" is both the title of chapter 29 and of an article Charles Eliot wrote shortly before his death. See Morgan, introduction to *Charles Eliot*, xxxi, and Charles Eliot, "What Would Be Fair, Must First Be Fit," *Garden and Forest* 9 (April 1896): 132–33.

32. Sylvester Baxter, "The Great Civic Awakening in America," *Century* 64 (July 1902): 255–63.

33. May, *End of American Innocence*, 154–56; Wilson, *City Beautiful Movement*, 41; Michael H. Frisch, "Urban Theorists, Urban Reform, and American Political Culture in the Progressive Period," *Political Science Quarterly* 97 (Summer 1982): 295–315.

34. Frederic Howe, *The Hope of Democracy* (New York: Charles Scribner's Sons, 1906), xii, 10.

35. Curt Meine, *Correction Lines: Essays on Land, Leopold, and Conservation* (Washington, DC: Island Press, 2004), 42–52.

36. In 1908 Pray followed Olmsted Jr. as chair of the landscape architecture department, a position he would hold for twenty years.

37. Simo, *Forest and Garden*, 9–11.

38. Nolen to Harris, January 25, 1904, box 69 NP.

39. Nolen and Strong, "Family Album," 20.

40. "Landscape Architecture I," box 38, NP.

41. Kenneth Clark, *Civilization* (New York: Harpers & Row, 1969), 269.

42. Lawrence Gowing, *Turner: Imagination and Reality*, exhib. cat. (New York: Museum of Modern Art with Doubleday, 1966), 1–9.

43. John Ruskin, *Modern Painters, Volume V* (New York: John W. Lovell, 1873), 12.

44. Schmitt, *Back to Nature*, 56–61.

45. Nolen to Harris, November 12, 1904, box 69, NP.

46. Nolen to Harris, January 25, 1904, box 69, NP.

47. "Landscape Architecture I," box 38, NP.

48. Simon Schama, *Landscape and Memory* (New York: Knopf, 1995), 526–34; John Hanson Mitchell, *The Wildest Place on Earth: Italian Gardens and the Invention of Wilderness* (Washington, DC: Counterpoint, 2001).

49. "Landscape Architecture I," box 38, NP.

50. Ibid.

51. Marie Frank, *Denman Ross and American Design Theory* (Lebanon, NH: University Press of New England, 2012), 3–5.

52. "Theory of Pure Design," box 38, NP.

53. John Nolen, *New Ideals in the Planning of Cities, Towns, and Villages* (New York: American City Bureau, 1919), 136; at Harvard, Nolen's only typed notes were for Ross's class.

54. Hancock, "Pioneer Planner," 49.

55. Nolen and Strong, "Family Album," 20.

56. Nolen to Harris, November 12, 1904, box 69, NP.

57. "Landscape Architecture II," box 38, NP.

58. Nolen to Harris, November 12, 1904, box 69, NP; Cecil Lavell to Nolen, June 12, 1904, box 18, NSP.

59. Nolen to Harris, November 12, 1904, box 69, NP.

60. Justin Martin, *Genius of Place: The Life of Frederick Law Olmsted* (Cambridge, MA: De Capo Press, 2011), 323–24.

61. "Landscape Architecture II," box 38, NP.

62. Frederick Law Olmsted Sr., "Preliminary Report upon the Proposed Suburb Village at Riverside," in *The Papers of Frederick Law Olmsted: Volume VI,* ed. David Schuyler and Jane Censer (Baltimore: Johns Hopkins University Press, 1992), 275.

63. "Landscape Architecture II," box 38, NP.

64. John Nolen, "What Is Needed in American City Planning?," Hearing Before the Committee on the District of Columbia United States Senate on the Subject of City Planning, 61st Congress, 2nd Session, Senate Document No. 422 (Washington, DC: Government Printing Office, 1910), 74.

65. Hancock, "Pioneer Planner," 47.

66. "Winthrop Square," box 38, NP.

67. Except for a piece by Mariana Griswold Van Rensselaer, no one had documented Olmsted Sr.'s accomplishments. See Van Rensselaer, "Frederick Law Olmsted," *Century Illustrated Monthly Magazine* 46 (October 1893): 860–67.

68. The installments appeared in the February, March, May, and July 1906 issues of *House and Garden.*

69. John Nolen, "Frederick Law Olmsted and His Work," *House and Garden* 9 (February 1906): 73–75.

70. Ibid., *House and Garden* 10 (July 1906): 11.

71. Samuel P. Hays, *Conservation and the Gospel of Efficiency: The Progressive Conservation Movement* (Cambridge: Harvard University Press, 1959), 1–4; Stephen J. Diner, *A Very Different Age: Americans of the Progressive Era* (New York: Hill and Wang, 1998), 176–99, 426.

72. Frederick Law Olmsted Jr. and John Nolen, "The Normal Requirements of American Towns and Cities in Respect to Public Open Space," *Charities and the Commons: A Weekly Journal of Philanthropy and Social Advance* 16 (July 7, 1906): 411–26.

73. Nolen to Harris, August 16, 1905, box 69, NP.

3. CHARLOTTE, LETCHWORTH, AND SAVANNAH, 1905–1907

1. Mary Norton Kratt and Thomas W. Hanchett, *Legacy: The Myers Park Story* (Charlotte, NC: Myers Park Foundation, 1986), 21–26; Nolen to Alan Harris, August 16, 1905, box 69, NP.

2. Stephens was building a new subdivision adjacent to the site in conjunction with a trolley line extension, and he promised to donate land to the new park if the city created a public board to oversee its construction and maintenance. Thomas Hanchett, *Sorting Out the New South City: Race, Class, and Urban Development in Charlotte, 1875–1975* (Chapel Hill: University of North Carolina Press, 1998), 152–53.

3. Daniel Augustus Tompkins (1851–1914) earned an engineering degree from Rensselaer Polytechnic Institute and applied his skills to the booming textile industry, eventually

building and operating a conglomeration of cotton mills, many of which were accompanied by mill villages that he designed. A leading industrialist and publisher of the *Charlotte Observer,* Tompkins made a point of studying public parks on his business trips to the Northeast and Europe. According to Henry W. Grady, editor of the *Atlanta Constitution,* Tompkins "did more for the industrial South than any other man." Hanchett, *New South City,* 152–53; Paul M. Gaston, *The New South Creed: A Study in Southern Myth-Making* (Baton Rouge: Louisiana State Press, 1970), 50.

4. Hanchett, *New South City,* 153–54.
5. Nolen to Barbara Nolen, June 19, 1905, box 7, NSP.
6. Hanchett, *New South City,* 116–21.
7. Nolen to Barbara Nolen, June 20, 1905, box 7, NSP.
8. Ibid.
9. *Charlotte Observer,* June 26, 1905. box 23, NP.
10. Ibid.
11. Nolen to Barbara Nolen, June 22, 1905, box 7, NSP.
12. Nolen to Harris, August 16, 1905, box 69, NP.
13. Ibid.
14. Nolen to Barbara Nolen, October 7, 1905, box 7, NSP.
15. Nolen to Barbara Nolen, October 8, 1905, box 7, NSP.
16. Charles E. Beveridge and Paul Rocheleau, *Frederick Law Olmsted: Designing the American Landscape* (New York: Rizzoli, 1995), 193–219.
17. Nolen to Barbara Nolen, October 9, 1905, box 7, NSP.
18. The plan for Independence Park was lost sometime before 1909.
19. Kratt and Hanchett, *Legacy,* 30–31.
20. Brian W. C. Sturm, "The Evolution of Greenspace: A History of Urban Landscape in Charlotte, North Carolina, 1890–1990" (honors thesis, University of North Carolina, 2000).
21. Kratt and Hanchett, *Legacy,* 155–56; Nolen to Harris, August 16, 1905, box 69, NP.
22. Hancock, "The Background of a Pioneer Planner," in *The American Planner: Biographies and Recollections,* ed. Donald Krueckeberg (New York: Methuen, 1983), 50.
23. Thomas F. Dixon Jr. (1864–1946) was educated at Wake Forest and the Johns Hopkins Graduate School. By his late twenties, he had become a leading Baptist minister in New York City, but decided to strike out on his own to earn a living as a lecturer and author. Maintaining segregation, he preached, would procure economic equality for the downtrodden white working class. By 1902 he had addressed five million people. After publication of *The Clansman,* Dixon came to see himself as a prophet capable of reuniting North and South and solving the problems of industrial society.
24. Nolen to Barbara Nolen, October 11, 1905, box 7, NSP.
25. Nolen to Barbara Nolen, October 13, 1905, box 7, NSP.
26. *Charlotte Observer,* October 11, 1905, box 23, NP.
27. Nolen to Barbara Nolen, October 13, 15, 1905, box 7, NSP.
28. Hanchett, *New South City,* 90–95.
29. Kratt and Hanchett, *Legacy,* 27.
30. *Charlotte Observer,* October 11, 1905, box 23, NP.
31. John Whiteclay Chambers II, *The Tyranny of Change: America in the Progressive Era, 1900–1917* (New York: St. Martin's, 1980), 110–12.
32. *Charlotte Observer,* October 11, 1905, box 23, NP.
33. *Charlotte Observer,* January 13, 1906, box 23, NP.
34. *Greenville Daily News,* January 17, 1906, box 23, NP.
35. David Potter, "The Enigma of the South," in *Myth and Southern History: The New South Edition,* ed. Patrick Gerster and Nicholas Cords (Champaign: University of Illinois

Press, 1989), 33–42; David Goldfield, "The Urban South: A Regional Framework," *American Historical Review* 86 (December 1981): 1009–34.

36. Thomas Jefferson, "Notes on the State of Virginia," in *Thomas Jefferson Writings*, ed. Merrill Peterson (New York: Library of America, 1984), 301.

37. Greenville folder, box 69, NP; Dean Sinclair, "'Some Maps and a Lot of Trouble': Town Planner John Nolen in South Carolina," *South Carolina Historical Magazine* 105 (October 2004): 258–81.

38. *Boston Evening Transcript*, February 23, 1906, box 7, NP.

39. Nolen to Harris, March 12, 1906, box 69, NP.

40. *Newark Adviser*, October 27, 1906, box 7, NP.

41. *Charlotte Observer*, May 2, 1906, box 23, NP.

42. Bill Alexander, *Around Biltmore Village* (Charleston, SC: Arcadia, 2008), 27–48.

43. Nolen to Harris, April 6, 1906, box 69, NP.

44. John Nolen, introduction to Humphry Repton, *The Art of Landscape Gardening*, ed. John Nolen (Boston: Houghton Mifflin, 1907), xv.

45. Ibid., xviii.

46. Nolen, introduction to Repton, *Art of Landscape Gardening*, xix.

47. Nolen to Harris, December 24, 1907, box 69, NP; Charles E. Beveridge, "Olmsted: His Essential Theory," *Nineteenth Century* (Victorian Society in America) 20 (Fall 2000): 32–37.

48. Thomas Warren Sears (1880–1966), an amateur photographer, had completed his B.S. in landscape architecture at Harvard that spring. After his trip with Nolen, Sears spent two years working for Olmsted Brothers and gained additional experience in Rhode Island before opening his own successful practice in Philadelphia in 1913. Catherine Howett, *A World of Her Own Making: Katharine Smith Reynolds and the Landscape of Reynolda* (Amherst: University of Massachusetts Press in association with Library of American Landscape History, 2007), 192–95.

49. Hancock, "Pioneer Planner," 48–49.

50. Ebenezer Howard (1850–1928) immigrated to the United States in 1871. He spent a year homesteading on the Nebraska plains before moving to Chicago and finding work as a court reporter. After reading Edward Bellamy's *Looking Backward*, Howard helped obtain the English copyright for the book and gained standing with the Nationalization of Labor Society (NLS), a group formed to promote Bellamy's ideas in Britain. The NLS gave Howard a platform to articulate his interest in urban reform. In the early 1890s, he developed an outline for building an interlocking system of towns founded on communal land ownership and dedicated to simple, healthy living. Howard's garden city drew from Bellamy's utopianism as well as from land reforms advocated by Thomas Spence, Henry George, and Alfred Wallace. The second edition of *To-morrow* was retitled *Garden Cities of To-morrow* (1902) to reflect the garden city's central role in advancing "real reform." See Evan D. Richert and Mark B. Lapping, "Ebenezer Howard and the Garden City," *Journal of the American Planning Association* 64 (Spring 1998): 125–32. For an overview of the garden city, see Stephen V. Ward, ed., *The Garden City: Past, Present, and Future* (London: E. & F. N. Spon, 1992); Stanley Buder, *Visionaries and Planners: The Garden City Movement and the Modern Community* (New York: Oxford University Press, 1990); Kermit C. Parsons and David Schuyler, eds., *From Garden City to Green City: The Legacy of Ebenezer Howard* (Baltimore: Johns Hopkins University Press, 2002); and Robert Fishman, *Urban Utopias in the Twentieth Century: Ebenezer Howard, Frank Lloyd Wright, Le Corbusier* (Cambridge: MIT Press, 1982).

51. Howard quoted in Parsons and Schuyler, *From Garden City to Green City*, 5.

52. Stanley Buder, "Ebenezer Howard: The Genesis of a Town Planning Movement," *Journal of the American Planning Association* 35 (November 1969): 390–98; Standish Meacham, *Regaining Paradise: Englishness and the Early Garden City Movement* (New Haven: Yale University Press, 2002), 56.

53. Ebenezer Howard, *Garden Cities of To-morrow* (London: Swan Sonnenschein, 1902), 22.

54. Parsons and Schuyler, *From Garden City to Green City,* 7.

55. Stephen V. Ward, "The Howard Legacy," in Parsons and Schuyler, *From Garden City to Green City,* 222–44; Eugenie Birch, "Five Generations of the Garden City: Tracing Howard's Legacy in Residential Planning," in Parsons and Schuyler, *From Garden City to Green City,* 171–200; Mervyn Miller, "Garden Cities at Home and Abroad," *Journal of Planning History* 1 (January 2002): 6–28.

56. Fishman, *Urban Utopias,* 40–63.

57. Vincent Scully, *Architecture: The Natural and the Manmade* (New York: St. Martin's, 1991), 314.

58. Buder, *Visionaries and Planners,* 96–115.

59. John Nolen, *Montclair: The Preservation of Its Natural Beauty and Its Improvment as a Residence Town* (Montclair, NJ: Montclair Municiple Art Commission, 1909), 97; Nolen and Strong, "Family Album," 22.

60. Nolen to Barbara Nolen, August 13, 17, and 31, 1906, box 7, NSP.

61. Nolen to Barbara Nolen, September 10, 1906, box 7, NSP.

62. Nolen and Strong, "Family Album," 22, NP.

63. Nolen to Harris, April 4, 1906, box 69, NP.

64. George John Baldwin (1856–1927) had contacted Nolen on a recommendation from Edward Griggs, who lectured regularly in Savannah. A leading voice in Savannah's plans for urban expansion, Baldwin served on the board of the Augusta and Savannah Railroad and was a founding member of the Savannah Parks and Tree Commission. See Thomas Hanchett, "John Nolen and the Planning of Savannah's Daffin Park, 1906–1909," *Georgia Historical Quarterly* 78 (Winter 1994): 810–14.

65. George Baldwin to Nolen, May 1, 1906, box 75, NP.

66. Nolen to Barbara Nolen, November 25, 1906, box 7, NSP.

67. Nolen to Baldwin, December 10, 1906, box 75, NP.

68. John Williams Reps, *The Making of Urban America: A History of City Planning in the United States* (Princeton, NJ: Princeton University Press, 1965), 199.

69. Nolen to Baldwin, December 10, 1906, box 75, NP.

70. Philip Dickinson Daffin to Nolen, March 1, 1907, box 75, NP.

71. Baldwin to Nolen, April 9, 1907, box 75, NP.

72. Paul Boyer, *Urban Masses and Moral Order in America, 1820–1920* (Cambridge: Harvard University Press, 1978), 242–51.

73. Galen Cranz, *The Politics of Park Design: A History of Urban Parks in America* (Cambridge: MIT Press, 1982), 58–64.

74. *Charlotte Observer,* April 20, 1907, box 23, NP.

75. Boyer, *Urban Masses,* 242–51; Cranz, *Politics of Park Design,* 40–67.

76. *Charlotte Observer,* April 20, 1907, box 23, NP.

77. Hanchett, "Daffin Park," 815–17.

78. Baldwin to Nolen, June 6, 1907, box 75, NP.

79. Hanchett, "Daffin Park," 818–20.

80. The park is the product of community investment and "John Nolen's vision," as the Daffin Park Centennial Committee proclaimed in 2007. *Savannah Morning News,* February 14, 2007.

4. CITY PLANNER, 1907–1908

1. Roosevelt quoted in John Whiteclay Chambers II, *The Tyranny of Change: America in the Progressive Era, 1900–1917* (New York: St. Martin's, 1980), 141.
2. Jon A. Peterson, *The Birth of City Planning in the United States, 1840–1917* (Baltimore: Johns Hopkins University Press, 2003), 177–98.
3. John Nolen, *Remodeling Roanoke* (Roanoke, VA: Stone Printing, 1907), 9, box 20, NP.
4. Rand Dotson, *The Magic City of the New South: Roanoke, Virginia, 1882–1912* (Knoxville: University of Tennessee Press, 2007), 221–25.
5. Kevan Frazier, "Big Dreams, Small Cities, John Nolen, the New South, and the City Planning Movement" (PhD diss., University of West Virginia, 2000), 48–51.
6. Nolen to Barbara Nolen, August 23, May 1, and July 1, 1907, box 8, NSP.
7. Dotson, *Magic City*, 1–221.
8. Adam Rome, "Gender and Environmental Reform," *Environmental History* 11 (July 2006): 451.
9. Nolen, "Roanoke 1907 Preliminary Survey," box 10, NP.
10. *Roanoke News*, April, 30, 1907, box 23, NP.
11. Nolen to Barbara Nolen, July 3, 1907, box 8, NSP.
12. Nolen and Strong, "Family Album," 23, NP.
13. Nolen, *Remodeling Roanoke*, 17.
14. Ibid., 14.
15. Ibid.
16. Christopher Silver, "John Nolen: Planner for the New South" *Journal of Planning Education and Research* 15 (Spring 1996): 80–81; Dewey W. Grantham, *Southern Progressivism: The Reconciliation of Progress and Tradition* (Knoxville: University of Tennessee Press, 1983), 126–27.
17. Nolen, *Remodeling Roanoke*, 18.
18. The reformer's belief in the ability to engineer behavior through physical planning is discussed in William Wilson, *The City Beautiful Movement* (Baltimore: Johns Hopkins University Press, 1990), 92–95.
19. Nolen, *Remodeling Roanoke*, 22.
20. Ibid., 28.
21. Nolen, *Remodeling Roanoke*, 26.
22. Ibid., 28.
23. Ibid., 30.
24. Ibid., 29.
25. Ibid., 10, 29.
26. Nolen and McFarland had met at the inaugural American Civic Association (ACA) conference held in Boston in 1904. Nolen had impressed McFarland, who began to regularly write letters of reference for the aspiring landscape architect. In reciprocation, Nolen served as an officer in the association, demonstrating his knack for organizational outreach. McFarland put his skills to good use. Nolen delivered the keynote address at the 1909 ACA conference in Cincinnati, sat on the ACA executive board, and was named first vice president in 1915. See Peterson, *Birth of City Planning*, 131–34, 140–44, and Ernest Morrison, *J. Horace McFarland: A Thorn for Beauty* (Harrisburg: Pennsylvania Historical and Museum Commission, 1996). John L. Hancock, "John Nolen and the American City Planning Movement" (PhD diss., University of Pennsylvania, 1964), 140–41.
27. Peterson, *Birth of City Planning*, 131–34, 140–44.
28. Wilson, *City Beautiful Movement*, 126–46.
29. Peter J. Schmitt, *Back to Nature: The Arcadian Myth in Urban America* (New York: Oxford University Press, 1969), 71.

30. Frazier, "Big Dreams, Small Cities," 52–57.
31. Dotson, *Magic City,* 232–34.
32. Ibid., 235–38.
33. Patrick Geddes, *Cities in Evolution* (London: Williams & Norgate, 1915), 233.
34. Nolen to Barbara Nolen, January 18, 1908, box 9, NSP.
35. Roanoke folder, box 33, NP.
36. Roanoke City Planning Division, *Vision 2001–2020: The City's Comprehensive Plan* (Roanoke, VA: Roanoke City Council, 2001). Nolen's plans are in the introduction.
37. "Rebirth of the Roanoke River," *Roanoke Times,* September 16, 2007; Greenways Inc., *Conceptual Greenway Plan: Roanoke Valley Virginia* (Roanoke, VA: Roanoke Valley Open Space Steering Committee, 1995).
38. George Marston to Nolen, May 28, 1907, box 94, NP. George Marston (1850–1946) arrived in San Diego in 1870 as a bookkeeper, but within the year he had bought out his employer. A decade later, he owned San Diego's first department store. On his buying trips to New York, Marston regularly visited Central Park, and his admiration for Olmsted Sr. led him to champion public parks in San Diego. After the San Diego project, Marston hired Nolen to design the gardens for his grand hillside estate.
39. Nolen to Marston, June 3, 1907, box 94, NP.
40. John L. Hancock, "Smokestacks and Geraniums: Planning and Politics in San Diego," in *Planning and the Twentieth-Century American City,* ed. Mary Corbin Sies and Christopher Silver (Baltimore: Johns Hopkins University Press, 1996), 161–63.
41. Nolen to Alan Harris, December 24, 1907, box 69, NP.
42. Edward Griggs to Nolen, June 1907, box 18, NSP.
43. Wilson, *City Beautiful Movement,* 99–125.
44. "John Nolen Praises Park System," *Kansas City Post,* November 25, 1907, box 7, NP.
45. Nolen to Barbara Nolen, June 7, 1914, box 12, NSP; William S. Worley, *J. C. Nichols and the Shaping of Kansas City* (Columbia: University of Missouri Press, 1993), 236–37.
46. John Nolen and Henry Hubbard, *Parkways and Land Values* (Cambridge: Harvard University Press, 1937), 41–71.
47. Nolen to Barbara Nolen, October 9, 1907, box 12, NSP.
48. Nolen to Barbara Nolen, October 12, 14, and 15, 1907, box 12, NSP.
49. Nolen and Strong, "Family Album," 23.
50. Hancock, "Nolen and the American City Planning Movement," 504; George Marston, "Address to the San Diego Art Association," box 94, NP.
51. John Nolen, *San Diego: A Comprehensive Plan for Its Improvement* (Boston: George Ellis, 1908), 4.
52. Hancock, "Nolen and the American City Planning Movement," 506.
53. Nolen, *San Diego,* 1–2.
54. Ibid., 3.
55. Nolen quoted in Hancock, "Nolen and the American City Planning Movement," 507.
56. Nolen, *San Diego,* 10.
57. Lucinda Eddy, "Visions of Paradise: The Selling of San Diego," *Journal of San Diego History* 41 (Summer 1995): 170–75; Richard F. Pourade, *The History of San Diego: The Glory Years* (San Diego: Union-Tribune Publishing Co., 1964), 175–226.
58. Nolen, *San Diego,* 7.
59. Ibid., 7.
60. Catherine Cocks, *Doing the Town: The Rise of Urban Tourism in the United States, 1859–1915* (Berkeley: University of California Press, 2001), 1–7.
61. Nolen to Harris, October 1, 1907, box 69, NP.
62. Nolen, *San Diego,* 45.
63. Ibid., 78, 81.

64. Nolen to Barbara Nolen, October 24, 1908, box 12, NSP.
65. Ibid., 75.
66. Ibid., 62.
67. Ibid., 62–70.
68. Nolen to Charles Van Hise, February 20, 1909, box 79, NP.
69. "Quote File," box 7, NP.
70. Hancock, "Smokestacks and Geraniums," 165–67.
71. Marston to Nolen, December 23, 1907, box 94, NP.
72. Julius Wangenheim to Nolen, July 31, 1908, box 94, NP.
73. Hancock, "Smokestacks and Geraniums," 167–69.
74. Uldis Ports, "Geraniums vs. Smokestacks: San Diego's Mayoralty Campaign of 1917," *Journal of San Diego History* 21 (Summer 1975): 50–56.
75. Melanie Macchio, "John Nolen and San Diego's Early Residential Planning in the Mission Hills Area," *Journal of San Diego History* 52 (Summer/Fall 2006): 131–50.
76. Hancock, "Smokestacks and Geraniums," 170–86.

5. CITY PLANNING IN AMERICA AND EUROPE, 1908–1911

1. A law professor, John M. Olin (1892–1982) dedicated himself to making Madison the "Athens of the West," a city devoted to culture, beauty, and education. Olin earned his undergraduate degree from Williams College, where he was a student of the noted sociologist John Bascom. In 1874 Bascom assumed the presidency of the University of Wisconsin. Eager to raise the school's standards to match the top eastern universities, he brought in idealistic young New Englanders like Olin. Only twenty-three on arriving in Madison, Olin taught, earned a law degree, and built a profitable practice. By 1908, in large part thanks to his efforts, the Madison Park and Pleasure Drive Association had raised $250,000 and acquired 269 acres of parkland, and the University of Wisconsin stood at the forefront of educational reform. Olin to Nolen, January 14, 1908, box 28, NP; Nolen to Griggs, January 18, 1908, box 28, NP.

2. Olin came to personify the Wisconsin Idea, dividing his duties between teaching and spearheading urban beautification projects during a period of rapid growth. In 1894 the Madison Improvement Association became the Madison Park and Pleasure Drive Association, and Olin was elected its president. When he stepped down in 1909, the organization had grown to a thousand members and sponsored the new park commission. Charles McCarthy, *The Wisconsin Idea* (New York: Macmillan, 1912). On the Wisconsin Idea and progressive reform, see David Hoeveler Jr., "The University and the Social Gospel: The Intellectual Origins of the Wisconsin Idea," *Wisconsin Magazine of History* 59 (Summer 1976): 282–98.

3. Nolen to Griggs, January 18, 1908, box 28, NP.

4. Nolen to Olin, January 28, 1908, box 28, NP; Nolen to Griggs, April 9, 1908, box 28, NP.

5. Nolen to Olin, March 11, 1908, box 28, NP.

6. La Follette's much-heralded refusal to take bribes made his reputation. The journalist Lincoln Steffens, intent on raking the muck on a man he assumed to be a wily demagogue, found instead an honest politician: "His enemies convinced me that I was on the track of the best story yet, the story of a straight, able, fearless individual who was trying to achieve not merely good but representative government and this in a State, not a city." Lincoln Steffens, *The Autobiography of Lincoln Steffens* (New York: Literary Guild, 1931), 456.

7. Carl R. Burgchardt, *Robert M. La Follette, Sr.: The Voice of Conscience* (New York: Greenwood Press, 1992), 53–72; David P. Thelen, *Robert M. La Follette and the Insurgent Spirit* (Boston: Little, Brown, 1976), 32–51.

8. Thelen, *La Follette*, 108–17.

9. By 1912 thirty-seven professors had served on committees established by the state legislature, resulting in significant advancements. Wisconsin established the nation's first workers' compensation program and instituted factory safety regulations, farm cooperatives, a state income tax, and limited work hours for women and children. In reform circles, the University of Wisconsin earned the title "The University That Runs the State." Merle Curti and Vernon Carstensen, *The University of Wisconsin: A History, 1848–1925*, vol. 2 (Madison: University of Wisconsin Press, 1949), 3–43; Henry Farnham May, *The End of American Innocence: A Study of the First Years of Our Own Time, 1912–1917* (New York: Knopf, 1959), 99–101.

10. Nolen to Barbara Nolen, April 24, 1908, box 9, NSP.

11. John Nolen, "Beauty and Order in State and City," *Madison Parks and Pleasure Drive Association Annual Report* (Madison: MPPDA, 1908), 75–78.

12. Ibid.

13. *Wisconsin State Journal,* April 28, 1908.

14. Nolen to Barbara Nolen, April 24, box 9, NSP.

15. Barbara Jo Long, "John Nolen: The Wisconsin Activities of an American Landscape Architect, 1908–1937" (master's thesis, University of Wisconsin, 1978), 30.

16. Nolen to Barbara Nolen, November 26, 1908, box 10, NSP.

17. Nolen, "Parks and the City Plan," *Madison Park and Pleasure Drive Association Annual Report* (Madison, WI: MPPDA, 1910), 58.

18. David V. Mollenhoff, "The Realism of Visionary Planning: Nolen's Comprehensive Plan for Madison, Wisconsin, 1907–1911," *Historic Madison: Journal of the Four Lakes Region* 12 (1995): 346.

19. John Nolen, "Madison: A Model Capital City," in *Madison Park and Pleasure Drive Association Annual Report* (Madison, WI: MPPDA, 1909), 87–91.

20. Nolen to Barbara Nolen, May 6, 1908, box 10, NSP.

21. Nolen to Barbara Nolen, May 19, 1908, box 10, NSP.

22. In 1878 the Wisconsin state legislature set aside a 760-square-mile reserve in the northern part of the state, but two decades later the property was sold to lumber interests. Minnesota and Wisconsin joined forces in 1900 to create Interstate Park and preserve the picturesque scenery along their common boundary on the St. Croix River. When Robert La Follette assumed the governorship a year later, the protection of natural resources became policy. Charles Van Hise, a geologist by training, chaired the new state Conservation Commission. The university president was a nationally recognized conservationist who would later write *The Conservation of Natural Resources in the United States* (1909). Under his leadership, the commission established regulations to rein in private mining and lumber operations. Van Hise also proposed that the state establish a system of parks and forests. The Wisconsin legislature adopted the commission's agenda and, in 1907, established the State Park Commission. John Nolen, *State Parks for Wisconsin* (Madison, WI: State Park Board, 1908), 53; Thomas C. Chamberlain, *Charles Richard Van Hise, 1857–1918* (Washington, DC: Government Printing Office, 1924); William H. Tishler, *Door County's Emerald Treasure: A History of Peninsula State Park* (Madison: University of Wisconsin Press, 2006), 56.

23. Nolen, *State Parks for Wisconsin*, 6.

24. Donald Worster, *A Passion for Nature: The Life of John Muir* (New York: Oxford University Press, 2008), 212–14, 366–69.

25. Robert Sullivan, *The Thoreau You Don't Know: What the Prophet of Environmentalism Really Meant* (New York: HarperCollins, 2009), 298.

26. Douglas Brinkley, *The Wilderness Warrior: Theodore Roosevelt and the Crusade for America* (New York: HarperCollins, 2009).

27. Theodore Roosevelt, "Opening Address by the President," in *Proceedings of a Conference of Governors* (Washington, DC: Government Printing Office, 1909), 3–13.

28. Nolen, *State Parks for Wisconsin*, 12–13.

29. Ibid., 18, 50.

30. Ibid., 20.

31. Ibid., 23–34.

32. After convincing legislators of the need for parks, Reynolds and Nolen played a crucial role in creating Peninsula Park in Door County, "arguably the premier park in the entire state." Tishler, *Emerald Treasure,* 72. A remnant of the Dells of the Wisconsin River was established as a state preserve in 1994.

33. John Nolen, "The Parks and Recreation Facilities in the United States," *Annals of the American Academy of Political and Social Science* 35 (January 1910): 219. Nolen's report documented the country's public open space, from urban playgrounds to national parks. While principally descriptive, the article called for the protection of Yosemite National Park's Hetch Hetchy Valley, which was at the center of a debate over the sanctity of national parks. The controversy began after the catastrophic 1906 San Francisco earthquake, during which firefighters ran out of water and entire sections of the city burned to the ground. Municipal officials lobbied the federal government to dam the Tuolumne River and turn the Hetch Hetchy Valley into a reservoir. John Muir headed the opposition, which Olmsted Jr. and Horace McFarland later joined, in a fight pitting "preservationists" against "conservationists." Muir believed Yosemite was a sacred reserve of spiritual purity that human use would defile. But Secretary of the Interior Gifford Pinchot and the conservationist philosophy of utility—the "greatest good for the greatest number"—won out. In 1913 the Tuolumne River was dammed, and Hetch Hetchy became an impoundment basin supplying San Francisco with water. See Robert W. Righter, *The Battle over Hetch Hetchy: America's Most Controversial Dam and the Birth of Modern Environmentalism* (New York: Oxford University Press, 2005), 191–215; Melanie Louise Simo, *Forest and Garden: Traces of Wildness in a Modernizing Land, 1897–1949* (Charlottesville: University of Virginia Press, 2003), 148–49.

34. Tishler, *Emerald Treasure,* xiii, 68. Today, Wisconsin holds title to ninety-three parks encompassing 139,000 acres, attracting more than fourteen million visitors a year to some of the most scenic areas in the Midwest.

35. C. H. Schaffer to Nolen, December 11, 1936, box 58, NP.

36. Jon A. Peterson, *The Birth of City Planning in the United States, 1840–1917* (Baltimore: Johns Hopkins Unversity Press, 2003), 247–49.

37. Harvey Kantor, "Benjamin C. Marsh and the Fight over Population Congestion," in *The American Planner: Biographies and Recollections,* ed. Donald A. Krueckeberg (New York: Methuen, 1983), 58–74.

38. Benjamin Marsh, "Economic Aspects of City Planning," *Proceedings of the First National Conference on City Planning Senate Documents* 49 (422), 61st Cong., 2nd sess. (Washington, DC, 1910), 105.

39. Mel Scott, *American City Planning since 1890: A History Commemorating the Fiftieth Anniversary of the American Institute of Planners* (Berkeley: University of California Press, 1969), 99.

40. Susan L. Klaus, *A Modern Arcadia: Frederick Law Olmsted Jr. and the Plan for Forest Hills Gardens* (Amherst: University of Massachusetts Press in association with Library of American Landscape History, 2002), 32–33.

41. Frederick Law Olmsted Jr., "The Scope and Results of City Planning in Europe," *Proceedings of the First National Conference on City Planning Senate Documents,* 70.

42. Scott, *American City Planning,* 95–96.

43. Nolen to Barbara Nolen, May 22 and 23, 1909, box 10, NSP.

44. Nolen to Barbara Nolen, July 22, 1909, box 10, NSP.

45. John Nolen, "City Making in Wisconsin: What Must Be Done to Create Healthful, Beautiful, and Convenient Cities," *La Follette's Magazine* 1 (November 1909): 9.

46. Nolen, "What Is Needed in American City Planning?," *Proceedings of the First National Conference on City Planning Senate Documents*, 74–75.

47. "John Nolen Talked on Art and the Civic Spirit," *New London (Connecticut) Day*, June 10, 1908, box 7, NP.

48. Stuart Meck and Rebecca C. Retzlaff, "A Familiar Ring: A Retrospective on the First Conference for City Planning," *Planning & Environmental Law Commentary* 41 (April 2009): 3.

49. Peterson, *Birth of City Planning*, 243–53; Kantor, "Benjamin C. Marsh," 71–72.

50. Nolen to Barbara Nolen, May 23, 1909, box 10, NSP.

51. Steffens, *Autobiography*, 598. An early confidant of the self-educated department store magnate was Louis D. Brandeis, the future Supreme Court justice. Acquainted through their Jewish faith, the two men experimented with new methods of applying social science to improve business–labor relations. Their effort led to the institution of worker compensation and the forty-hour work week in Massachusetts. Kim McQuaid, "An American Owenite: Edward A. Filene and the Parameters of Industrial Reform, 1890–1937," *American Journal of Economics and Sociology* 35 (January 1976): 77–94.

52. Steffens, *Autobiography*, 598–600.

53. Ibid., 600–613.

54. Edward A. Filene, "Immigration, Progress, and Prosperity," *Saturday Evening Post*, July 28, 1923, box 7, NP.

55. Christiane C. Collins, *Werner Hegemann and the Search for Universal Urbanism* (New York: Norton, 2005), 24–28.

56. John Nolen, "City Planning and Civic Consciousness," *New Boston* 1 (May 1911): 7–8.

57. Daniel T. Rodgers, *Atlantic Crossings: Social Politics in a Progressive Age* (Cambridge: Belknap Press of Harvard University Press, 1998), 138–45.

58. Collins, *Werner Hegemann*, 29, 85–145.

59. Ibid., 31.

60. May, *End of American Innocence*, 20–21. The Boston-1915 exhibition provided the impetus for the chamber of commerce to sponsor the Boston Metropolitan Planning Commission. In 1911 Nolen joined Filene, Coolidge, and Mayor John Fitzgerald on its inaugural board. Eight years later, the Metropolitan Sewerage Commission, the Metropolitan Water Board, and the Metropolitan Park Commission combined to form the Boston Metropolitan District Commission, the first regional planning commission in the nation. John L. Hancock, "John Nolen and the American City Planning Movement" (PhD diss., University of Pennsylvania, 1964), 143–44.

61. Nolen to Barbara Nolen, July 28, 1909, box 9, NSP.

62. Mollenhoff, "Realism," 350–52; John Nolen, *Replanning Small Cities: Six Typical Studies* (New York: Huebsch, 1912), 175–76. For Nolen's role in the passage of the 1909 Wisconsin Planning Enabling Act, see Brian F. O'Connell and Dan Dyke, "The Wisconsin Planning Enabling Act of 1909," *Planning History Present* 5 (1992), 1–6.

63. John Nolen, *Madison: A Model City* (Boston, 1911), 137, 151.

64. Ibid., 35–44.

65. Ibid., 69–71; Nolen to Van Hise, February 20, 1909, box 28, NP. On the Madison park system, see John Nolen, "Parks and the City Plan," in *Madison Park and Pleasure Drive Association Annual Report* (Madison, WI: MPPDA, 1910).

66. Nolen, *Madison*, 121–23.

67. Nolen, "City Making in Wisconsin," 14.
68. Nolen, *Madison*, 128–32.
69. Ibid, 136–37.
70. Ibid, 146–47.
71. Carl Smith, *The Plan of Chicago: Daniel Burnham and the Remaking of the American City* (Chicago: University of Chicago Press, 2006), 146.
72. Charles E. Beveridge and Paul Rocheleau, *Frederick Law Olmsted: Designing the American Landscape* (New York: Rizzoli, 1995), 155–64.
73. Eric A. McDonald, Arnold R. Alanen, and Holly Smith, *Wisconsin's Capitol Park, 1838–2000: A Landscape History* (Madison, WI: State Department of Administration), 30–33.
74. Mollenhoff, "Realism," 334.
75. Mollenhoff, "Realism," 58–60; Franklin E. Court, *Pioneers of Ecological Restoration: The People and Legacy of the University of Wisconsin Arboretum* (Madison: University of Wisconsin Press, 2012), 5–8.
76. Frederic Howe, "The Remaking of the American City," *Harper's Monthly* 127 (July 1913): 193.
77. Hancock, "Nolen and the American City Planning Movement," 295–96.
78. Sonja Dümpelmann, "The Park International: Park System Planning as an International Phenomenon at the Beginning of the Twentieth Century," *Bulletin of the German Historical Institute Bulletin* 37 (Fall 2005), 5–11.
79. Nolen to Griggs, May 26, 1911, box 95, NP; Rodgers, *Atlantic Crossings,* 71–74.
80. Nolen to Barbara Nolen, July 11, 1911, box 11, NSP.
81. The first zoning law in the United States, this ordinance established building height and setback controls and identified industrial uses deemed to be incompatible with residential districts. See Frank B. Williams, "The German Zone Building Regulations," *Report of Heights of Buildings Commission* (New York: Board of Estimate and Apportionment, 1913), 94–119; and Russell Van Nest Black, *Planning and the Planning Profession: The Past Fifty Years, 1917–1967* (Washington, DC: American Institute of Planners, 1967), 47–48.
82. Nolen to Barbara Nolen, July 13, 1911, box 11, NSP.
83. R. Bruce Stephenson, "The Roots of the New Urbanism: John Nolen's Garden City Ethic," *Journal of Planning History* 1 (May 2002): 105–10; Pierre-Yves Saunier, "John Nolen: Atlantic Crosser," *Planning History* 21 (Spring 1999): 28–29; see also "Unwin File," box 8, NP.
84. Nolen to Barbara Nolen, July 11, 1911, box 11, NSP.
85. Steffens, *Autobiography,* 652–53; Nolen to Barbara Nolen, July 13, 1911, box 11, NSP.
86. Saunier, "John Nolen," 23–31; Christiane C. Collins, "Camillo Sitte across the Atlantic: Raymond Unwin, John Nolen, and Werner Hegemann," in *Sitte, Hegemann, and the Metropolis: Modern Civic Art and International Exchanges,* ed. Charles C. Bohl and Jean-François Lejeune (London: Routledge, 2009), 177–80; Stanley Buder, *Visionaries and Planners: The Garden City Movement and the Modern Community* (New York: Oxford University Press, 1990), 133–42.
87. Stephenson, "New Urbanism," 111–20.
88. Saunier, "Atlantic Crosser," 25–26.
89. John Nolen, "The Basis of German City Planning Procedure: An Example from Düsseldorf," *Landscape Architecture* 2 (October 1911): 52–57.
90. Rodgers, *Atlantic Crossings,* 179–99.
91. In 1911 only Harvard and the University of Illinois offered courses in city planning. See Peterson, *Birth of City Planning,* 283.
92. Nolen to Thomas Adams, February 15, 1911, box 8, NP.
93. Michael Simpson, *Thomas Adams and the Modern Planning Movement* (London: Man-

sell, 1985), 122–23; Frank Jackson, *Sir Raymond Unwin: Architect, Planner, and Visionary* (London: Zwemmer, 1985), 111–12.

94. Klaus, *Modern Arcadia*, 31–53.

6. MODEL SUBURBS AND INDUSTRIAL VILLAGES, 1909–1918

1. John Nolen, *Montclair: The Preservation of Its Natural Beauty and Its Improvement as a Residence Town* (Montclair, NJ: Montclair Municipal Art Commission, 1909), 16.

2. Ibid.

3. Christiane C. Collins, "Camillo Sitte across the Atlantic: Raymond Unwin, John Nolen, and Werner Hegemann," in Charles C. Bohl and Jean-François Lejeune, *Sitte, Hegemann, and the Metropolis: Modern Civic Art and International Exchanges* (London: Routledge, 2009), 177–80; Nolen, *Montclair*, 36.

4. Nolen, *Montclair*, 10, 35, 73–75.

5. John Nolen, *Comprehensive Planning for Small Towns and Villages* (Boston: American Unitarian Association, 1910), 2. On the Social Gospel, see Susan Curtis, *A Consuming Faith: The Social Gospel and Modern American Culture* (Baltimore: Johns Hopkins University Press, 1991).

6. Nolen is quoting John Stuart Mills. See *Comprehensive Planning for Small Towns and Villages*, 2, 6.

7. Herbert Croly, *The Promise of American Life* (New York: Macmillan, 1909), 399–400, 406, 421, 454. For his comments on city planning, see Herbert Croly, "The Promised City of San Francisco," *Architectural Record* 20 (June 1906): 425–36; and Herbert Croly, "Civic Improvements: The Case for New York," *Architectural Record* 21 (May 1907): 347–52.

8. The "promise of American life" refrain was common to speeches Nolen made between 1909 and 1919. See John L. Hancock, "John Nolen and the American City Planning Movement" (PhD diss., University of Pennsylvania, 1964), 231.

9. Grosvenor Atterbury, *Model Towns in America* (New York: National Housing Association, 1913), 1.

10. John Nolen, *Replanning Small Cities: Six Typical Studies* (New York: Huebsch, 1912), 1–2.

11. Mary Norton Kratt and Thomas W. Hanchett, *Legacy: The Myers Park Story* (Charlotte, NC: Myers Park Foundation, 1986), 30–36; Thomas W. Hanchett, *Sorting Out the New South City: Race, Class, and Urban Development in Charlotte, 1875–1975* (Chapel Hill: University of North Carolina Press, 1998), 171.

12. Nolen to Barbara Nolen, March 18, 1911, box 11, NSP.

13. Kratt and Hanchett, *Legacy*, 37–38; John Nolen, *New Towns for Old: Achievements in Civic Improvement in Some American Small Towns and Neighborhoods* (1927; reprint, Amherst: University of Massachusetts Press in association with Library of Landscape History, 2005), 100.

14. Kratt and Hanchett, *Legacy*, 52–53.

15. Charles D. Warren, introduction to *New Towns for Old*, lxxxviii.

16. Draper to Nolen, March 7 and May 3, 1915, box 73, NP; Frank Waugh to Nolen, March 19, 1915, box 73, NP.

17. Kratt and Hanchett, *Legacy*, 41.

18. Nolen to Ray Dennis, March 5, 1917, box 26, NP.

19. Nolen to George Stephens, February 27, 1917, box 23, NP.

20. Nolen to Stephens, March 2, 1917, box 23, NP.

21. Stephens to Nolen, March 2, 1917, box 23, NP. Stephens would work with Nolen on the plan for Asheville, NC, in the mid-1920s.

22. Any breach in the two men's relationship was repaired; Nolen later wrote to Stephens that "if at any time you should desire our services, you can be sure that we shall respond heartily"; Nolen to Stephens, March 23, 1917, box 23, NP.

23. Nolen also came into conflict with Draper on this project. See Warren, introduction to *New Towns for Old*, lxxxix.

24. Thomas W. Hanchett, *Sorting Out the New South City: Race, Class, and Urban Development in Charlotte, 1875–1975* (Chapel Hill: University of North Carolina Press, 1998), 219–20.

25. George Stephens to Arthur E. Morgan, June 5, 1933, box 65, NP. Myers Park declined in the 1960s and 1970s but regained its prominence in the 1980s. In 1987 the National Register of Historic Places designated most of Myers Park a National Historic District, and by 2000 the streetcar suburb had been recognized as a model of what planners called transit-oriented development. Kratt and Hanchett, *Legacy*, 201–4.

26. In 2005, as city planners reconfigured Charlotte to accommodate a new rail and streetcar system, the Levine Museum of the New South sponsored the exhibit "John Nolen: Neighborhood Maker." The exhibit, and a three-day symposium, "New Urbanism in Charlotte: The Legacy of John Nolen," showed how Myers Park and other streetcar suburbs illustrated Nolen's lessons of thoughtful planning. City officials, citizens, practitioners, scholars, and public planners analyzed and discussed the attributes of each community. Drawing on the past, they came away with a better understanding of how to build a system of transit-oriented neighborhoods. By 2009 private development valued at $232 million had been built within a quarter mile of the new rail line. Once again, Charlotte won recognition for its unique style of development, earning the Environmental Protection Agency's Smart Growth Achievement Award. Richard Jackson, *Designing Healthy Communities* (Washington, DC: Island Press, 2012), 125; Environmental Protection Agency, *2009 National Award for Smart Growth Achievement* (Washington, DC: EPA, 2009).

27. Nolen to Barbara Nolen, March 14, 1911, box 11, NSP.

28. Ibid.

29. Ibid.

30. John Nolen, J. Randolph Coolidge Jr., and Edward Filene, *Report of the Metropolitan Plan Commission* (Boston: Metropolitan Plan Commission, 1912), 10–13, box 71, NP.

31. Mel Scott, *American City Planning since 1890: A History Commemorating the Fiftieth Anniversary of the American Institute of Planners* (Berkeley: University of California Press, 1969), 116–17.

32. Margaret Crawford, *Building the Workingman's Paradise: The Design of American Company Towns* (New York: Verso, 1995), 46–61.

33. *Proceedings of the First National Conference of the National Housing Association* (Washington, DC: National Academy of Political Science, 1912).

34. Lawrence Veiller, *Housing Reform* (New York: Charities Publication Committee, 1910), 15.

35. John Nolen, "The Factory and the Home," in *Proceedings of Second National Conference*, National Housing Association (Washington, DC: National Academy of Political Science, 1913).

36. Ibid., 115–19.

37. John Nolen, "City Planning and Civic Consciousness," *New Boston* 2 (May 1911), 10.

38. John Nolen, "Factory and Home," 117.

39. For discussion of the plan, see *Proceedings of the Fifth National Conference on City Planning* (Boston: National Conference on City Planning, 1913), 189–209.

40. Crawford, *Workingman's Paradise*, 156–59. The New York City architectural firm of Horace B. Mann and Perry Robinson MacNeille designed the housing. Francis William Park's mix of bucolic landscape and active recreational areas remains largely as Nolen

envisioned: a sequestered space for play set within "sun-swept meadows" and "shadowed glades." Nolen, Francis William Park, box 37, NP.

41. "Hobart College Inaugural," November 14, 1913, box 5, NP.

42. Nolen and Strong, "Family Album," 26–30.

43. Hancock, "Nolen and the American City Planning Movement," 298.

44. Harland Bartholomew quoted in Eldridge Lovelace, *Harland Bartholomew: His Contributions to American Urban Planning* (Urbana: Department of Urban and Regional Planning, University of Illinois, 1993), 17.

45. Jon A. Peterson, *The Birth of City Planning in the United States, 1840–1917* (Baltimore: Johns Hopkins University Press, 2003), 264.

46. Nolen to Patrick Geddes, January 17, 1923, box 76, NP.

47. *New York Sun*, June 30, 1912, box 69, NP.

48. *Springfield Republican*, June 30, 1912, box 69, NP.

49. Nolen to Barbara Nolen, June 11, 1914, box 12, NSP.

50. Nolen and Strong, "Family Album," 26–30, NP.

51. John L. Hancock, *John Nolen, Landscape Architect, Town, City, and Regional Planner: A Bibliographical Record of Achievement* (Ithaca, NY: Program in Urban and Regional Studies, Cornell University, 1976), 58–59.

52. William S. Worley, *J. C. Nichols and the Shaping of Kansas City: Innovation in Planned Residential Communities* (Columbia: University of Missouri Press, 1990), 237; Charles Bohl, *Place-Making: Developing Town Centers, Main Streets, and Urban Villages* (Washington, DC: Urban Land Institute, 2002), 40–47.

53. John Mosier, *The Myth of the Great War: A New Military History of World War I* (New York: Harper Perennial, 2002), 303–6.

54. Warren, introduction to *New Towns for Old*, lxxiv–lxxvii.

55. John Nolen, *The Industrial Village* (New York: National Housing Association, 1918), 18–22.

56. Crawford, *Workingman's Paradise*, 160–63.

57. Nolen, *New Towns for Old*, 73–74.

58. Nolen quoted in *A Symposium on War Housing* (New York: National Housing Association, 1918), 18.

59. John Nolen, *New Ideals in the Planning of Cities, Towns, and Villages* (New York: American City Bureau, 1919), 87; Crawford, *Workingman's Paradise*, 163.

60. Nolen, *Industrial Village*, 5.

61. John Nolen, *A Good Home for Every Wage-Earner* (Washington, DC: American Civic Association, 1917), 1–7.

62. Nolen, *Industrial Village*, 8.

63. Hancock, *John Nolen*, 4–6.

64. Charles Harris Whitaker, Frederick L. Ackerman, Richard S. Childs, and Edith Wood, *The Housing Problem in War and Peace* (Washington, DC: American Institute of Architects, 1918); Daniel T. Rodgers, *Atlantic Crossings: Social Politics in a Progressive Age* (Cambridge: Belknap Press of Harvard University Press, 1998), 285–89.

65. Nolen to Barbara Nolen, November 11, 1914, box 11, NSP.

66. Nolen to Barbara Nolen, March 1, 1916, box 11, NSP.

67. Nolen to Hamilton Holt, March 3, 1932, box 20, NP.

68. Robert Macieski, "'The Home of the Workingman Is the Balance Wheel of Democracy': Housing Reform in Wartime Bridgeport," *Journal of Urban History* 26 (September 2000): 716–21.

69. John Nolen and Frank Williams, *Better City Planning: Some Fundamental Proposals to the City of Bridgeport, Connecticut* (Bridgeport, CT: Bridgeport City Planning Commission, 1916), 66–68.

70. Nolen, *A Good Home,* 10; John Nolen, *More Houses for Bridgeport: A Report to the Chamber of Commerce* (Bridgeport, CT: Bridgeport Housing Authority, 1916).

71. Macieski, "'The Home of the Workingman,'" 722.

72. Garden City Movement Hearing, *Senate Resolution 305 Sixty-Fourth Congress* (Washington, DC: Government Printing Office, 1917), 43.

73. Ibid.

74. The hearing report listed fifty communities that had been either built or planned. Ibid., 39, 50–53.

75. Peter Pennoyer and Anne Walker, *The Architecture of Grosvenor Atterbury* (New York: Norton, 2009), 190; Alexander Garvin, *The American City: What Works, What Doesn't* (New York: McGraw-Hill, 2002), 407–17.

76. Whitaker et al., *Housing Problem,* 17–68.

77. Ray Lubove, "Homes and 'A Few Well Placed Fruit Trees': An Object Lesson in Federal Housing," *Social Research* 27 (Winter 1960): 468–86; Scott, *American City Planning,* 170–73; Kristin M. Szylvian, "Industrial Housing Reform and the Emergency Fleet Corporation," *Journal of Urban History* 25 (July 1999): 647–89; Daniel Brook, "Unnecessary Excellence: What Public Housing Can Learn from Its Past," *Harper's,* March 2005, 76–79.

78. Nolen to Thomas Adams, January 17, 1918, box 8, NP.

79. Hancock, "Nolen and the American City Planning Movement," 275–78.

80. Scott, *American City Planning,* 163–65; John L. Hancock, "Planners in the Changing American City: 1900–1940," *Journal of the American Institute of Planners* 30 (September 1967): 295.

81. Szylvian, "Industrial Housing Reform," 657; Michael Simpson, *Thomas Adams and the Modern Planning Movement* (London: Mansell, 1985), 94–117.

82. *Symposium on War Housing,* 17–18, 46–47.

83. Crawford, *Workingman's Paradise,* 170.

84. Nolen, *New Towns for Old,* 89.

85. Nolen and Strong, "Family Album," 33.

86. Crawford, *Workingman's Paradise,* 168–73; Lang, *Designing Utopia,* 144–50.

87. Nolen, *New Towns for Old,* 91–93.

88. Eric J. Karolak, "Shaping Housing and Enhancing Consumption: Hoover's Interwar Housing Policy," in *From Tenements to the Taylor Homes: In Search of an Urban Housing Policy in Twentieth-Century America,* ed. John F. Bauman, Roger Biles, and Kristin Szylvian (University Park: Pennsylvania State University Press, 2000), 69; William E. Groben, "Union Park Gardens: A Model Garden Suburb for Shipworkers at Wilmington, Delaware," *Architectural Record* 45 (January 1919): 22–23.

89. Ballinger and Perrot, "Cost Data for Wilmington Housing Company," April 1918, box 17, NP.

90. Szylvian, "Industrial Housing Reform," 667–68.

91. Groben, "Union Park Gardens," 23; Nolen, *A Good Home,* 9.

92. Nolen, *New Ideals,* 26.

93. Nolen to Patrick Geddes, July 15, 1919, box 95, NP.

94. Nolen, *New Ideals,* 10, 58.

95. Ibid., 23.

96. Ibid., 135–38.

97. Brian F. O'Connell and Dan Dyke, "The Wisconsin Planning Enabling Act of 1909," *Planning History Present* (1992), 1–6.

98. Nolen, *New Ideals,* 18–19.

7. KINGSPORT AND MARIEMONT, 1919–1926

1. Horace McFarland, "New Ideals in the Planning of Cities, Towns and Villages," *National Municipal Review* 9 (September 1921): 568.

2. "Invitation to attend 'Meeting at City Club, January 3, 1919,' Industrial Housing and Related Subjects," December 21, 1918, box 77; Felix Frankfurter to Nolen, January 6, 1919, box 77, NP.

3. For a more detailed history of Kingsport, see Margaret Ripley Wolfe, *Kingsport, Tennessee: A Planned American City* (Lexington: University Press of Kentucky, 1987), 13–25.

4. Nolen to Ray Dennis, January 6 and February 10, 1916, box 26, NP.

5. D. Appleton published a second edition in 1929.

6. Wolfe, *Kingsport*, 35–36.

7. Nolen to Dennis, January 6 and February 7, 1916, box 26, NP.

8. John Nolen, *New Towns for Old: Achievements in Civic Improvement in Some American Small Towns and Neighborhoods* (1926; reprint, Amherst: University of Massachusetts Press in association with Library of Landscape History, 2005), 54.

9. Earle Draper to Nolen, April 15, 1916, box 26, NP.

10. Nolen to Dennis, April 10, 1916, and February 3, 1917, box 26, NP.

11. Wolfe, *Kingsport*, 39; Nolen to Dennis, August 8, 1917, box 26, NP.

12. Nolen to Grosvenor Atterbury, November 4, 1919, box 26, NP.

13. Clinton McKenzie, "The Work of Clinton McKenzie, Kingsport, Tennessee," *Southern Architect and Building News* 33 (March 1927): 2.

14. Peter Pennoyer and Anne Walker, *The Architecture of Grosvenor Atterbury* (New York: Norton, 2009), 207.

15. Nolen to Dennis, August 8, 1917, box 26, NP.

16. Wolfe, *Kingsport*, 51.

17. Kingsport folder, box 9, NP.

18. John L. Hancock, "John Nolen and the American City Planning Movement" (PhD diss., University of Pennsylvania, 1964), 466.

19. Blaine A. Brownell, *The Urban Ethos in the South, 1920–1930* (Baton Rouge: Louisiana State University Press, 1975), 182–84; Hancock, "Nolen and the American City Planning Movement," 466.

20. Wolfe, *Kingsport*, 84–115.

21. Floyd Parsons, "A New Kind of Town," *Saturday Evening Post*, October 25, 1919, 44.

22. Nolen, *New Towns for Old*, 28.

23. Wolfe, *Kingsport*, 70–78.

24. William H. Stone, "Kingsport: An Industrial City Built on a Foundation of Sound Practical Ideals," *Manufacturers Record* 78 (March 3, 1921), box 26, NP; F. Gould, "Kingsport," *Manufacturers Record* 90 (December 10, 1925), 77; John Piquet, "Low Cost Methods and High Cost Men: The Story of Kingsport, a Tennessee Hill Town," *Industrial Management* 71 (May 1926): 317–23; John Nolen, "Kingsport, Tennessee: An Industrial City Made to Order," *American Review of Reviews* 74 (March 1927), 286–92; Mary Frances Hughes, "Where Planned Beauty Blossoms in an Industrial Community," *American City* 22 (December 1930): 140–41.

25. Nolen to Dennis, November 15, 1919, box 26, NP.

26. Nolen to Fred Johnson, April 20, 1922, box 26, NP. Upon Nolen's death in 1937, approximately one-sixth of the city did not conform to the 1919 plan. Hancock, "Nolen and the American City Planning Movement," 477–78.

27. See William Fulton, "The Garden City and the New Urbanism," in *From Garden City to Green City: The Legacy of Ebenezer Howard*, ed. Kermit C. Parsons and David Schuyler (Baltimore: Johns Hopkins University Press, 2002), 163. Mumford was critical of Earle

Draper's design for Norris, Tennessee, the Tennessee Valley Authority's only significant planned community, commenting that "the TVA had no urban policy whatever."
According to Mumford, "had the original directors paid more attention to the success
of the small industrial town of Kingsport, Tennessee, planned in 1915 by John Nolen
under the direction of private enterprise, they would have coordinated their superb
regional improvements with the renewal and extension of the existing small communities, and the building of new ones." See Lewis Mumford, *The City in History: Its
Origins, Its Transformations, and Its Prospects* (New York: Harcourt, Brace, 1961), 432.
28. Daniel Brook, "Unnecessary Excellence: What Public Housing Can Learn from Its
Past," *Harper's*, March 2005, 76–79; Margaret Crawford, *Building the Workingman's
Paradise: The Design of American Company Towns* (New York: Verso, 1995), 172–73.
29. "The Garden City has been on my mind since the war," Nolen wrote to John Glenn,
the executive director of the Russell Sage Foundation; Nolen wanted Glenn to fund the
planning and construction of a model community. Nolen to Glenn, December 14, 1920,
box 31, NP. On the end of progressive reform, see John Whiteclay Chambers II, *The
Tyranny of Change: America in the Progressive Era, 1900–1917* (New York: St. Martin's,
1980), 233–73; Henry F. May, "What Happened to the Progressive Movement in the
1920s," *Mississippi Valley Historical Review* 64 (December 1959): 406–27; David Gold-
berg, *Discontented America: The United States in the 1920s* (Baltimore: Johns Hopkins
University Press, 1999), 40–65; and Harold Stearns, ed., *Civilization in the United
States: An Inquiry by Thirty Americans* (New York: Harcourt, Brace, 1922), iii–viii.
30. Two years later, The Russell Sage Foundation funded "New York and Its Environs," a
plan for the twenty-two-county New York City region. Nolen served on the advisory
board of the New York Regional Plan Committee, joining a group that included Olmsted Jr., Henry Hubbard, and Frank Williams. Raymond Unwin was brought in as a
consultant, and Thomas Adams left his post in Canada to oversee the effort.
31. Nolen to Unwin, December 28, 1920, box 8, NP.
32. Nolen's daughter Barbara spent a summer with the Unwin family in England; she wrote
her Stanford University master's thesis on the wartime effects of English housing policy.
Edward Unwin would work in the Nolen office in 1926. Hancock, "Nolen and the
American City Planning Movement," 439–40.
33. Mervyn Miller, *Raymond Unwin: Garden Cities and Town Planning* (Leicester, UK:
Leicester University Press, 1992), 161–88; Daniel T. Rodgers, *Atlantic Crossings: Social
Politics in a Progressive Age* (Cambridge: Belknap Press of Harvard University Press,
1998), 381–83.
34. Nolen, "Project List," *New Towns for Old*, 191–99.
35. John L. Hancock, *John Nolen, Landscape Architect, Town, City, and Regional Planner:
A Bibliographical Record of Achievement* (Ithaca, NY: Program in Urban and Regional
Studies, Cornell University, 1976), 13–14.
36. Sam Bass Warner and Andrew H. Whittemore, *American Urban Form: A Representative
History* (Cambridge: MIT Press, 2012), 84–101: Ellis Hawley, *The Great War and the
Search for a Modern Order, 1917–1933* (New York: St. Martin's, 1979), 70–91; Nathan
Miller, *New World Coming: The 1920s and the Making of Modern America* (New York:
Simon & Schuster, 2003), 341–64; Leland Roth, *American Architecture: A History*
(Boulder, CO: Westview Press), 341–43.
37. Nolen, "The Place of the Beautiful in the City Plan," Paper delivered to the National
City Planning Conference, Springfield, MA, 1922, box 7, NP.
38. Nolen, "Regional Planning," n.d., box 241, NP.
39. John Nolen, "Madison: A Model Capital City," in *Madison Park and Pleasure Drive
Association Annual Report* (Madison, WI: MPPDA, 1909), 95.
40. Hancock, "Nolen and the American City Planning Movement," 424–26.

41. Olmsted became increasingly disillusioned after the failure to extend the gains made during World War I and the death of John Charles Olmsted in 1920. He shifted his emphasis to state and national park commissions and maintained only a peripheral interest in planning. See Susan L. Klaus, "Frederick Law Olmsted Jr.," in *Pioneers of American Landscape Design*, ed. Charles A. Birnbaum and Robin Karson (New York: McGraw-Hill, 2000), 275.

42. Russell Van Nest Black, *Planning and the Planning Profession: The Past Fifty Years, 1917–1967* (Washington, DC: American Institute of Planners, 1967), 44.

43. Lewis Mumford, *The Story of Utopias* (New York: Boni & Liveright, 1922), 35, 290, 300.

44. Nolen to Mumford, January 11, 1923, box 76, NP.

45. Nolen to Raymond Unwin, July 20, 1922, box 8, NP; John Nolen, "Mariemont: A Demonstration American Town," paper presented at the International Cities and Town Planning Conference, Gothenburg, Sweden, August 3–10, 1923, box 1, NP.

46. Nolen to Patrick Geddes, January 10, 1923, box 76, NP.

47. Millard F. Rogers Jr., *John Nolen and Mariemont: Building a New Town in Ohio* (Baltimore: Johns Hopkins University Press, 2001), 8–72; Nolen to Fred Johnson, April 20, 1922, box 26, NP.

48. Marc Weiss, *The Rise of the Community Builders* (New York: Columbia University Press, 1987), 64–68; Andrés Duany, Elizabeth Plater-Zyberk, and Jeff Speck, *The Suburban Nation: The Rise of Sprawl and the Decline of the American Dream* (New York: North Point Press, 2000), 100–103.

49. Rogers, *Nolen and Mariemont,* 50.

50. Nolen, *New Towns for Old,* 121; John Nolen, "Mariemont, Ohio—A New Town Built to Produce Local Happiness," *American Civic Annual* (Washington, DC: American Civic Association, 1929), 235–37.

51. Millard Rogers Jr., "John Nolen and Mariemont: A Town Planner's Reverence for the Site," Paper presented to the Society for American City and Regional Planning History, Miami, FL, October 15, 2005; R. Bruce Stephenson, "The Roots of the New Urbanism: John Nolen's Garden City Ethic," *Journal of Planning History* 1 (May 2002): 109–10.

52. These included greens, urban squares, athletic fields, nature preserves, neighborhood parks, playgrounds, and allotment gardens. See Nolen, "Mariemont," 4–5.

53. Charles Livingood quoted in Rogers, *Nolen and Mariemont,* 147.

54. Nolen, *New Towns for Old,* 128.

55. John Nolen Jr. to Nolen, July 7, 1923, box 13, NSP.

56. Rogers, *Nolen and Mariemont,* 72, 176.

57. Nolen to Livingood, October 13, 1922, box 29, NP.

58. Livingood to Nolen, October 16, 1922, box 29, NP.

59. Rogers, *Nolen and Mariemont,* 144–45; Hancock, *John Nolen,* 378–80; Pennoyer and Walker, *Grosvenor Atterbury,* 208.

60. Warren W. Parks, *The Mariemont Story: A National Exemplar of Town Planning* (Cincinnati, OH: Creative Writers and Publishers, 1967), 30–35.

61. Rogers, *Nolen and Mariemont,* 176.

62. Nolen, *New Towns for Old,* 127–30.

63. Rogers, *Nolen and Mariemont,* 119–21.

64. Ibid., 130.

65. Ibid., 121–30.

66. Grosvenor Atterbury designed the houses in an Elizabethan style. Sheldon Close was the last project built by the Mariemont Company. After 1925, emphasis shifted from renting units to selling single-family home lots. See Rogers, *Nolen and Mariemont,* 165–68.

67. "Mariemont, America's Demonstration Town," *American City* 27 (October 1922): 309–10; Nolen, "Mariemont," 2–13; John Nolen and Sylvester Baxter, "Modern City Planning Principles Applied to a Small Community: Mariemont, a New Town in the Cincinnati District," *National Real Estate Journal* 24 (March 26, 1923): 21–27; Glenn Hall and John Nolen, "Carrying Out Mariemont Plans for a Self-Contained Town," *Engineering News Record* 92 (April 3, 1924): 580–82; Charles J. Livingood and John Nolen, *A Descriptive and Pictured Story of Mariemont—A New Town: A National Exemplar* (Cincinnati, OH: Mariemont Co., 1925), 39–44.

68. Livingood to Nolen, December 8, 1925, box 29, NP.

69. Livingood quoted in Rogers, *Nolen and Mariemont*, 182.

70. After the presentation, Nolen went on to hold a number of leadership positions in the organization, eventually assuming its presidency in 1931. Nolen, "Mariemont," 10.

71. Charles D. Warren, introduction to *New Towns for Old*, lvi–lviii.

72. Henry Wright, "Review of 'New Towns for Old,'" *New York Times*, November 13, 1927; see Hancock, *John Nolen*, 28.

73. Nolen, *New Towns for Old*, 120.

74. Ibid., 141.

75. Calvin Coolidge to Nolen, May 9, 1927, box 6, NP; In 1921, after a report revealed that a third of the country's population lived in substandard conditions, Hoover established a division of housing. A noted efficiency expert, he believed that inadequate housing offered "thriving food for Bolshevism" and led a federal initiative to standardize home construction. William E. Leuchtenburg, *Herbert Hoover* (New York: Henry Holt, 2009), 54–55; Ellis Hawley, *Herbert Hoover as Secretary of Commerce* (Iowa City: Iowa University Press, 1981), 22–73.

76. Pennoyer and Walker, *Grosvenor Atterbury*, 208.

77. Hancock, "Nolen and the American City Planning Movement," 379.

78. Ibid., 381.

79. H. I. Brock, "A New Experiment in Town Planning to Fit the Motor Age," *New York Times Magazine*, August 24, 1924, 7–8; Rogers, *Nolen and Mariemont*, 212–14.

80. When road rage became an issue in the 1990s, the town's human-scaled environs captured national attention. *ABC World News Tonight with Peter Jennings*, July 21, 1999, ran a three-minute piece contrasting Mariemont's pedestrian urbanism to life in the automobile-oriented subdivisions of nearby Florence, Kentucky. Teens in Mariemont fared especially well; their ability to walk and bike to destinations resulted in what Nolen called "local happiness." By contrast, their counterparts in Florence struggled to find meaning in a maze of disconnected subdivisions.

81. Duany, Plater-Zyberk, and Speck, *Suburban Nation*, 103; Robert Davis, Andrés Duany, and Elizabeth Plater-Zyberk, *The Lexicon of the New Urbanism* (Miami, FL: DPZ, 1999), 24.

82. Stephen Litt, "Great Neighborhoods," *Planning* 74 (December 2008): 4.

83. "Greetings," *Mariemont Messenger*, March 19, 1926, box 30, NP.

8. FLORIDA, 1922–1931

1. John Nolen, "Common Places and Ideals of City Planning," address delivered to the City Planning Exhibition, Jacksonville, FL, October 29, 1925, box 14, NP.

2. Lewis Mumford, "The Intolerable City: Must It Keep Growing," *Harper's Monthly* 152 (February 1926): 292.

3. T. H. Weigall, *Boom in Paradise* (New York: Alfred H. King, 1932), xi; Frederick Lewis Allen, *Only Yesterday: An Informal History of the 1920s* (New York: Harper & Row, 1935) 225–35.

4. *St. Petersburg Times,* June 22, 1925, box 94, NP.

5. R. Bruce Stephenson, *Visions of Eden: Environmentalism, Urban Planning, and City Building in St. Petersburg, Florida, 1900–1995* (Columbus: Ohio State University Press, 1997), 38.

6. Walter P. Fuller, *This Was Florida's Boom* (St. Petersburg: Outdoor Publishing, 1954), 21–29; George Tindall, "The Bubble in the Sun," *American Heritage* 16 (August 1965): 83–111; David Nolan, *Fifty Feet in Paradise: The Booming of Florida* (New York: Harcourt Brace Jovanovich, 1984), 156–230.

7. *St. Petersburg Times,* August 9, 1921.

8. William Straub, *History of Pinellas County, Florida, Narrative and Biographical* (St. Augustine, FL: Record Printers, 1930), 11.

9. Stephenson, *Visions of Eden,* 17–29.

10. Ibid., 20–29, 46–47.

11. *St. Petersburg Times,* March 7 and 9, 1922.

12. Stephenson, *Visions of Eden,* 52.

13. John Nolen, Nolen, "City Planning in Florida," *Suniland* 3 (November 1925), 28; Nolen to Frank Williams, March 22, 1922, box 99, NP.

14. Nolen, "City Planning in Florida," 28–29.

15. During the 1920s, Miami's population grew by 274.1% and St, Petersburg's increased by 183.9%. U.S. Bureau of the Census, *Fifteenth Census of the United States* (Washington, DC: Government Printing Office, 1930).

16. Edward M. Bassett, "Review of 'The Law of City Planning and Zoning,'" box 99, NP. Nolen helped expedite the book's publication by meeting with Macmillan editor Richard Ely; Williams to Nolen, August 1, 1921, box 99, NP.

17. Nolen to Williams, January 15, 1923, box 99, NP. On the British Planning Act, see Stanley Buder, *Visionaries and Planners: The Garden City Movement and the Modern Community* (New York: Oxford University Press, 1990), 105–7; and Mervyn Miller, *Raymond Unwin: Garden Cities and Town Planning* (Leicester, UK: Leicester University Press, 1992), 9, 126.

18. Nolen to Orrin Randolph, January 3, 1923, box 38, NP.

19. On the relationship between planning and zoning in this period, see Emily Talen, *City Rules: How Regulations Affect Urban Form* (Washington, DC: Island Press, 2012), 19–36.

20. Williams to Nolen, January 16, 1923, box 99, NP.

21. Mel Scott, *American City Planning since 1890* (Berkeley: University of California Press, 1969), 192–95; Stuart Meck, "Model Planning and Zoning Enabling Legislation: A Short History," in *Modernizing State Planning Statutes: The Growing Smart Working Papers* (Chicago: American Planning Association, 1996), 1–3.

22. E. C. Garvin to Nolen, June 4, 1922, box 75, NP.

23. Nolen, *St. Petersburg Today, St. Petersburg Tomorrow* (St. Petersburg: St. Petersburg City Commission, 1923), 15, box 99, NP.

24. Nolen, *St. Petersburg Today,* 25.

25. Ray Arsenault, *St. Petersburg and the Florida Dream, 1888–1950* (Gainesville: University of Florida Press, 1988), 206–7; Robert N. Pierce, *A Sacred Trust: Nelson Poynter and the St. Petersburg Times* (Gainesville: University Press of Florida, 1993), 38–39.

26. *St. Petersburg Times,* April 3, 1923.

27. Nolen to Williams, January 2, 1923, box 99, NP.

28. Williams to Nolen, January 3 and February 2, 1923, box 99, NP. On racial zoning, see Christopher Silver, "The Racial Origins of Zoning: Southern Cities from 1910–1940," *Planning Perspectives* 6 (Winter 1991): 189–205.

29. Straub to Nolen, January 16, 1923, box 75, NP.

30. Ibid., 137; David Edgell, "John Nolen and the New Urbanists in Florida: The Cases

of Seaside, Venice, and West Palm Beach" (master's thesis, Cornell University, 1995), 109–11.

31. West Palm Beach folder, box 66, NP.
32. "Minutes of the Joint Meeting of the West Palm Beach City Commission and Planning Board," December 15, 1922, box 37, NP.
33. Karl Riddle to Nolen, December 14, 1922, box 66, NP.
34. Nolen to Orrin Randolph, January 3, 1923, box 38, NP.
35. Nolen to Riddle, September 6, 1923, box 66, NP.
36. John Nolen, "West Palm Beach, Florida, City Planning Proposals," 25, box 20, NP.
37. Jack E. Davis, "Whitewash in Florida: The Lynching of Jesse James Payne and Its Aftermath," *Florida Historical Quarterly* 68 (January 1990): 277–80.
38. *Baltimore Daily Herald*, April 19, 1919.
39. David R. Colburn, "Rosewood and America in the Early Twentieth Century," *Florida Historical Quarterly* 76 (Fall 1997): 175–92.
40. Michael D'Orso, *Like Judgment Day: The Ruin and Redemption of a Town Called Rosewood* (New York: Grosset/Putnam, 1996), 19–20; Jon Wilson, *St. Petersburg's Historic African American Neighborhoods* (Charleston, SC: History Press), 61–66.
41. Arsenault, *St. Petersburg*, 207–8.
42. *St. Petersburg Times*, July 25, 1984.
43. *St. Petersburg Times*, January 21, 1929.
44. *St. Petersburg Independent*, August 21, 1923.
45. *St. Petersburg Independent*, July 23, 1923.
46. John F. Eades, "City Planning in West Palm Beach during the 1920s," *Florida Historical Quarterly* 75 (Winter 1997): 283–86.
47. Randolph to Nolen, November 5, 1923, box 23, NP.
48. Nolen to Riddle, November 3, 1923, box 66, NP.
49. Nolen to Riddle, October 10, 1923, box 66, NP.
50. Nolen to H. L. Freeman, October 1, 1924, box 65, NP.
51. Nolen, "City Planning in Florida," box 99, NP.
52. Nolen and Strong, "Family Album," 40.
53. Nolen Jr. to Nolen, June 4, 1925, box 95, NP.
54. David McCally, *The Everglades: An Environmental History* (Gainesville: University Press of Florida, 1999), 121–22; Gail M. Hollander, *Raising Cane in the 'Glades: The Global Sugar Trade and the Transformation of Florida* (Chicago: University of Chicago Press, 2008), 92–96.
55. Alfred Wagg to Nolen, October 22, 1922, and June 18, 1923, box 38, NP; "Clewiston, Florida, Project 264," box 1, NP.
56. Hollander, *Raising Cane*, 79–96.
57. McNally, *Everglades*, 26–30.
58. "Clewiston, Florida, Project 264," box 1, NP.
59. Bror Dahlberg to Nolen, June 3, 1925, box 23, NP.
60. Jeffrey R. Brown, Eric A. Morris, and Brian A. Taylor, "Planning for Cars in Cities," *Journal of the American Planning Association* 75 (Spring 2009): 163–64.
61. Warren S. Thompson and P. K. Whelpton, "Changes in Regional and Urban Patterns of Population Growth," *American Sociological Review* 5 (December 1940): 921–29.
62. Philip Foster, "Clewiston Report," July 1925, box 24, NP.
63. *Miami Herald*, September 15, 1925, box 58, NP.
64. Hale Walker and John Nolen Jr., "Recommendations and Program, Clewiston, Florida," March 1926, box 39, NP.
65. "Details of How Clewiston, Florida, Escaped Storm," *St. Louis Star*, October 14, 1926, box 100, NP.

66. See box 95, NP, esp. Nolen Jr. to Nolen, August 8, 1925; Nolen to Foster, September 17 and 30, 1925; and Foster to Nolen, September 23, 1925.

67. Foster to Nolen, October 3, 1925, box 95, NP.

68. Nolen memorandum, January 7, 1926; Foster to Nolen, February 2, 1926, box 95, NP; Nolen to Foster, October 5, 1932, box 76, NP.

69. Nolen to Straub, August 6, box 94, NP.

70. Stephenson, *Visions of Eden*, 87.

71. Straub to Nolen, August 18, 1925, box 94, NP.

72. Stephenson, *Visions of Eden,* 72–74; Raymond Vickers, *Panic in Paradise: Florida's Banking Crash of 1926* (Tuscaloosa: University Alabama Press, 1994), 17–31.

73. Justin Hartzog, "St. Petersburg, Florida: Report on City Planning Proposals," box 19, NP.

74. "The City's Great Need," *St. Petersburg Times,* April, 1926, box 94, NP.

75. Russell Conklin to Nolen, August 27, 1924, box 71, NP.

76. Kelly Reynolds, *Henry Plant: Pioneer Empire Builder* (Cocoa: Florida Historical Press, 2003), 159–86.

77. Vincent Scully, "A Dream of Coral Gables," in *Coral Gables: An American Garden City,* ed. Roberto M. Behar and Maurice G. Culot (Paris: Norma Editions, 1997), 31–64.

78. Russell Conklin to Nolen, August 27, 1924, box 71, NP.

79. Nolen to Charles Cheney, February 23, 1924, box 8, NP.

80. Fukuo Akimoto, "Charles H. Cheney of California," *Planning Perspectives* 18 (July 2003): 253–75.

81. Fukuo Akimoto, "California Garden Suburbs: St. Francis Wood and Palos Verdes Estates," *Journal of Urban Design* 1 (February 2007): 43–72.

82. Robert Fogelson, *Bourgeois Nightmares: Suburbia, 1870–1930* (New Haven: Yale University Press, 2005), 16–20.

83. Nolen to Conklin, October 6, 1924, box 71, NP.

84. Visiting Belleair in the spring of 1925, Nolen was gratified to find the plan being followed with only minor exceptions. Conklin to Nolen, October 7, 1924, box 71, NP. Nolen to Cheney, March 11, 1925, box 8, NP.

85. *Clearwater Sun,* October 22, 1925, box 94, NP.

86. Janet Snyder Matthews, *Venice: Journey for Horse and Chaise* (Sarasota, FL: Pineapple Press, 1989), 209–26.

87. Nolen convinced the Kansas City developer J. C. Nichols to tour the property. Nichols thought the plan was well conceived and promised to put $250,000 into Venice if its "development was carried on in a very high class manner." J. J. Ruppert, the owner of the New York Yankees, also visited Venice in April 1925 and expressed a similar interest. Roger Rice to Nolen, April 11, 1925, box 37, NP.

88. Fred Albee to Nolen, June 29, 1925, box 37, NP.

89. Nolen to Straub, August 6, 1925, box 94, NP.

90. Nolen to H. A. Paddock, May 5, 1926, box 37, NP.

91. *Venice News,* June 1927, box 37, NP.

92. Rexford Newcomb, *Mediterranean Domestic Architecture in the United States* (Cleveland, OH: J. H. Jansen, 1928); Justin Nylander, *Casas to Castles: Florida's Historic Mediterranean Revival Architecture* (Atglen, PA: Schiffer, 2010).

93. This property was later named John Nolen Park.

94. Nolen to C. B. Purdom, January 16, 1925, box 70, NP.

95. "Brochure" folder, box 37, NP.

96. "Brotherhood of Locomotive Engineers Memorandum," September 28, 1929, box 37, NP.

97. Nolen to the Brotherhood of Locomotive Engineers, September 29, 1926, box 37, NP.

98. Nolen to George Webb, June 23, 1926, box 37, NP.

99. Ibid.

100. Nolen to R. Brearky, June 30, 1926, box 37, NP.

101. Nolen to Webb, June 15, 1926, box 37, NP.

102. Prentiss French to Nolen, March 22, 1926, box 37, NP.

103. Nolen to French, August 23, 1926, box 37, NP.

104. Nolen to Unwin, July 29, 1926, box 8, NP. Nolen considered Venice his best work, aside from Mariemont; Nolen to Joseph Hudnut, May 13, 1936, box 70, NP.

105. Jessica Seymour to Nolen, March 19 and 25, 1925, box 58, NP; Nolen to Nolen Jr., August 11, 1925, box 74, NP; *Miami Herald,* October 7, 1925, box 58, NP; Nolen to John Orr, October 13, 1925, box 58, NP. Before moving to Miami after World War I, Seymour had studied with Patrick Geddes in St. Paul; after this experience, she became a vocal city planning advocate. In Miami, Marjory Stoneman Douglas was one of her disciples; see Jack Davis, *An Everglades Providence: Marjory Stoneman Douglas and the American Environmental Century* (Athens: University of Georgia Press, 2009), 283–90.

106. Seymour to Nolen, March 19, March 25, and May 29, 1925, box 58, NP.

107. *St. Petersburg Times,* April 2, 1926, box 94, NP.

108. Stephenson, *Visions of Eden,* 88–92.

109. Nolen to N. Cauchon, March 16, 1926, box 6, NP.

110. Davis, *Everglades Providence,* 293–300.

111. Vickers, *Panic in Paradise,* 60–113.

112. Nolen, *St. Petersburg Today,* 13–14.

113. *St. Petersburg Times,* May 29, 1932.

114. Stephenson, *Visions of Eden,* 99–100.

115. Nolen to Seymour, January 16, 1927, box 59, NP.

116. Nolen to Nolen Jr., April 24, 1928, box 16, NP; Nolen and Strong, "Family Album," 41.

117. *St. Petersburg Times,* December 12, 1927, box 94, NP.

118. "If you ever saw reaction they are having it now," the city manager reported. H. Richards to Nolen, February 2, 1928, box 72, NP.

119. Rudolph Weaver to Nolen, November 8, 1932, box 76, NP.

120. Nolen to George Gallup, January 23, 1931, box 8, NP.

121. Nolen's confidence was not misplaced. In 2007 the Venice city council outlined the parameters for drafting a new plan to create a "unified community character based on the design, architecture, master planning, and building standards reflected in John Nolen's 1926 plan." With completion of the new plan in 2010, local officials were once again implementing a civic vision that valued a human-scaled urbanism. Venice Planning Department, *Future Land Use and Design Element of the Comprehensive City Plan* (Venice, FL, 2010), 1.

122. Nolen to Nolen Jr., April 24, 1928, box 16, NP.

123. Prentiss French to Nolen, September 15 and October 10, 1928, box 37, NP.

124. Matthews, *Venice,* 308.

125. Nolen to Webb, May 14, 1929, and May 16, 1931, box 37, NP; Nolen to Frank Jonesburg, 1927–28, box 34, NP.

126. Nolen to Barbara Nolen, December 18, 1928, box 14, NSP.

127. Hollander, *Raising Cane,* 96.

128. "Florida's relative 'emptiness' provided Dahlberg with a political frontier," the historian Gail Hollander notes. "He was intent on not only restructuring the physical landscape of the Everglades but also the political-economic landscape of Florida, and more generally, of the nation." Ibid., 110.

129. Jonathan Grunwald, *The Swamp: The Everglades, Florida, and the Politics of Paradise* (New York: Simon & Schuster, 2006), 197.

130. "Clewiston, Florida, Project File 365B, Canal Point Town Site, Project File 375," box 1, NP.

131. "Clewiston Celebration," *West Palm Beach Post,* January 30, 1929, box 24, NP.

132. Ibid. The previous fall another hurricane had decimated the region, and 2,000 people died when Lake Okeechobee flooded Belle Glade. Grunwald, *Swamp,* 189–94.

133. Hollander, *Raising Cane,* 109–12.

134. Grunwald, *Swamp,* 199–201; Davis, *Everglades Providence,* 331–32.

135. Joseph J. McGovern, *Clewiston: The First Fifty Years* (Clewiston, FL: U.S. Sugar Corporation, 1981), 1.

136. Nolen to Deane Duff, August 29, 1930, box 24, NP.

137. Nolen to Duff, May 16, 1932, box 24, NP.

138. Nolen to Amy Bridgeman, March 22, 1932, box 36, NP.

9. THE DEAN OF AMERICAN CITY PLANNING, 1931–1937

1. Gustav Oberlaender, a Pennsylvania businessman, founded the trust in 1931 to accelerate the flow of knowledge between the world's largest industrial republics. *Milwaukee Sentinel,* June 22, 1931, 2.

2. Howard and Unwin preceded Nolen as president.

3. Richard J. Evans, *The Coming of the Third Reich* (New York: Penguin, 2004), 252–54.

4. Ibid, 255.

5. "Harvard University Lectures," 1935, box 15, NP.

6. Nolen to Barbara Nolen, August 6, 1931, box 14, NSP; John Nolen, "Housing Needs of a Modern Family," paper presented at the Annual Meeting of the American Home Economics Association, Denver, CO, June 25, 1930, box 14, NP.

7. John Nolen, "'Germany's Bad Faith,'" *Boston Herald,* October 29, 1931.

8. Evans, *Coming of the Third Reich,* 255.

9. John Kenneth Galbraith, *The Great Crash, 1929* (Boston: Houghton Mifflin, 1954), 3–11; Richard Florida and Marshall Feldman, "Housing in the United States, Fordism," *International Journal of Urban and Regional Research* 12 (June 1988): 187–210; Robert S. McElvaine, *The Great Depression: America 1929–1941* (New York: Three Rivers, 1984), 72–94; William E. Leuchtenburg, *Perils of Prosperity, 1914–1932* (Chicago: University of Chicago Press, 1958), 241–64.

10. John Nolen, "Economy and Security through Planning," paper presented to the Pennsylvania Association of Planning Commissioners, Wilkes-Barre, PA, March 22–23, 1932, box 14, NP.

11. Richard Ely to Nolen, August 23, 1932, box 58, NP.

12. Mark Luccarelli, *Lewis Mumford and the Ecological Region: Politics of Planning* (New York: Guilford Press, 1997), 72–111.

13. Daniel Schaffer, *Garden Cities for America: The Radburn Experience* (Philadelphia: Temple University Press, 1981), 223–25.

14. Ibid., 145–66; Chang-Moo Lee and Barbara Stabin-Nesmith, "The Continuing Value of a Planned Community: Radburn in the Evolution of Suburban Development," *Journal of Urban Design* 6 (June 2001): 151–56; Eugenie L. Birch, "Radburn and the American Planning Movement," *Journal of the American Planning Association* 46 (October 1980): 424–39.

15. John Nolen, "Recreation Planning," *Recreation* 25 (May 1931), 69–70.

16. Schaffer, *Garden Cities,* 164.

17. Nolen to Charles Beard, January 14, 1932, box 73, NP.

18. Nolen to Russell Black, February 8, 1933, box 8, NP. Like many reformers, Nolen read Stuart Chase's *The New Deal,* David Cushman Coyle's *The Irrepressible Conflict: Business*

vs. Finance, and George Soule's *A Planned Society* to gain insight into the thinking of the new administration.

19. Nolen to Howard Strong, May 19, 1933, box 14, NP.

20. Nolen to Robert Luce, April 29, 1933, box 65, NP.

21. Aelred Gray and David Johnson, *The TVA Regional Planning and Development Program: The Transformation of an Institution and Its Mission* (London: Ashgate, 2005), 3–17.

22. Nolen to Earle Draper, June 23, box 65, NP.

23. Felix Frankfurter to David Lilienthal, July 5, 1933, box 65, NP.

24. George Marston to Arthur Morgan, July 10, 1933, box 65, NP.

25. Lawrence Veiller to Morgan, n.d., box 65, NP.

26. George Stephens to Morgan, July 5, 1933, box 65, NP.

27. Although Mumford and Stein had misgivings about Draper, Nolen never voiced such concerns. In fact, he thought Draper well qualified. See Stein to Benton MacKaye, June 22, 1933, cited in *The Writings of Clarence S. Stein: Architect of the Planned Community,* ed. Kermit C. Parsons (Baltimore: Johns Hopkins University Press, 1998), 249.

28. Cathy Knepper, *Greenbelt, Maryland: A Living Legacy of the New Deal* (Baltimore: Johns Hopkins University Press, 2000); Joseph L. Arnold, *The New Deal in the Suburbs: A History of the Greenbelt Town Program, 1935–1954* (Columbus: Ohio State University Press, 1971).

29. William Fulton, "The Garden Suburb and the New Urbanism," in *From Garden City to Green City: The Legacy of Ebenezer Howard,* ed. Kermit C. Parsons and David Schuyler (Baltimore: Johns Hopkins University Press, 2002), 167–68; Carol A. Christensen, *The American Garden City and the New Towns Movement* (Ann Arbor: University of Michigan Research Press, 1986), 105–25; Andrés Duany, Elizabeth Plater-Zyberk, and Robert Alminana, *New Civic Art: Elements of Town Planning* (New York: Rizzoli, 2003), 292.

30. Daniel T. Rodgers, *Atlantic Crossings: Social Politics in a Progressive Age* (Cambridge: Belknap Press of Harvard University Press, 1998), 384–87, 455; Lewis Mumford, *The Culture of Cities* (New York: Harcourt, Brace, 1938), 31. Robert Fishman, *Urban Utopias in the Twentieth Century: Ebenezer Howard, Frank Lloyd Wright, Le Corbusier* (New York: Basic Books, 1977), 184–204; Eric Mumford, *The CIAM Discourse on Urbanism, 1928–1960* (Cambridge: MIT Press, 2000), 75–95.

31. In 1934 Nolen earned a small commission at Muscle Shoals, AL, but it was not the position he had hoped for. Muscle Shoals folder, box 30, NP.

32. William Fulton, "Portrait of a Consultant in Hard Times"; Justin Hertzog, Geoffrey Platt, and John Nolen, *State Planning in New Hampshire* (Washington, DC: National Resources Board, 1935).

33. Nolen to Russell Bourne, September 13, 1935, box 30, NP.

34. In the early 1930s Elliot was staff director for the National Capital Planning Commission and reported to Frederick A. Delano. John Nolen Jr., after scoring first on the civil service exam, replaced Elliot at the commission. Nolen Jr. would head the NCPC until his retirement in 1958. Nolen to Edward Griggs, January 6, 1934, box 14, NP.

35. Alan Brinkley, "The National Resources Planning Board and the Reconstruction of Planning," in *The American Planning Tradition: Culture and Policy,* ed. Robert Fishman (Baltimore: Johns Hopkins University Press, 2000), 173–87.

36. John L. Hancock, "The New Deal and American Planning: The 1930s," in *Two Centuries of American Planning,* ed. Daniel Schaffer (Baltimore, Johns Hopkins University Press), 197–230.

37. By 1940 the investment reached $10 million, an unusually high amount for a midsize city. R. Bruce Stephenson, *Visions of Eden: Environmentalism, Urban Planning, and*

City Building in St. Petersburg, Florida, 1900–1995 (Columbus: Ohio State University Press, 1997), 103–4.

38. "San Diego's New Civic Center on Waterfront Gets Underway," *Christian Science Monitor,* May 5, 1937, 7.

39. John L. Hancock, "Smokestacks and Geraniums: Planning and Politics in San Diego," in *Planning and the Twentieth-Century American City,* ed. Mary Corbin Sies and Christopher Silver (Baltimore: Johns Hopkins University Press, 1996), 182.

40. Brinkley, "National Resources Planning Board," 174.

41. Paul Conkin, *Tomorrow a New World: The New Deal Community Program* (Ithaca, NY: Cornell University Press, 1959).

42. Ibid., 277–93.

43. Schaffer, *Garden Cities,* 224–27; Hancock, "The New Deal and American Planning," 219–24.

44. Nolen to Unwin, February 23, 1934, box 8, NP.

45. Mumford cited in Rodgers, *Atlantic Crossings,* 409.

46. Nolen to E. Russell Bourne, February 14, 1936, box 30, NP.

47. Rodgers, *Atlantic Crossings,* 461.

48. Millard F. Rogers Jr., *John Nolen and Mariemont: Building a New Town in Ohio* (Baltimore: Johns Hopkins University Press, 2001), 198.

49. Michael Simpson, *Thomas Adams and the Modern Planning Movement: Britain, Canada, and the United States, 1900–1940* (London: Mansell, 1985), 162–64.

50. "Newest Profession Is Recognized by Harvard City Planning School," *Christian Science Monitor,* October 21, 1929, 1–2; Anthony Alofsin, *The Struggle for Modernism: Architecture, Landscape Architecture, and City Planning at Harvard* (New York: Norton, 2002), 70–71.

51. Alfonsin, *Struggle for Modernism,* 65–66.

52. Henry Hubbard to Nolen, September 12, 1929, box 15, NP; Nolen to Thomas Adams, December 17, 1929, box 71, NP; Alofsin, *Struggle for Modernism,* 7.

53. Alofsin, *Struggle for Modernism,* 74–75.

54. Nolen to Adams, December 17, 1929, NP.

55. Ian McHarg, *A Quest for Life: An Autobiography* (New York: Wiley, 1996), 67–91.

56. Alofsin, *Struggle for Modernism,* 124.

57. John Nolen, "Cities Fit to Live In," *Technology Review* 32 (April 1930): 7.

58. Lewis Mumford, *The Culture of Cities* (New York: Harcourt, Brace, 1938), 255.

59. Harland Bartholomew, *Urban Land Uses* (Cambridge: Harvard University Press, 1932), v.

60. Stephenson, *Visions of Eden,* 107–16. On Bartholomew, see Eldridge Lovelace, *Harland Bartholomew: His Contributions to American Urban Planning* (Urbana: Department of Urban and Regional Planning, University of Illinois, 1993); Norman Johnston, "Harland Bartholomew: Precedent for the Profession," in *The American Planner: Biographies and Recollections,* ed. Donald A. Krueckeberg (New York: Methuen, 1983), 289–99; Joseph Heathcott, "'The Whole City Is Our Laboratory': Harland Bartholomew and the Production of Urban Knowledge." *Journal of Planning History* 4 (December 2005): 322–55; Jeffrey Brown, "A Tale of Two Visions: Harland Bartholomew, Robert Moses, and the Development of the American Freeway," *Journal of Planning History* 4 (2005): 3–32.

61. *Santa Barbara Press,* March 2, 1929.

62. "Harvard University Lectures 1935," box 15, NP.

63. Most likely Nolen adopted this idea from Mumford; see Lewis Mumford, "The Next Twenty Years in City Planning," *Proceedings of the Nineteenth Conference on City Planning* (Washington, DC: American Institute of City Planning, 1927), 43–58.

64. "Harvard University Lectures 1935."

65. Ibid.

66. "Harvard University, Lectures, Assignments, Syllabus," 1935, box 15, NP.

67. Mark S. Foster, *From Streetcar to Superhighway: American City Planners and Urban Transportation, 1900–1940* (Philadelphia: Temple University Press, 1981), 117; Nolen to Bernard DeVoto, March 3, 1932, box 14, NP.

68. Nolen to Russell Black, May 31, 1927, box 71 NP.

69. "Harvard Lectures 1935."

70. Stanley Buder, *Visionaries and Planners: The Garden City Movement and the Modern Community* (New York: Oxford University Press, 1990), 148–49; Mumford, *CIAM Discourse on Urbanism*, 55–64.

71. Buder, *Planners and Visionaries*, 149–51.

72. John Nolen, "Meeting the Housing Needs of the Modern Family," paper presented at the Annual Meeting of the New England Home Economic Association, Boston, May 16, 1931, box 14, NP.

73. "Le Corbusier," *Technology Review* 32 (April 1930): 1–3; Peter Calthorpe, *Urbanism in the Age of Climate Change* (Washington, DC: Island Press, 2010), 51.

74. John L. Hancock, "John Nolen and the American Planning Tradition" (PhD diss., University of Pennsylvania, 1964), 440–44.

75. Buder, *Visionaries and Planners*, 154–55.

76. John Nolen, "The Landscape Architect in Regional and State Planning," *Landscape Architecture* 27 (July 1935): 200.

77. *Christian Science Monitor*, June 19, 1934, 3.

78. John Nolen, *Madison: A Model City* (Boston, 1911), 71.

79. Nancy D. Sachse, *A Thousand Ages: The University of Wisconsin Arboretum* (Madison: University of Wisconsin Press, 1974), 17–18.

80. Joseph Jackson to Nolen, September 7, 1933, box 28, NP; Jackson to Martin J. Gillen, March 10, 1933, box 1, Arboretum Papers, University of Wisconsin–Madison (hereafter AP); Curt Meine, *Aldo Leopold: His Life and Work* (Madison: University of Wisconsin Press, 1991), 301–7.

81. Jackson to Jay "Ding" Darling, August 13, 1933, box 2, AP.

82. Aldo Leopold, "Arboretum Policy," March 28, 1934, William Longenecker files, box 10, AP.

83. Interview with Nina Leopold Bradley, July 20, 2004, Baraboo, WI. For Fassett's role in laying the groundwork for prairie restoration at the University of Wisconsin–Madison Arboretum, see Sachse, *A Thousand Ages*, 49–50. For Fassett's pioneering work in plant ecology, see Robert L. Burgess, "John T. Curtis: Botanist, Ecologist, and Conservationist," in *John T. Curtis: Fifty Years of Wisconsin Plant Ecology*, ed. James Fralish, Robert McIntosh, and Orie Loucks (Madison: Wisconsin Academy of Sciences, Arts & Letters, 1993), 7–9; Aldo Leopold, "Grass, Brush, Timber, and Fire," in *The River of the Mother of God and Other Essays by Aldo Leopold*, ed. Susan Flader and J. Baird Callicott (Madison: University of Wisconsin Press, 1991), 114–22.

84. Jackson to Nolen, November 23, 1933, box 28, NP.

85. John Nolen, "Address at the University of Wisconsin Arboretum and Wildlife Refuge Dedication," box 1, AP.

86. Aldo Leopold, "What Is the University of Wisconsin Arboretum and Wild Life Refuge?" box 1, AP; see also J. Baird Callicott, "'The Arboretum and the University': The Speech and the Essay," *Transactions of the Wisconsin Academy of Science, Arts and Letters* 87 (1999), 5–21.

87. Ecology was a peripheral field for Leopold before he took on his responsibilities at the arboretum, but after 1934 he immersed himself in the subject. Leopold's shift from conservation to ecology has received much scholarly attention; see Max Oelschlaeger,

The Idea of Wilderness: From Prehistory to the Age of Ecology (New Haven: Yale University Press, 1991), 205–42.

88. For a review of language describing Leopold as a "prophet" and the *Sand County Almanac* as the "bible" of the environmental movement, see Flader and Callicott, introduction to *River of the Mother of God*, 30.

89. Girard College owned property outside the city that could be used for field studies. John Nolen, "Stephen Girard: An Educational Pioneer," *Steel and Garnett* (June 1936): 71–73.

90. Herrick to Nolen, May 28, 1936, box 14, NP.

91. Nolen to Herrick, June 3, 1936; Herrick to Nolen, May 28, 1936, box 14, NP.

92. "Regional" was added to the title the year before.

93. Hubbard to Nolen, May 28, 1936, box 15, NP.

94. Alofsin, *Struggle for Modernism*, 118–28.

95. Ibid., 130.

96. Hubbard to Nolen, May 28, 1936; Hubbard to Nolen, June 19, 1936, box 15, NP.

97. John Nolen and Henry Vincent Hubbard, *Parkways and Land Values* (Cambridge: Harvard University Press, 1937), xi.

98. Jeffrey Brown, Eric Morris, and Brian Taylor, "Planning for Cars in Cities: Planners, Engineers, and Freeways in the 20th Century," *Journal of the American Planning Association* 75 (Spring 2009): 163–64.

99. Hubbard to Nolen, May 28, 1936, box 15, NP.

100. Nolen to Henry Sturgis Dennison, June 18, 1936, box 15, NP.

101. Nolen to Edward Filene, June 3, 1936, box 15, NP.

102. B. W. Connors (secretary to Filene) to Nolen, June 29, 1936, box 15, NP.

103. Hubbard to Nolen, June 27, 1936, box 15, NP.

104. Nolen to Hubbard, July 6, 1936, box 15, NP.

105. Alofsin, *Struggle for Modernism*, 137, 172.

106. Vincent Scully, "The Architecture of Community," in *The New Urbanism: Toward an Architecture of Community*, ed. Peter Katz (New York: McGraw-Hill, 1994), 226.

107. Nolen to Hartzog, July 10, 1936, box 15, NP.

108. Charlotte Parsons to Guy W. Hayler, April 6, 1937, box 58; NP; Nolen to Herrick, August 18, 1936, box 14, NP.

109. John Nolen, "Need for Regional Analysis and Planning in the Southeast," in *The Importance of Planning in the Southeast* (Washington, DC: National Resources Board, 1936), 6–14.

110. Nolen to George Merrick, November 3 and December 19, 1936; Merrick to Nolen, November 27 and December 14, 1936; *Miami Daily News*, May 23, 1937, box 59, NP.

111. Nolen to Barbara Nolen, November 18, box 15, NSP.

112. Nolen to Duff, November 28, 1936; Justin Hartzog to Bror Dahlberg, December 28, 1937, box 24, NP.

113. George Gallup to Nolen, August 20, 1930, box 8, NP.

114. John C. Gifford, "All-Florida Corridor," 4, box 58, NP.

115. C. H. Schaffer to Nolen, December 11, 1936, box 58, NP.

116. Davis, *Everglades Providence*, 363–68.

117. Clara Thomas to Ray Green, January 28, 1934, box 58, NP; "Highland Hammock File," box 58, NP.

118. Charlotte Parsons to George Merrick, December 8; Merrick to Nolen, December 14, 1936, box 59, NP.

119. Nolen to Herrick, December 10, 1936, box 14, NP.

120. Nolen and Strong, "Family Album," 48.

121. Nolen to David Coyle, January 7, 1930, box 30, NP.

122. Parsons to Hayler, April 7, 1937 box 59, NP; Nolen and Strong, "Family Album," 48.

123. Nolen to Dana Dotson, February 5, 1937, box 59, NP.

124. Ibid.

125. Unwin to Nolen, February 2, 1937, box 8, NP.

126. Straub thought Nolen had already died when he wrote this editorial; *St. Petersburg Times,* September 26, 1936, 4.

127. Jackson to Nolen, February 13, 1937, box 59, NP.

128. "John Nolen," *American Magazine of Art* 27 (March 1937): 3, 6.

EPILOGUE

1. R. Bruce Stephenson, "A 'Monstrous Desecration': Dredging and Filling in Boca Ciega Bay," in *Paradise Lost: An Environmental History of Florida,* ed. Jack Davis and Raymond Arsenault (Gainesville: University of Florida Press, 2005), 326–32.

2. R. Bruce Stephenson, *Visions of Eden: Environmentalism, Urban Planning, and City Building in St. Petersburg, Florida, 1900–1995* (Columbus: Ohio State University Press, 1997), 107–13.

3. Stephenson, "A 'Monstrous Desecration,'" 340–46.

4. Stephenson, *Visions of Eden,* 152–58.

5. Ibid., 187–90.

6. William Fulton, "The Garden Suburb and the New Urbanism," in *From Garden City to Green City: The Legacy of Ebenezer Howard,* ed. Kermit C. Parsons and David Schuyler (Baltimore, Johns Hopkins University Press, 2002), 166.

7. James Kunstler, *The Geography of Nowhere: The Rise and Decline of America's Man-made Landscape* (New York: Simon & Schuster, 1993), 254–55.

8. Fulton, "Garden Suburb." On Nolen and New Urbanism, see R. Bruce Stephenson, "The Roots of the New Urbanism: John Nolen's Garden City Ethic," *Journal of City Planning History* 1 (May 2002), 100–125; David Mohney and Keller Easterling, *Seaside: Making a Town in America* (New York: Princeton Architectural Press, 1990); Emily Talen, *New Urbanism and American Planning* (New York: Routledge, 2005); and Kenneth Helphand and Cynthia Girling, *Yard, Street, Park: The Design of Suburban Open Space* (Chicago: APA Press, 1994).

9. Ruth Knack, "Repent, Ye Sinners, Repent," *Planning* 44 (August 1989): 4–9; William Fulton, *The New Urbanism: Hype or Hope for American Communities?* (Cambridge, MA: Lincoln Institute of Land Policy, 1996).

10. Thomas E. Low and Tom Hanchett, *Civic by Design: John Nolen's Lessons and the New Urbanism* ([Charlotte, NC]: DPZ Charlotte, 2008).

11. Congress for the New Urbanism, *Charter of the New Urbanism* (New York: McGraw-Hill, 2000).

12. John Nolen, *New Ideals in the Planning of Cities, Towns, and Villages* (New York: American City Bureau, 1919).

13. John A. Dutton, *New American Urbanism: Re-forming the Suburban Metropolis* (Milan: Skira, 2001), 49–68.

14. Ellen Dunham-Jones and June Williamson, *Retrofitting Suburbia: Urban Design Solutions for Redesigning Suburbs* (New York: Wiley, 2010); Henry Cinceros and Lora Engdahl, eds., *From Despair to Hope: Hope VI and the Promise of Public Housing in American Cities* (Washington, DC: Brookings Institute Press, 2009); Douglas Farr, *Sustainable Urbanism: Urban Design with Nature* (New York: Wiley, 2008); Thomas Low, *Light Imprint: Integrating Sustainability and Community Design* (Charlotte, NC: Civic by Design, 2009); Andrés Duany, Jeff Speck, and Mike Lydon, *The Smart Growth Manual* (New York: McGraw-Hill, 2010); Emily Talen, "Affordability in New Urban-

ist Development: Principle, Practice, and Strategy," *Journal of Urban Affairs* 32 (April 2010): 489–510; Peter Calthorpe, *Urbanism in an Age of Climate Change* (Washington, DC: Island Press, 2010).

15. Duany quoted in David Mohney and Keller Easterling, *Seaside: Making a Town in America* (New York: Princeton Architectural Press, 1991), 87.

16. Nolen to Orrin Randolph, January 3, 1923, box 38, NP.

17. Emily Talen, *City Rules: How Regulations Affect Urban Form* (Washington, DC: Island Press, 2010), 185–93.

18. Robert Davis, the developer of Seaside, was especially noteworthy in this regard. See Robert Davis, "Marinated in Modernism," in *Views of Seaside: Commentaries and Observations on a City of Ideas* (New York: Rizzoli, 2008), 15–24.

19. D. R. Bryan and James Earnhardt, "Southern Village, a New Old Town," paper delivered to the Chapel Hill Historic Preservation Society, November 12, 2006, Chapel Hill, NC; Rosemary Waldorf, "Southern Village's Center Defied Recession Gloom," *New Urban News* 15 (January/February 2010): 3; Tim Padgett, "Saving Suburbia," *Time,* August 16, 1999, 50–51; "A Place of Grace," *U.S. News & World Report,* June 2, 2003, 68; *Wall Street Journal,* August 4, 1999; "Tomorrow's Hope Today," *Builder* 23 (January 2000): 56.

20. Philip R. Berke et al., "Greening Development to Protect Watersheds: Is New Urbanism the Answer?," *Journal of American Planning Association* 69 (Winter 2003): 397–413; Asad Khattak and Daniel Rodriquez, "Travel Behavior in Neo-Traditional Neighborhood Developments: A Case Study in USA," *Transportation Research: Policy and Practice* 39 (June 2005): 481–500.

21. For more on the documentary "Moving Forward by Looking Back," see Keid Benfield, "A tale of two cities in Florida, where walkability trumps sprawl," Natural Resources Defense Council blog, March 2010, http://switchboard.nrdc.org.

22. R. Bruce Stephenson, "Halting Suburban Sprawl," *Forum* 31 (Fall 2007): 6–10.

23. Neil Heinen, "Nolen's Vision, 100 Years Later," *Madison* 8 (January 2011), 66.

24. Stephen Litt, "Great Neighborhoods," *Planning* 74 (December 2008): 4. Union Park Gardens celebrated John Nolen Day on August 29, 2010.

25. William R. Jordan III, "Ecological Restoration: Reflections on a Half Century of Experience at the University of Wisconsin–Madison Arboretum Restoration," in *Biodiversity,* ed. E. O. Wilson (Washington, DC: National Academy of Sciences, 1988), 311–16.

26. Richard Jackson and Stacy Sinclair, *Designing Healthy Communities* (San Francisco: Jossey-Bass, 2012); Peter Newman, Timothy Beatley, and Heather Boyer, *Resilient Cities: Responding to Peak Oil and Climate Change* (Washington, DC: Island Press, 2009).

27. John Nolen, "Cities Fit to Live In," *Technology Review* 32 (April 1930): 7.

INDEX

Page references to illustrations are in italics.

Aaronson, Caleb (stepfather), 8, 19
Ackerman, Frederick L., 141
Adams, Charles Francis, 32
Adams, Thomas: in city planning education,
217; as Garden City Association
secretary, 59; on garden city for
suburban housing, 115; on housing,
141–42, 209; as Massachusetts
Institute of Technology instructor,
217; Nolen sends him questionnaire on
comprehensive planning, 114; Nolen's
give-and-take correspondence with, 132;
Nolen visits home of, 111, *112,* 113
Addams, Jane, 72
African Americans: lynching, 179–80; in
Nolen's Kingsport, Tennessee, plan,
151, 154–55; in Nolen's St. Petersburg,
Florida, plan, 176–81; in Nolen's
Venice, Florida, plan, 198; racism, 5,
179–80, 181; restrictive covenants,
191–92, 198; in Roanoke, Virginia,
72, 72–73, 78–79; Rosewood, Florida,
attacks on, 180; Tuskeegee Institute,
3, 127–28, 155; in West Palm Beach,
Florida, 178. *See also* segregation
"Aid from University Extension Methods"
(Nolen), 34
Albee, Fred H., 192–93
Alliot, Lucien Charles, 169–70, *170*
American Cast Iron Pipe Company, 136

American City (journal), 114
American City Planning Institute, 141, 159,
200, 217, 226
American Civic Association (ACA): on
Charlotte, North Carolina, planning,
127; on garden cities, 140–41;
McFarland as president of, 47; Nolen
and McFarland meet at 1904 meeting
of, 246n26; Nolen as member of, 114;
Nolen lectures on housing to, 136;
Nolen's "Comprehensive Planning for
Small Towns and Villages" address at,
118; Nolen's keynote address at 1909
conference, 99; and Nolen's *Remodeling
Roanoke,* 79; Nolen's *Replanning Small
Cities* drawn from addresses to, 119;
Nolen writes for proceedings of, 146
American Gardens (Lowell), 36
American Historic Towns (Powell), 131
American Metal Company, 136
American Planning Association, 79, 172,
234
American Society for the Extension of
University Teaching (ASEUT), 16,
19–21, 23, 31, 35, 41, 50
American Society of Landscape Architects,
57, 114
*American Vitruvius, The: An Architect's
Handbook of Civic Art* (Hegemann and
Peets), 103

Gompers, Samuel, 149

Good Home for Every Wage-Earner, A
(Nolen), 141

Great Depression, 171, 207, 209

Greenbelt (Maryland), 212

Greenbelt Program, 212–13

greenbelts: in Nolen's Kingsport, Tennessee, plan, 153, 157; in Nolen's Roanoke, Virginia, plan, 74; in Nolen's St. Petersburg, Florida, plan, 176, 188; in Nolen's Venice, Florida, plan, 193

Greenhills (Ohio), 212

Greenville (South Carolina), 54–55

gridiron plans, 4, 107

Griggs, Edward Howard: Baldwin referred to Nolen by, 245n64; loans money to Nolen, 81; "The Ministry of Nature," 25; in Montclair, New Jersey, 55; on nature, 76; *The New Humanism*, 25; Nolen discusses Wisconsin work with, 93; on Nolen going to Harvard, 35; Nolen lecture arranged by, 55; Nolen recommended for San Diego commission by, 79; Nolen's friendship with, 20, 24–25; Nolen's *Remodeling Roanoke* quotes, 72; photograph of, *24*

Gropius, Walter, 226

Gutheim, Frederick "Fritz," 229

Haldeman, B. A., 129

Hampstead Garden Suburb (England): Housing and Town Planning Act inspired by, 129; Mariemont, Ohio, modeled on, 161, 168; Nolen and party visit in 1911, 111, *112*, 113; Nolen encourages his students to study, 219; picturesque building styles in, 115; as sister city to Mariemont, 172

Harris, Alan, 38, 41, 61

Harrisburg (Pennsylvania), 78

Hartzog, Justin: in Florida office, 183; in Foster–Nolen Jr. conflict, 187; in Greenbelt Program, 212, 213; Greenhills, Ohio, plan, 212; National Resources Board position, 213; Nolen as mentor to, 159; Nolen maintains contact with, 213; on Nolen relating to others, 5; returns to Cambridge from St. Petersburg, 201; St. Petersburg, Florida, office opened by, 187; works as independent contractor, 205; works on

Nolen's St. Petersburg, Florida, plan, 188

Harvard University: City Planning Studies series, 217–18, 225; Department of Landscape Architecture, 34, 35–36, 217; Nolen lectures at, 132, 218–19; Nolen studies at, 34–46; School of City and Regional Planning, 217, 224–26, 268n92

Haskins, Charles H., 93

Haussmann, Charles-Eugène, 26–27

Hegemann, Werner, 103, 111, 132

Herrick, Cheesman, 16, 224, 228

Highlands Hammond State Park (Florida), 228

Hollander, Gail, 264n128

Hook, Charles Christian, 124

Hoover, Herbert, 171, 175, 204, 205, 207, 208, 260n75

Hoover Dike, 205, 227

housing: federal involvement in, 141, 146–48, 209, 210; Hoover establishes division of, 260n75; International Federation of Housing and Town Planning, 207, 220; International Housing Association, 220; International Housing Congress, 27; New Deal policy on, 216; Nolen and reform of, 128–29; in Nolen's Mariemont, Ohio, plan, 165–66; Philadelphia symposium on wartime, 141–42; Radburn, New Jersey, as laboratory for, 209; United States Housing Corporation, 141, 148; Wilmington, Delaware, protests for better, *142. See also* National Housing Association; working-class housing

Housing and Town Planning Act (Britain), 129, 175

Housing Reform (Veiller), 128

Howard, Ebenezer: cooperative ownership model of, 60, 130, 244n50; *Garden Cities of Tomorrow*, 59, 244n50; garden city idea of, 6, 59, 157, 160, 244n50; Letchworth built according to plans of, 59, 60; Nolen influenced by, 129, 130; in Nolen's international network, 6; Nolen visits, 111; *Tomorrow: A Peaceful Path to Real Reform*, 59, 244n50

Howe, Frederic C., 37, 110, 111

Hubbard, Henry Vincent: in federal government's housing construction

America, 209; *Report of the Board of Metropolitan Park Commissioners* of 1893 inspires, 34; *The Story of Utopias*, 160; on Tennessee Valley Authority, 216

Munich (Germany): competition for new plan for, 26, 27, 113; Nolen visits in 1911, 113

Municipal League, 114

Muscle Shoals (Alabama), 266n31

Myers, John, 119

Myers Park suburb (Charlotte, North Carolina), 119–27; Colonial Revival home, *125*; DPZ firm establishes office in, 232; Draper works at, 124, 127, 212; Edgehill Park, 121, *121*; entrance plan, *122*; envisioned as model, 115; intimate scale of, 117; Levine Museum exhibit on, 254n26; as National Historic District, 254n25; Neponset Garden Village, Massachusetts, compared with, 130; in Nolen's *New Towns for Old*, 171; plan, *120*; Queens College, 122–24; Southern Village, North Carolina, influenced by, 233; tree canopy, *120, 126*

National Association of Manufacturers, 136

National Capital Planning Commission, 266n34

National Conference on City Planning: Adams and Unwin speak at, 115; American City Planning Institute established by, 141; Croly attends, 119; Marsh–Olmsted debate at, 99–102; Nolen addresses, 96, 119, 136; Nolen joins, 114; Nolen's "The Place of the Beautiful in the City Plan" read at, 158–59; Nolen writes for proceedings of, 146; Olmsted Jr. as chairman of, 102, 129; prototype housing plan of, 139; on regional planning, 146–47; St. Petersburg meeting of 1926, 199–200, 209

National Housing Association: Committee on Wartime Housing, 141; Nolen addresses and submits reports to, 136; Nolen as founding member of, 5, 114, 128; Nolen encourages it to support planning legislation, 129; Nolen writes for proceedings of, 146

National Planning Board, 213

National Resources Board, 213, 214, 216, 226

Neponset Garden Village (Massachusetts), 129–31, *130*

Neville, Ralph, 59

New Deal, 210, 212, 213, 214, 216, 217, 228

New Hampshire state planning board, 213

New Humanism, The (Griggs), 25

New Ideals in the Planning of Cities, Towns, and Villages (Nolen), 146, 147, 149, 157, 160, 169

New Jersey: Glen Ridge, 117, 119; Radburn, 209, 210, 219. *See also* Montclair (New Jersey)

New Towns for Old (Nolen), 3, 4, 171, 188, 210

New Urbanism, 232–33, 234

New York City: Central Park, *30*, 31, 40, 41, *45*; Committee on the Congestion of Population in New York, 100; Forest Hills Gardens, Queens, 115, 219; Long Meadow, Prospect Park, Brooklyn, 41, *42*; Sage Foundation's "New York and Its Environs" plan, 258n30; zoning ordinance of 1916, 111, 175, 252n81

New York Regional Plan Association, 217

New York State Commission on Housing and Regional Planning, 209–10

Nice (France), 86, *86*

Nichols, J. C., 82, 133, 134, 225, 263n87

Nineteenth Conference on Urban Planning, 5

Nolen, Barbara (daughter), 35, 132, 258n30

Nolen, Barbara Schatte (wife): Avon Place home in Cambridge, 61–62, *62*; children of, 23, 35, 46, 132; Garden Terrace home in Cambridge, 132–33; honeymoon in Europe, 22; hospitality of, 23; Mexico trip of 1936, 226–27; in Munich, 26, 29, 226; Nolen begins romance with, 12, 18; Nolen proposes to, 19–20; partnership with Nolen, 23; relatives in Germany, 22, 25, 239n78; wedding of, 21–22

Nolen, Humphrey (son), 226

Nolen, John

—commissions: Belleair, Florida, work, 188–92; Bridgeport, Connecticut, work, 136, 137–40; Charlotte, North Carolina, work, 46, 47–54, 64, 127,

Nolen's visit of 1906, 61; Nolen urges his students to visit, 219

Parker, Barry, 59–60, 111

parks: for celebrating natural conditions, 56; in comprehensive planning, 69; as element of Nolen plans, 4; Everglades National Park, 227–28; Highlands Hammond State Park, Florida, 228; in Kansas City, 79, 82; in Madison, Wisconsin, 94; Marston and San Diego's, 84; Nolen and publishing of works on design of, 57; Nolen and state parks for Wisconsin, 96–99, 228, 249n22; Nolen on changing conception of, 64; Nolen on Olmsted-designed, 56; Nolen's Charlotte, North Carolina, work, 46, 47–54, 64; in Nolen's city planning lectures, 219; in Nolen's Clewiston, Florida, plan, 184; in Nolen's Kingsport, Tennessee, plan, 150, 153, 157; in Nolen's *Madison: A Model City,* 106, 221; in Nolen's Mariemont, Ohio, plan, 161, 170, 172, 259n52; in Nolen's Montclair, New Jersey, plan, 118; in Nolen's *Remodeling Roanoke,* 72, *76,* 76–77, *77,* 78; in Nolen's St. Petersburg, Florida, plan, 178, 231; in Nolen's San Diego plan, 87, 92; Nolen's Savannah, Georgia, work, 62–67; in Nolen's Venice, Florida, plan, 194, *195,* 201; Olmsted and Nolen's "Normal Requirements of American Towns and Cities in Respect to Public Open Space" on, 46; Olmsted Brothers plan for St. Petersburg, Florida, 174; in Roanoke, Virginia, 70; Roosevelt on, 97; segregated, 180

"Parks and Recreation Facilities in the United States, The" (Nolen), 99, 250n33

parkways: "All Florida Corridor" project, 228; in Buffalo, 40; in Eliot's "Emerald Metropolis" plan, 33; in Kansas City, 82, *82,* 133, *133,* 225; in Nolen's *Madison: A Model City,* 105; in Nolen's Mariemont, Ohio, plan, 169; in Nolen's St. Petersburg, Florida, plan, 176, 179; in Nolen's San Diego plan, 89; in Nolen's Venice, Florida, plan, 194, 198; Olmsted and Nolen's "Normal Requirements of American Towns and Cities in Respect to Public Open

Space" on, 46; in Union Park Gardens, Wilmington, Delaware, 144, *144*

Parkways and Land Values (Nolen and Hubbard), 82, 220, 225

Parsons, Charlotte, 133, 205, 228

Parsons, Samuel B., Jr., 57, 79, 84

Pastorale (Corot), *39*

Patten, Simon Nelson: Ely as classmate of, 94; German doctorate for, 11; Marsh as student of, 100; Nolen's *Remodeling Roanoke* quotes, 72; Nolen's "The Parks and Recreation Facilities in the United States" written for, 99; on social history, 11, 236n18

pedestrians: as element of Nolen plans, 4; in Nolen's Mariemont, Ohio, plan, 260n80; walkable urban environments, 219, 232

Peets, Elbert, 103

Penderlea Homesteads (North Carolina), 214, *215,* 216

Peninsula State Park (Wisconsin), 96, *97,* 99, *99,* 250n32

Pennsylvania: Erie, 136; Harrisburg, 78; Langeloth, 136; Marcus Hook, 136; Mount Union, 134–36; Philadelphia, 7

Perot family, 18, 20, 22, 41

Perrot, Emile G., 143, 144

Peterson, Jon, 35

Pinchot, Gifford, 250n33

"Place of the Beautiful in the City Plan, The" (Nolen), 158–59

Plant, Henry, 190

Plater-Zyberk, Elizabeth, 232

Playground Association of America, 63

playgrounds: in Chicago, 82, 106; in Düsseldorf, 113; in Madison, Wisconsin, 95; in Nolen's Charlotte, North Carolina, plan, 64; in Nolen's *Madison: A Model City,* 106; in Nolen's Mariemont, Ohio, plan, 170; in Nolen's San Diego plan, 91, 92; Olmsted and Nolen's "Normal Requirements of American Towns and Cities in Respect to Public Open Space" on, 46; Playground Association of America, 63; Roanoke, Virginia, lacks, 70

Polyzoides, Stefanos, 232

Pope, Alexander, 38

Poussin, Nicolas, 38

Powell, Lyman Pierson, 131

Pray, James Sturgis, 37, 241n36

progressivism, 37, 69, 118–19, 132, 157
Promise of American Life, The (Croly), 119
property rights, 100, 102, 119, 129, 209
Prospect Park (Brooklyn), 40, 41, *42*
Public Works Administration (PWA), 213

Queens College (Myers Park, North
    Carolina), 122–24, *123, 124, 125*

racism, 5, 179–80, 181
Radburn (New Jersey), 209, 210, 219
Randolph, Orrin, 179, 181
Rauschenbusch, Walter, 128
recreation: democracy of, 44; Nolen on areas
    for, 63–64, *64*; in Nolen's Clewiston,
    Florida, plan, 184; in Nolen's St.
    Petersburg, Florida, plan, 176; in
    Nolen's San Diego plan, 91; Olmsted
    Sr. on re-creating, 44, 63. *See also*
    playgrounds
Recreation Magazine, 63, 114
Red Scare, 157
reform: for African Americans, 73; Bird
    as reformer, 129; in Boston, 36–37;
    in Charlotte, 54; Filene as reformer,
    102; garden cities and land reform,
    244n50; Girard as reformer, 8; housing,
    128–29, 158; on land stewardship, 37;
    Letchworth not a model for social, 60;
    in Madison, Wisconsin, 94, 95, 96;
    National Conference on City Planning
    on, 102; Nolen as reformer, 11, 18, 20–
    21, 54, 161; Nolen on education and,
    101; Olmsted Jr. on, 100; Olmsted Sr.
    as reformer, 45; Philadelphia as center
    of, 8; Red Scare and, 157; in Roanoke,
    Virginia, 70–71; Straub as reformer,
    173–74; as technical challenge,
    107; Wharton School in, 10, 11; in
    Wisconsin, 94, 248n9
regional planning: Boston Metropolitan
    District Commission in, 251n60;
    federal housing programs and, 146–48;
    New York Regional Plan Association,
    217; New York State Commission
    on Housing and Regional Planning,
    209–10; Nolen on New Deal and, 210;
    Nolen's Dubuque, Iowa, plan, 210, *211*;
    in Nolen's *New Towns for Old*, 171;
    Nolen's St. Petersburg, Florida, plan,

174, 176, 179; Nolen's state regional
    planning reports, 213; Nolen's Venice,
    Florida, plan, 193; Regional Planning
    Association of America, 209; *Report
    of the Board of Metropolitan Park
    Commissioners* of 1893 as prototype for,
    34; Sage Foundation's "New York and
    Its Environs" plan, 258n30
Regional Planning Association of America,
    209
Remington Arms Company, 137, 138–39
Remodeling Roanoke (Nolen), 71–79; on
    African American housing, 72–73,
    154; civic center in, 72, *73*, 73–74, 76,
    78; the comprehensive plan, *74, 80*;
    influence of, 79; parks in, 72, *76*, 76–
    77, *77*, 78; reception of, 78; on street
    trees, *75*, 75–76; transportation in, 72,
    74–75, 76, 78
Renaissance, Italian. *See* Italian Renaissance
Renaissance, The (Schaff), 12
Replanning Small Cities: Six Typical Studies
    (Nolen), 119, 132
*Report of the Board of Metropolitan Park
    Commissioners* (1893), 33–34
*Report of the Metropolitan Planning
    Commission* (Nolen, Coolidge, and
    Filene), 128
Repton, Humphry: *The Art of Landscape
    Gardening*, 57, *58*; highlights site's
    definitive features, 43; Nolen studies
    work of, 21; *Observations on the Theory
    and Practice of Landscape Gardening*,
    57; Olmsted Jr. lectures on, 40; Sears'
    photographs of landscapes of, *58,
    60*; *Sketches and Hints on Landscape
    Gardening*, 57
Resettlement Administration, 212, 213, 214
restrictive covenants, 191–92, 198
Reynolds, Thomas, 99, 250n32
Riddle, Karl, 178–79, 181
Riis, Jacob, 96
Ripley, Hubert G., 165, 166
Riverside (Illinois), *43*, 43–44, 121, 129
Roanoke (Virginia): African Americans in,
    72, 72–73, 78–79; comprehensive plan
    of 1928, 79; downtown, *71*; location,
    69–70, 71; Market Square, *70*, 71, 79;
    Nolen's work in, 69–79, *80*, 103, 234;
    population growth, 70
Roanoke River Greenway, 79, *81*
Roberts, R. D., 18

Nolen as consultant to, 93, 94; Nolen lectures at, 132; in Nolen's Madison plan, 105, 106, 109; power in state of Wisconsin, 249n9

Unwin, Edwin, 200

Unwin, Raymond: as deputy director of housing in Britain, 158; friendship with Nolen, 6, 113, 158; housing as concern of, 209; Letchworth, England, designed by, 59–60, 161; meets Nolen in Letchworth, 111; National Conference on City Planning speech, 115; and New York Regional Plan Committee, 258n30; and Nolen on New Deal housing policy, 216; Nolen's give-and-take correspondence with, 132; on Nolen's Mariemont, Ohio, plan, 164; Barbara Nolen spends summer with family of, 258n30; and Nolen's questionnaire about comprehensive planning, 114; and Nolen's Venice, Florida, plan, 198; Sitte as influence on, 27; son Edwin, 200; and working-class housing during World War I, 137

Urban Land Uses (Bartholomew), 218

urban planning. *See* city planning

Vance Square (Charlotte, North Carolina), 47, 51, *52*

Vanderbilt, George Washington, 51

Van Hise, Charles, 94, 96, 249n22

Vaux, Calvert, 41

Veiller, Lawrence, 128, 141, 142, 209, 212

Venice (Florida): aerial view, c. 1930, *202*; beachfront park, c. 1950, *202*; business district frontages, *194*; city plan of 1926, *194*; documentary on Nolen's enduring legacy in, 234; downtown, *196*; financial crisis, 201–3; Grand Apartments, *196*; in Great Recession of 2008, 233–34; Greenbelt towns contrasted with, 212; Harlem Village proposal, 198, *199*; Historic District, *203*; industrial zone, 197; landscaping, 198; Mediterranean Revival architecture, 194, 201; memorial to Nolen in, 234; new plan of 2007, 264n121; New Urbanism influenced by, 232; Nichols on, 263n87; Nolen's financial loss in, 203; Nolen's work in, 192–98, 201, 234; promotional brochure, *197*; Venice Hotel, *195*

Vienna, 27

Virginia: University of Virginia, 74; Williamsburg, 73. *See also* Roanoke (Virginia)

Wagg, Alfred, 181, 183

walkable urban environments, 219, 232

Walker, Hale: and Clewiston, Florida, plan, 185; in Florida office, 183; in Foster-Nolen Jr. conflict, 187; Greenbelt, Maryland, plan, 212; in Greenbelt Program, 212, 213; Nolen as mentor to, 159; Nolen lets him go, 205; returns to Cambridge from St. Petersburg, Florida, 201; St. Petersburg office opened by, 187

Walker, Stewart, 193

Walpole (Massachusetts), 129–31, 171

Wangenheim, Julius, 91

Waterbury (Connecticut), 136, 137

Watrous, Richard B., 140–41

Weaver, Rudolph, 201

Weese, Arthur, 26

West Palm Beach (Florida): city plan of 1923, *179*; Nolen's work in, 178, 181

Wharton School Bulletin, 13

Wharton School of Finance and Economy, 10–13, 37

Wheeler, Candace, 13, 14, 15

Williams, Frank B.: and Bridgeport, Connecticut, plan, 138; on European tour of 1911, 111; on Hoover's planning advisory committee, 175; legal work for St. Petersburg, Florida, planning, 174, 175; and New York Regional Plan Committee, 258n30; and New York zoning ordinance of 1916, 111; on racial zoning, 178; on a state planning agency, 200; zoning code for Kingsport, Tennessee, drawn up by, 157

Williamsburg (Virginia), 73

Wilmington (Delaware): housing market, 143; housing protest in, *142*; Union Park Gardens, 143–46

Wilmington Housing Company, 143

Wilson, Richard, 38

Wilson, Woodrow, 20, 22, 141

Winthrop Square (Cambridge, Massachusetts), 44–45

Wisconsin: City Planning Act, 104, 147; Nolen and state parks, 96–99, 228,